CRUISING SAILBOAT KINETICS

Cruising Sailboat Kinetics

THE ART, SCIENCE AND MAGIC OF CRUISING BOAT DESIGN

Text Illustrations by the Author

Including 62 of the best Cruising Boat Designs of the past decade from the pages of *Cruising World* magazine

by **Danny Greene**, N.A.

SEVEN SEAS PRESS, INC.
Newport, R.I.

Published by Seven Seas Press, Inc., Newport, Rhode Island, 02840

Copyright © 1984 by Danny Greene

Library of Congress Cataloging in Publication Data
Greene, Danny, 1949–
    Cruising boat kinetics.

    1. Sailboats—Design and construction.   I. Title.
VM351.G695   1985   623.8′223   84-13989
ISBN 0-915160-69-2

Designed by Irving Perkins Associates
Printed in the United States of America
Edited by James R. Gilbert

Acknowledgments

FIRST AND foremost I would like to thank all the designers whose work appears in this book, for submitting their designs to *Cruising World* and for updating information and drawings. While I am a naval architect myself, I also consider myself a student of all other naval architects. I thank them for their enlightenment. Though the designs are obviously the work of many individual architects, the conclusions drawn and all other material are my own.

Very soon after I started work on this book aboard my cutter *Frolic,* I lost the boat in an accident. Murray Davis graciously offered me a place to live and work for a few months and I am very grateful to him for that. What could have been a very painful and difficult period was made much easier and more comfortable.

This is my first effort at writing a book, and my editor Jim Gilbert deserves credit for piloting me through this long and danger-ridden passage. Thanks also to Noreen Barnhardt for typing the manuscript and naval architect Roger Martin for checking the technical content. Dan Spurr, Herb McCormick and George Day, fellow *Cruising World* editors and recent book authors, offered me encouragement and consolation when I needed it most.

I find the study of cruising boats and their design both challenging and fascinating. My intention with this book is to make these subjects both understandable and enjoyable to the cruising sailor. If I have been successful in doing this, all the work and effort has been worthwhile.

Preface

WE'RE NOT just marking time when we celebrate milestones in our travels through life. The act of pausing to rejoice or to reflect is a process more than an event. It's qualitative as much as quantitative.

We celebrate the Fourth of July, for example, not just to gloat over the fact we still are in existence after 200-plus years, but to marvel that we remain a free nation and to resolve to keep it that way. Sometimes we celebrate to reflect how much things have changed. Just as often we celebrate because things remain the same. When we can pin a date on a change, we call it revolution. When we can't, we call it evolution.

Celebrating the evolution of cruising sailboats poses somewhat of a problem for those of us whose lives are deeply affected by sailboat cruising and who remain emotionally attached to the boats that have given us so much pleasure over the years. We know where we are, but how did we get here?

Cruising Sailboat Kinetics is a celebration of the past 10 years of cruising boat design. The book might just as well be celebrating the past 25 years of evolution in the creation of cruising craft. It has, after all, been a quarter-century since the Pearson cousins, Everett and Clint, sold the first fiberglass production sailboat, the Triton, at the 1959 New York Boat Show.

We have chosen to celebrate a decade, because it has been only in the last 10 years that a forum has existed for designers and naval architects to showcase their creations and to subject their ideas to public and professional scrutiny. Not until the publication of *Cruising World* magazine in 1974 was there a communications medium dedicated solely to the concerns of cruising sailors. In a great many ways, the entire last 10 years has been an ongoing celebration.

That the cruising spirit has thrived and added many thousands of new members to the sailing family is due directly to the ability of designers and manufacturers to produce safe and comfortable boats within the means of so many.

And yet, if there exists a true "Never-Never Land," it exists in the world of boat designers and builders. We consumers demand that our boats be fast and yet be safe and comfortable. We want strength and yet we want our boats to be inexpensive. We want all the amenities of family living and yet we want boats that satisfy our cravings for adventure.

It is remarkable that these professionals have been able to deliver to us the boats of our dreams, boats that satisfy our often-conflicting yearnings, that still conform to the laws of nature—and that are beautiful to the eye. That they succeed as often as they do—a fact proven out in the designs section of this book—is a testament to the great creative impulse in humankind.

It is ironic that boat design has never been accorded status as an art form, as has architecture. And yet naval architecture is in many ways a more exacting and challenging endeavor, particularly when the goal is to produce a pleasing hullform. The designer can't ever sacrifice safety or performance for the sake of beauty and expect his designs to be hailed a success.

If there is any reason for naval architecture's rather low standing on the ascending ladder of art-forms, it is probably because sailboats today are generally used for recreation, and because, once designed, they often are produced in large numbers. This "a toy can't be art" attitude is odd in light of today's culture, which has come to admire and respect the economies of large-scale production, and which has come to worship its leisure time.

So it is fitting at this time and place, that we pause to celebrate past efforts that have helped us lead richer, more enjoyable lives. And, in keeping with the true cruising spirit, we hope readers will find in these pages information that will continue to enhance the sailing experience and that will continue the never-ending refinement and evolution of cruising boat design.

Murray Davis,
Seven Seas Press

Contents

Introduction

THE NOON sight has been taken and *Frolic*'s position is recorded in the log. We are six days and 700 miles out of St. Augustine, Florida, and 200 miles south of Newport, Rhode Island. In light reaching condition, *Frolic* seems to be slipping through the water so easily, driven by her faded red mainsail and huge multi-colored drifter.

I am sitting on the bowsprit, fascinated by the curl of the bow waves peeling away from the stem while my shipmate is below sleeping. The tiller is held in position with a rope across the cockpit. The self-steering wind vane on the stern is steering a perfect course, responding to every gust and wind shift.

A cat's paw of breeze is working its way slowly towards us and I anticipate *Frolic*'s reaction. Just before I feel the fresh breeze on my face, *Frolic* heels a few degrees. I see the drifter fill and strain at its light sheets, slowly but perceptively accelerating *Frolic*'s five tons. At the same time the wind vane flops to windward and brings the boat on course for the new wind.

"It feels like we're moving now." Dean calls to me from down below. She knows the sounds and motions well, and could probably have told me our speed and point of sail from her berth. "If this keeps up we'll make Newport for your birthday."

I am once again struck by the incredible uniqueness of the cruising sailboat. It is more than a home, a wind-driven vessel, a means of transportation; it is a marvelous combination of art and engineering, of design and construction, of sailor and machine. It is not human but it is alive. Whether at sea, at anchor or tied to a dock it is always moving, responding to all the many forces acting upon it from the sea and the air. It functions at the interface of these two fluids, the ocean and the atmosphere, supported by one and propelled by the other.

The manner in which a sailboat responds to the ever-varying forces of wind and water is a function of the design and construction of the boat. Hull shape, size and arrangement of the sails, weight and weight distribution of boat and contents, and the construction material and technique all affect the sailboat's behavior in the vast variety of conditions it experiences.

In designing a racing sailboat, the naval architect does not have to be concerned with many of these behavioral qualities, such as comfort on deck and below, ease of sail handling and steering by a small crew and seakindliness in general. His greater priority, far outweighing all others, is speed and windward ability. The degree of success of a racing sailboat is easily and clearly determined on the race course.

In the design of a cruising sailboat, however, the priorities are quite different and more complex. While speed and weatherliness are still major considerations, the naval architect also must design the boat as a home, considering comfort and safety in all conditions, the ability of the boat to steer itself, strength to survive collisions and groundings and even soundness of investment.

The past 10 years has seen a phenomenal growth, not only in the popularity of cruising under sail, but also in the variety of cruising boat designs. With new building materials and techniques, designers and builders have enjoyed great freedom to experiment with shapes and weights of boats that were difficult or impossible to construct in traditional methods.

Many new people are being attracted to cruising, people without traditional views of cruising and cruising boats. More specialized and diverse types of cruising have evolved, from trailer sailing and gunkholing to coastal cruising, ocean voyaging and singlehanded offshore passagemaking. Boat design has evolved to suit man's refined expectations for his boats.

With all these changes in cruising boats, cruising sailors and cruising in general, many of the long-held principles of what makes a good or poor cruising boat—and how they should be handled—no longer apply.

If the cruising sailor wants to be able to fairly evaluate boat designs, or to make the best choice in selecting a boat for himself or even to be able to sail a boat efficiently and safely, he must have an understanding of why a sailboat behaves the way it does.

Cruising boat kinetics is the study of the forces acting on a cruising sailboat and the manner in which it responds. What I have attempted to do in this book is to divide this seemingly complex subject into its fundamental principles, thus making it understandable to the non-technically oriented sailor.

To show how theory is transformed in practice, I have included 62 designs from the last 10 years of *Cruising World* magazine. Together, I hope they form an interesting and easily comprehended primer on modern cruising boat design and performance. It also is my hope that together, the fundamentals of cruising boat design and some of the best cruising boat designs of the past decade, will truly celebrate—as the book's subtitle implies—the science, art and magic of cruising boat design.

DANNY GREENE
Newport,
January, 1985

CRUISING SAILBOAT KINETICS

PART

I

THE ART, SCIENCE AND MAGIC OF CRUISING BOAT DESIGN

IF YOU want to know how to design a boat to perform in a certain way or, if you want to know how an existing boat will perform, you first must understand the concepts of weight and buoyancy. Thus, any discussion of the principles of naval architecture begins with a look at the work of the Greek scientist Archimedes.

According to legend, in the third century B.C. King Hieron asked Archimedes to determine if a crown made for him was solid gold or if it contained a percentage of silver. Archimedes was stumped by the problem until he stepped into the bath one day, causing water to spill out of the tub.

He realized that the volume of water that overflowed from the full bath, as he stepped into it, was equal to the volume of his own body. He could measure the volume of any object by immersing it in water and measuring the displacement. Since silver is lighter or less dense than gold, he deduced that a piece of silver would have a greater volume than a piece of gold of equal weight.

Archimedes, the story goes, was so thrilled with his revelation that he ran home naked from the baths, yelling, "Eureka, Eureka."

He measured the volume of the crown, plus the volumes of lumps of silver and gold with weights equal to that of the crown. If the crown were pure gold the water it displaced would equal that of the lump of gold.

The conclusion of this particular experiment is unknown, but it marks the beginning of the study of hydrostatics, or the behavior of objects floating or immersed in liquids. Archimedes discovered and recorded many laws of hydrostatics, the most basic of which is called Archimedes' Law which, simply stated, holds that a body immersed in a fluid "displaces" a volume of that liquid, and that a body either partially or fully immersed will experience an upward, buoyant force equal to the weight of the fluid displaced.

The hull of a boat forces water aside to form a "hole" in the water in the shape of the underwater portion of the hull. The volume of the hole is simply the displaced water. Saltwater weighs 64 pounds per cubic foot (freshwater weighs 62.4).

Figure 1 illustrates Archimedes' Law with a block of wood hanging from a scale. The weight

UNDERSTANDING WEIGHT AND BUOYANCY

Archimedes' Contribution

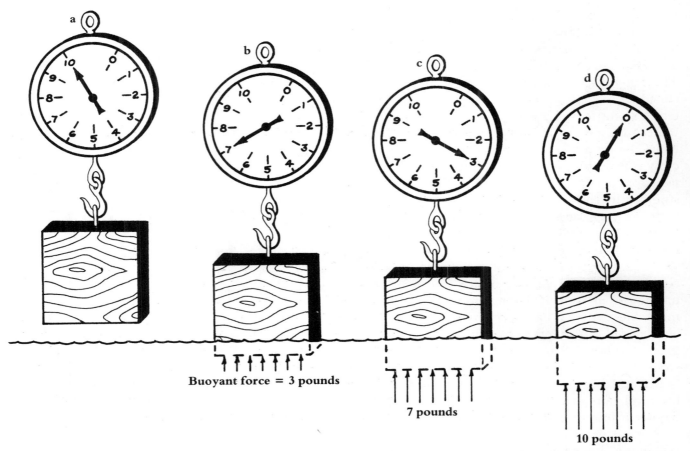

Buoyant force = 3 pounds

7 pounds

10 pounds

Figure 1. As a 10-pound block of wood is immersed in water, its buoyancy increases as its weight decreases. The two values always total 10 pounds. In 1d, the block is floating—entirely supported by buoyancy.

of the block, as shown by the scale in 1a is 10 pounds. As the block is lowered into the water (1b and 1c) it experiences a buoyant force equal to the weight of displaced water. At any stage of submersion the total of the weight shown on the scale and the buoyant force equals 10 pounds.

In 1d, the block of wood has reached equilibrium with the water; it is floating. The scale reads 0 pounds and the buoyant force is 10 pounds. This is the displacement of the block.

The same principle that applies to floating objects also applies to submerged ones, and here the concept of density is illustrated.

Density is the weight of an object divided by its volume.

$$\text{Density} = \frac{\text{Weight}}{\text{Volume}}$$

Figure 2 illustrates Archimedes' Law with a 10-pound block of granite in place of the block of wood. Since granite is much more dense than wood (175 pounds/cubic foot compared to about 30 pounds/cubic foot for wood, about ⅙th the size), it displaces ⅙th as much water, and experiences ⅙th of the buoyant force. When the block is fully submersed, its smaller volume develops only 3.6 pounds of buoyancy, so the scale still reads 6.4 pounds.

A 10-pound block of lead, which has a density of 700 pounds/cubic foot, is less than ¹⁄₂₀th the size of the wood block and ¼ the size of the granite. When it is fully submerged the scale will read about 9.1 pounds, with buoyancy less than one pound. See Figure 3.

Now, let's look at a sailboat floating in water. Figure 4 shows a 10,000-pound boat ready for launching. As it is lowered into the water it sinks until it displaces 10,000 pounds of water, or 156 cubic feet.

When the boat displaces 156 cubic feet of water

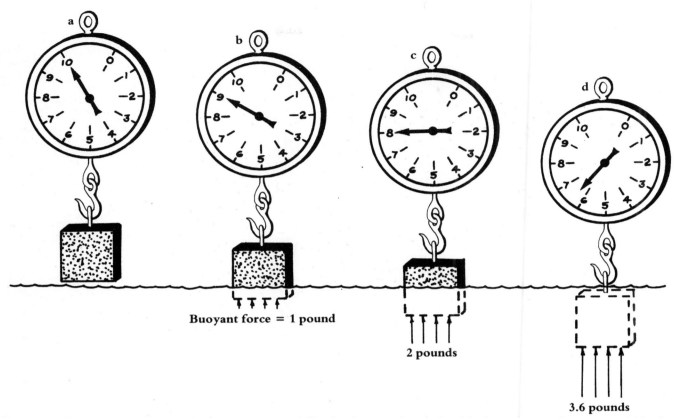

Buoyant force = 1 pound

2 pounds

3.6 pounds

Figure 2. Because of its greater density, a 10-pound block of granite has only ⅙th the volume of a 10-pound block of wood. Total weight and buoyancy is still 10 pounds, but when it is fully immersed, buoyancy is only 3.6 pounds and weight 6.4 pounds.

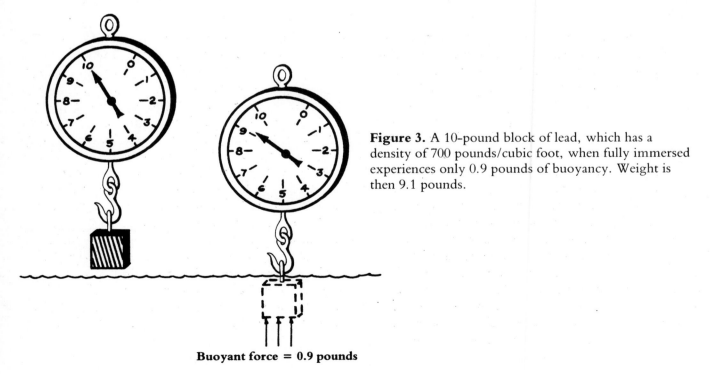

Figure 3. A 10-pound block of lead, which has a density of 700 pounds/cubic foot, when fully immersed experiences only 0.9 pounds of buoyancy. Weight is then 9.1 pounds.

Buoyant force = 0.9 pounds

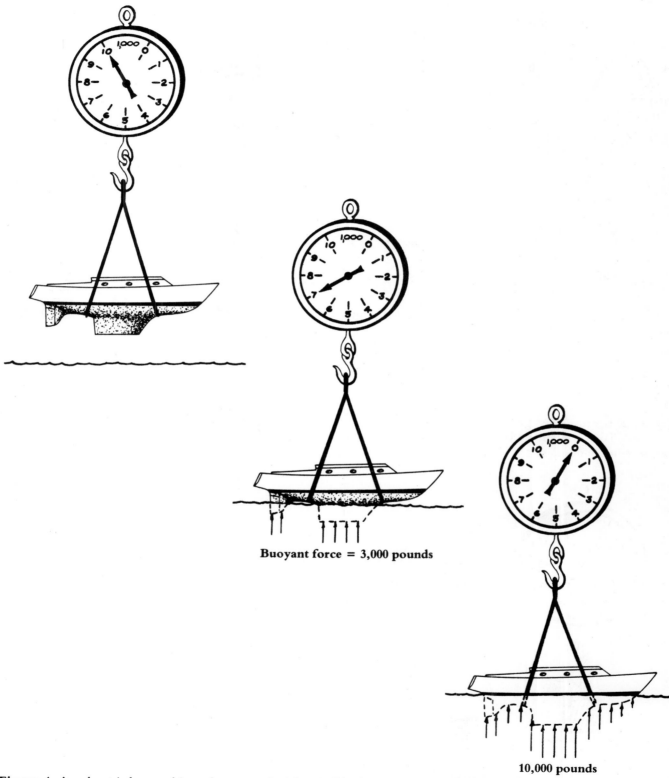

Figure 4. As a boat is lowered into the water, it sinks until its buoyancy, or weight of displaced water, equals the boat's dry weight.

$$\text{Volume of displacement} = \frac{\text{weight of boat}}{\text{density of water}} = \frac{10{,}000 \text{ pounds}}{64 \text{ pounds/cubic foot}} = 156 \text{ cubic foot}$$

the buoyant force of the water equals the weight of the boat. That's a condition we all know as "floating."

It's easier to visualize the forces of weight and buoyancy by considering them as single, distinct forces acting at single points;

Center of Gravity (CG)—This is the geometric center of weight of the boat and every item aboard it. The *Longitudinal Center of Gravity* is the point along the length of the boat at which it would balance if placed on a huge seesaw. The *Vertical Center of Gravity* is the height in the boat at which it would balance if laid on its side on the seesaw. The center of gravity is located on the centerline of the boat where the two lines intersect. See Figure 5.

Center of Buoyancy (CB)—This simply is the center of gravity of the water displaced by the boat. If somehow you could freeze solid the water displaced by the hull keeping intact the hull's underwater shape, you could place it on a seesaw much as in the above exercise. As in Figure 5, you could determine both the *Longitudinal Center of Buoyancy* and the *Vertical Center of Buoyancy*. Where the two lines intersect is located the boat's center of buoyancy.

What's crucial in the design process is not only knowing where centers of buoyancy and gravity are located, but how these two centers relate. The key principle to understand is that a boat—or any floating object—will always float with its center of

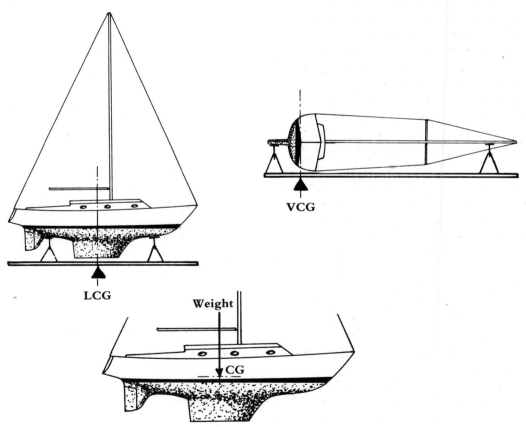

Figure 5. A boat's weight can be considered to be concentrated at the center of gravity (CG), which is at the intersection of the longitudinal center of gravity (LCG) and the vertical center of gravity (VCG).

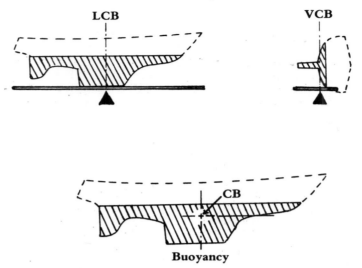

Figure 6. The underwater shape of the hull determines a boat's center of buoyancy (CB). Components of the center of buoyancy are the longitudinal center of buoyancy (LCB) and the vertical center of buoyancy (VCB).

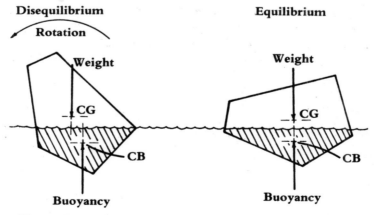

Figure 7. An object floating with its centers of weight and buoyancy out of vertical alignment forms a "couple", or force, that rotates the object until the centers are aligned.

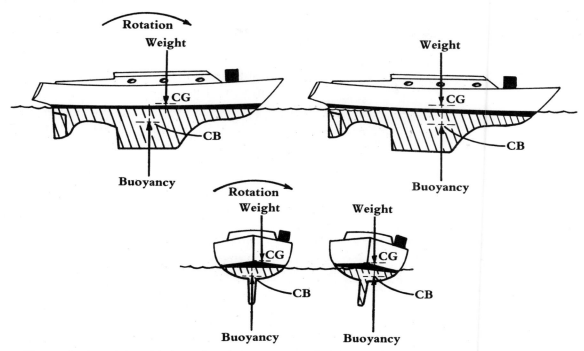

Figure 8. A weight added in a boat's bow moves the center of gravity forward and out of line with the center of buoyancy. The forces rotate the boat until the new center of buoyancy is forward and in line with the center of gravity. Likewise, a weight added to one side of a boat moves the center of gravity toward that side and the boat heels until the center of buoyancy moves to a position under the center of gravity.

buoyancy and center of gravity in the same vertical line. A boat will continue to change its position until this equilibrium is attained.

Figure 7 illustrates an object floating in water, with its center of gravity out of vertical line with its center of buoyancy. The two forces form a "couple," a pair of forces, which try to rotate the body until the centers are aligned vertically.

Figure 8 shows that a boat's tendency to balance its centers of buoyancy and gravity works on any axis. And, as you'll see in Chapter 3, the distance between a boat's center of gravity and center of buoyancy contributes to its ability to stay right-side up in varying conditions and to the boat's motion and the degree of comfort or discomfort imparted to those aboard.

Chapter

2

INTRODUCING THE LINES PLAN

Three dimensions in two

THE DISPLACEMENT of a floating object—the size of the hole it makes in the water—is only one consideration for the boat designer. More importantly, it's the shape and proportions of that hole that determine the speed, comfort and seakeeping abilities of the boat under scrutiny.

The task of creating a hull shape for a cruising sailboat is as unique and challenging an enterprise as exists anywhere. In a word, shape is everything. It determines speed, strength, stability, maneuverability, comfort, ease and cost of construction—even the boat's esthetic appeal. What makes the cruising boat design process particularly challenging is that the elements that determine the different characteristics of a boat often are in fundamental conflict. Those that increase stability, for example, usually are detrimental to speed. Making the design process even more difficult and complex is that frequently a boat must perform optimally in a wide variety of conditions, in port and at sea, in storm and in calm, in hot weather and in cold. A boat that is stable and maneuverable in normal sailing conditions can become dangerously unstable and impossible to control in a storm.

So, it is fair to say that few structures in this world are as complex and difficult to design as a cruising sailboat. It is both a home and a means of transportation. It functions in the two very different mediums of water and air. It is required to perform in an astonishing variety of conditions, with any lapse in performance having potentially serious consequences. In addition it is expected to be beautiful and graceful in appearance, an object of pride for both designer and owner.

The naval architect can learn all the technical aspects of boat design. But it is imagination, intuition and experience that distinguish his creations as noteworthy or successful. He must be not only an engineer but also an artist and an experienced sailor. He has to grasp intellectually all the conflicting and immeasurable considerations of a cruising sailboat, make the innumerable judgments and compromises and, finally, arrive at a hull shape that he believes will behave as required and please the eye.

The cruising sailor who wants to look at a design or a boat with a critical eye also faces a similarly formidable task. He or she has probably not been adequately educated or experienced to successfully pass judgment. And yet, ultimately, everyone who buys a boat must pass that judgment. So, now that the principles of flotation and balance have been explained, let's move on to the next step in unraveling the complexity of cruising boat design: hull shape.

To reach useful and accurate conclusions about hull shape the sailor must first understand the way in which hull shape is defined and determined. Here is a simple, step-by-step procedure a naval architect might use in designing a hull. In subsequent chapters I'll explain how the various aspects of hull shape affect the many characteristics of performance.

Ironically, hull shape is the part of the design least revealed by the drawings usually supplied by the designer and, because of its complex three-dimensional nature, the most difficult to illustrate. Designers often are reluctant to reveal the complete hull shape for fear that an unscrupulous builder will steal the design.

Before the naval architect can commence the design process he must establish some basic parameters: size, type, construction material, cruising purpose (including typical crew number) and approximate cost. If the design is commissioned by a client, a private buyer or, perhaps, a builder looking for a production boat, client and architect work out these parameters together. (See Chapter 10 for more information on hull materials and construction techniques.)

With these basic considerations formulated, the designer establishes certain boat characteristics to serve as starting points. Generally, these characteristics are ones that are easiest to establish in the preliminary design stage. Using information from the client, his own previous experience and from a study of other designs the architect can closely approximate the length and weight of boat that will best satisfy the established requirements. Length is closely related to the necessary accommodation space and weight is determined largely by construction technique, cost and performance.

Looking at other boats of generally the same length, materials and proportions, the architect settles on a weight of 16,000 pounds.

Of course, all design variables are interrelated.

But the designer has to begin somewhere, and whatever is most important in the client's mind (cost, speed, comfort, etc.) will be the controlling factor. In this case, the client wants to cruise comfortably with his family of four, and yet still have a boat small enough and competitive enough to sail in his club's weekly races. Working, too, within his client's budget, the architect chooses a fiberglass hull with an overall length of 40 feet, a waterline length of 32 feet, a beam of 12 feet and a five-and-a-half foot draft. In Chapters 3, 4 and 5 we'll look in finer detail at these specific design elements, their relationships to one another and how they determine various kinds of performance. Much as in learning algebra, you first must make the leap of faith that the various theorems work before you can fully understand how they work. For now, let's assume these values are consistent with the designer's assignment.

With the displacement and principle dimensions established, the designer's next step is to start defining the hull shape. From Archimedes' Law he knows that a boat that displaces 16,000 pounds will have an underwater volume of 16,000/64, or 250 cubic feet. The hull shape he draws must have this underwater volume if it is to float at its designed waterline.

The architect now determines the size and shape of the largest hull cross section—usually called the midship section, even though it often is not exactly at midlength. The shape of this section, given the constant of 250 cubic feet displacement, will be determined by the shape of the ends of the boat. The larger the midship section, the finer the ends. This relationship is called the prismatic coefficient (C_p). To measure it, the designer extends the midship section (without the keel) out to the boat's waterline length (See Figure 1) and then compares that volume with that of the designed hull. A barge with absolutely rectangular underwater shape would have a prismatic coefficient of 1.0. A fine-ended boat might have a coefficient of .45. Most cruising sailboats have prismatic coefficients between .52 and .65.

This coefficient is handy for determining a variety of things, from wave-making characteristics (more on this in Chapter 4) to the hull's ability to move in different conditions. A higher prismatic

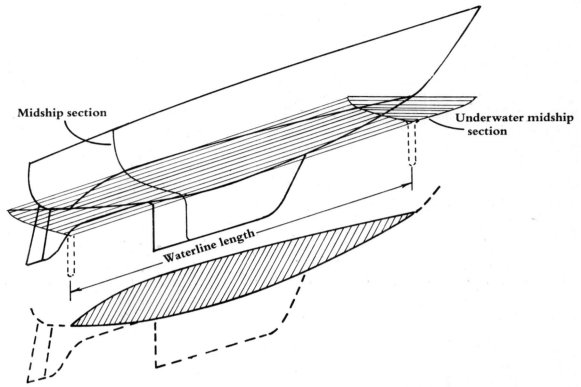

Midship section

Underwater midship section

Waterline length

Figure 1. Prismatic Coefficient (Cp) is the ratio between the actual underwater volume of the hull without the keel or skeg, and the volume of the cylinder (any shape with a constant cross section is called a cylinder) whose cross section is the boat's underwater midship section and whose length equals the boat's waterline length. It is a measure of the fullness of the ends of the underbody relative to the midsection.

coefficient, for example, will indicate better performance in higher wind, while a smaller value will indicate more speed in light wind.

In order to determine the midship section—the first line in the hull shape—the designer chooses a prismatic coefficient of .53. In his judgment this satisfies the speed and seakeeping qualities the client wishes in his boat. The keel is considered as an appendage to the hull and thus is not included in the calculations of prismatic coefficient. The designer estimates the volume of the keel and subtracts that from the required volume of the boat to arrive at the required volume of the hull itself, or "canoe body". He estimates the keel volume to be 15 cubic feet, so the hull volume must be 250 − 15, or 235 cubic feet. Given a waterline length of 32 feet, the only midship section area that will give him a .53 prismatic coefficient is one of 14 square feet.

This is perhaps the most creative stage of a boat design. At this point, the designer can start giving shape to his 14.0 square feet, playing with bilge shape and all the other underwater characteristics of the hull. This also is the time when the designer determines the position of the cabin sole, the height and sheer of the freeboard, and where he begins to establish the rough outlines of the cabin sole. Figure 2 shows three possible midship sections, all with the same beam, draft and underwater area. In this exercise, the architect selects 2b.

Now, on a large sheet of paper, the designer starts drawing the hull in three different views, as if looking at it from above, from the side and from ahead. Combining his artistic and technical experience, he draws the maximum section, the hull profile, the waterline and the sheer line (the top edge of the hull). Figure 3 shows these lines and how they appear in the three views. The end view

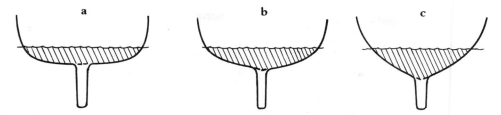

Figure 2. Three possible midship sections, all with the same beam, draft and underwater area.

is drawn as if the right side is the view looking from ahead and the left side is the view from astern.

These three views are, of course, three views of the same subject, so all measurements must agree from view to view. Distance(a), from the center-line to the intersection of the waterline and the midship section must be the same in the top and end views. Distance(b), the height of the sheer line at the midship section, must be the same in the side view and the end view. Any change of a point or line in one view requires a corresponding change in the other views.

The designer now further defines the hull shape

by drawing additional hull sections forward and aft of the maximum section, and more waterlines above and below the waterline at which the boat will float (called the designed waterline or DWL). Figure 4 shows the drawing, called the lines plan, with four more sections and two more waterlines. As the designer adds these lines he must constantly check the agreement of all points in all views and the fairness, or smoothness, of the lines drawn. This laborious process is called "fairing the lines."

To further define and check the fairness of the hull the designer adds two more types of lines, buttocks and diagonals. As shown in Figure 5, a buttock is a vertical plane parallel to the boat's

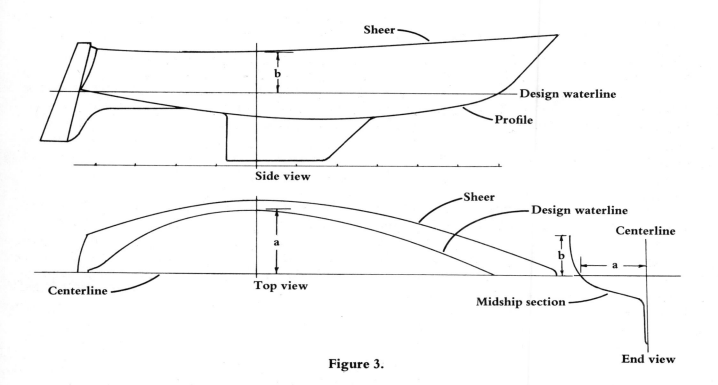

Figure 3.

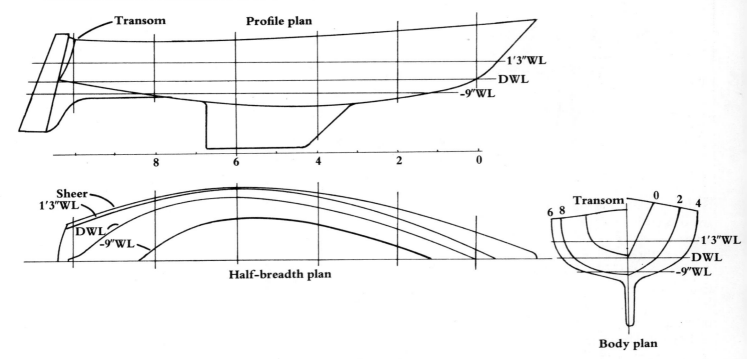

Figure 4.

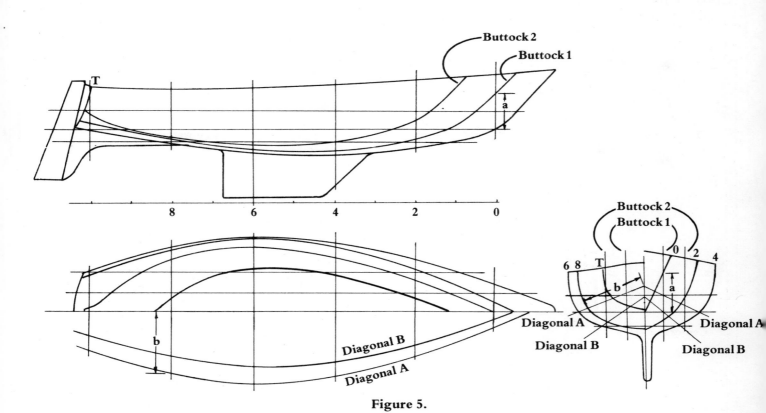

Figure 5.

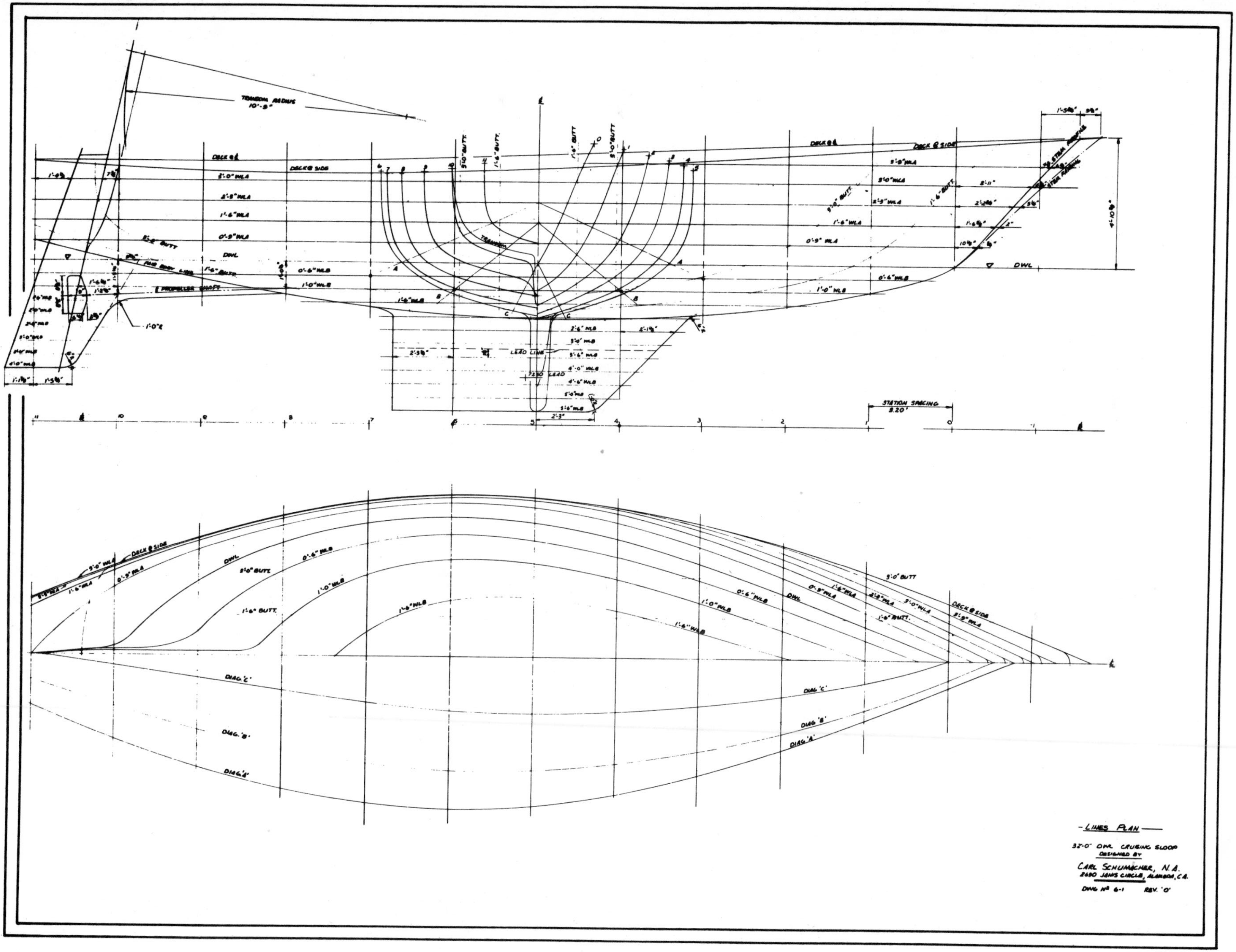

TRANSOM RADIUS 10'-9"
STATION SPACING 3.20'
-LINES PLAN-
32'-0" DWL CRUISING SLOOP
DESIGNED BY
CARL SCHUMACHER, N.A.
2690 JANIS CIRCLE, ALAMEDA, CA.
DWG Nº 6-1 REV. '0'

Figure 6.

centerline. It appears as a straight line in the body plan and the half-breadth plan, and as a curved line in the profile plan.

A diagonal is similar to a waterline, but instead of being horizontal it angles downward from the centerline. It is shown as a straight line in the body plan and as a curve opposite the half-breadth plan.

Diagonals and buttocks are particularly useful in areas of the hull which are intersected by the stations and waterlines at acute angles, which are inaccurate, or where there are significant changes in hull shape between waterlines and stations. By careful placement of buttocks and diagonals the designer can accurately define these areas.

At this stage, the architect is always looking at the shapes of the various sections, waterlines, buttocks and diagonals. If any one of these displeases him, if it indicates a shape he feels esthetically, hydrodynamically or structurally undesirable, he alters the offending shape. But then he must also alter the lines defining that particular shape in all the other views. It is a process of developing, refining and fine-tuning the hull shape to satisfy the designer's conceptions of what performs and looks best.

The designer continues to add sections, waterlines, buttocks and diagonals, always checking for agreement of points and fairness of lines, until the hull is completely defined and fair. He then measures the underwater areas of all the sections and calculates hull displacement and its center of buoyancy. He can also accurately approximate the boat's designed displacement and its center of gravity. This displacement and center of gravity includes not only the hull, deck and rig, but also the sails, anchors, deck hardware, engine, fuel, water, crew, personal effects, provisions, etc.—everything that will be aboard when the boat is cruising.

If the boat's estimated design displacement and the hull's calculated displacement differ significantly, the boat will not float at her designed waterline. If the boat's estimated center of gravity and the hull's calculated center of buoyancy do not occur in the same vertical line, the boat will not trim properly. A discrepancy in either case forces

Length overall (LOA)—The extreme length of the boat. On boats with extensions forward and aft (bowsprits and boomkins), length overall includes these extensions. Length on deck (LOD) is the length of the hull.

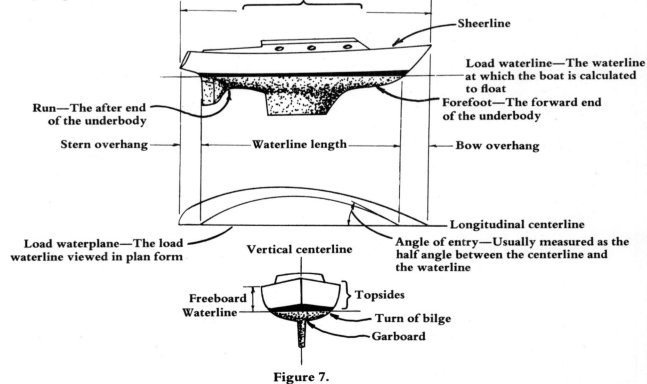

Figure 7.

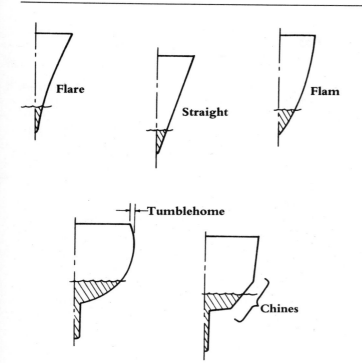

Figure 8. Sectional shapes

the designer either to alter the lines or to justify the new weight estimate.

It's this working back and forth between lines plan, weight estimation and considerations of performance and esthetics that best illustrates the marriage of art and science required in every successful cruising boat designer and shown in every good design. Figure 6 is the completed lines plan, as drawn by naval architect Carl Schumacher for his Ambra 40 (page 186).

The labor involved in producing a lines plan has been reduced in recent years by using computers to produce and fair lines plans, and to make all the tedious calculations. But the computer's output is only as good as the designer's input, so the machine is no substitute for skill or experience. It does, however, allow the designer to investigate many more possible hull shapes for a particular design, and to do so both quickly and accurately.

As we prepare now to move on from drawing the lines plan to a longer discussion of how hull shape affects performance, it's important to establish a good working vocabulary. Figures 7, 8 and 9 illustrate terms applied to various hull shapes that will be mentioned in succeeding chapters.

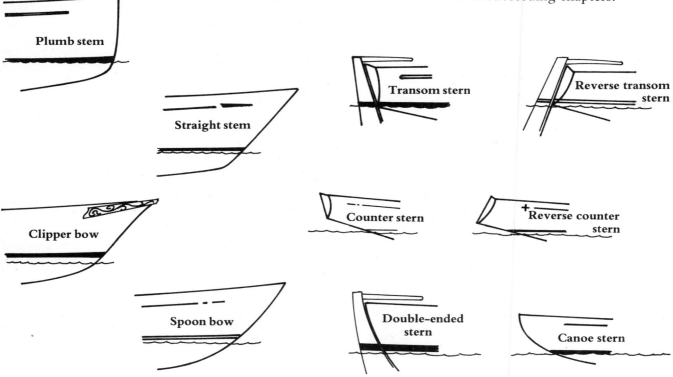

Figure 9. Bow and stern types

Chapter

3

THE BASICS OF TRANSVERSE STABILITY

Keeping the boat upright

EVERY SAILOR who's taken a novice out on their first sail in a stiff breeze remembers that wild-eyed look that grew from surprise into terror as the boat began to heel. At sea, one of the sailor's few sources of security—the landlubber's equivalent of terra firma—is the knowledge that the boat underfoot was designed to remain upright under nearly all conditions and will return to upright even if worse comes to worst and the boat is knocked down or rolled.

As was shown in Chapter 1, when a boat is sitting in the water it sits upright because its center of gravity is in a vertical line with its center of buoyancy, putting these forces in equilibrium.

But what happens when an outside force, such as the wind acting on the sails, disturbs this equilibrium? Look at Figure 1, where the upright boat (a) has been forced to a heeled position (b). Note how the change in the underwater shape causes the center of buoyancy to move to the right. The center of gravity, however, remains in a fixed position.

No longer aligned, the forces of gravity and buoyancy form a couple that tries to rotate the boat back to an upright position. The magnitude of the couple, or "righting moment" is equal to either force (remember they are equal) times the horizontal distance between them, or "righting arm."

It is possible, however, for these forces to capsize, rather than right, the boat. Figure 2 illustrates how an extreme angle of heel, a very narrow hull and/or a high center of gravity can cause such an unstable condition. Here the forces act to form a

Figure 1. When a boat heels, its center of buoyancy moves to leeward and forms a righting moment with the weight force.

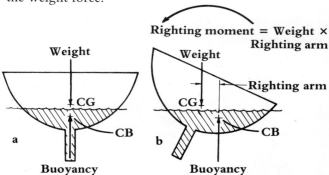

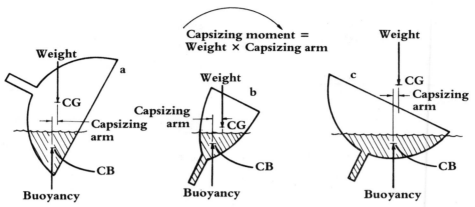

Figure 2. At extreme angles of heel (a), or with a very narrow hull (b), or with a high center of gravity (c), the forces of weight and buoyancy can result in a capsizing moment.

"capsizing moment" equal to either force multiplied by the horizontal distance between the forces, now called the "capsizing arm."

The beam and shape of the hull determine both the position of the center of buoyancy and the manner in which it shifts when the boat heels. The portion of the boat's stability contributed by the hull shape is called "form stability." The weight distribution in the boat, including the hull, ballast, deck rig and all other items on board, determines

the position of the center of gravity. The part of the total stability contributed by this factor is called "ballast stability." Together, form and ballast stability create a boat's "total stability."

Thus, one of the designer's challenges is to decide the right combination of form and ballast stability for the boat he is designing. As in every aspect of the design process, trade-offs exist. Stability must be balanced with considerations of speed, comfort, accommodation space, cost,

Figure 3. Form stability—A floating object relying entirely on form stability will show a maximum righting arm, and thus maximum stability, at an angle of heel of about 30°. Beyond this point righting arm decreases rapidly and becomes zero at 90°. At greater angles of heel a capsizing arm is formed and the vessel is unstable.

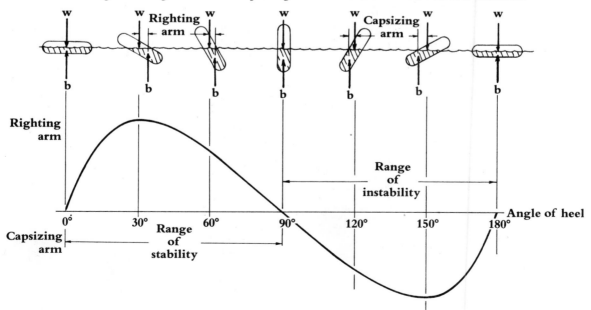

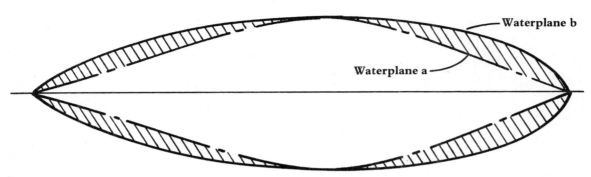

Figure 4. The greater waterplane area (shaded area) will give a boat with a full-ended waterplane (b) more form stability than a boat with a fine-ended waterplane (a).

strength and appearance. It's not just a question of how much weight, but where it is located. It's almost as hard for the sailor to look at a boat or lines plan and deduce the stability of the design.

FORM STABILITY

The characteristics of form stability are best exemplified by a flat-bottomed, unballasted vessel, such as the surfboard in Figure 3. If we heel the surfboard, we can determine the center of buoyancy as the center of underwater area, draw the forces of weight and buoyancy, and measure the arm between them. Since righting moment is equal to righting arm multiplied by displacement, we can plot the arms on a graph, as a function of the angle of heel. This is the same as plotting righting moment. So the graph of righting and capsizing arms at the bottom of Figure 3 is plotted on a

"stability curve" for the surfboard. It shows the righting arm is zero at 0° heel angle, increases to a maximum at about 30° heel, and returns to zero at about 90°. That is the surfboard's "range of stability," and explains why they are seen just as often capsized as right side up. If heeled beyond 90°, a surfboard is unstable and will not return to an upright position but will capsize instead. From 90° to 180° is its "range of instability," meaning it will remain capsized in that position.

Factors that enhance form stability are increased waterline beam and a high center of buoyancy. Distribution of beam as well as maximum waterline beam affects form stability. Figure 4 shows the waterplanes of two boats of equal beam and length. The fuller waterplane (b), with beam carried more into the ends than on the finer waterplane (a), is a more stable hull form.

A higher center of buoyancy shifts farther to the immersed side on heeling than a low center, as

Figure 5. When broad, shallow hull (a) heels, the center of buoyancy shifts farther to leeward than with narrower, deeper hull (b). The greater the shift in the center of buoyancy when heeled, the greater the form stability.

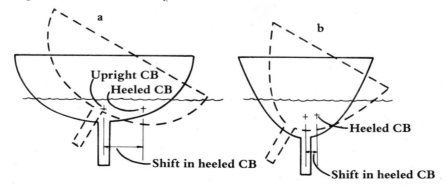

illustrated in Figure 5. When the broad, shallow hull (a) heels, its high center of buoyancy shifts farther to leeward than the center of buoyancy on the narrower, deeper hull (b). Thus it has greater form stability.

BALLAST STABILITY

To visualize the mechanics of ballast stability, picture a mooring pick-up buoy, a long stick with a lead weight at the bottom, a small float in the middle and a flag on top. The buoyancy of the stick and lead is negligible compared to that of the float, so we can consider the center of buoyancy to be fixed at the float. Thus the righting arm is simply the horizontal distance between the float and the center of gravity in the lead weight.

Figure 6 shows an analysis of the stability of the pick-up buoy. The righting arm, and thus the stability, increases very slowly at small angles of heel, then increases more rapidly to a maximum at 90° heel and diminishes to a value of zero at 180° heel. It is stable throughout all angles of heel, except at exactly 180° where it would remain inverted unless moved slightly to either side, when it would again become stable and return to the upright position.

Ballast stability increases for a given weight by lowering the center of gravity. Designers trying to increase ballast stability do so by increasing ballast and concentrating it as far down as possible. They also try to place heavy items on the boat, such as the engine, fuel and water tanks, as low as possible.

The center of gravity of most cruising boats is between the waterline and about 6″ above. Any weight that can be removed above this point or added below it will lower the center of gravity. An object's effect on the position of this center is a direct function of its vertical distance from it. A one-pound weight removed at the top of a mast, 40 feet from the center of gravity, lowers it as much as removing a 40-pound weight one foot above the center of gravity. A one-pound weight added at the bottom of a keel six feet from the center of gravity lowers it as much as a six-pound weight added one foot below it.

TOTAL STABILITY

A sailboat derives its overall stability from both form and ballast. Figure 7 compares the stability characteristics due to form and ballast. Except in extreme designs, the stability characteristics of a boat fall between the two, with the final stability

Figure 6. Ballast stability—A ballasted buoy exhibits pure ballast stability. Its righting arm, and thus its stability, increases slowly at small angle of heel, reaches a maximum at 90° and returns to zero at 180° of heel. It remains stable throughout the range of heel angles.

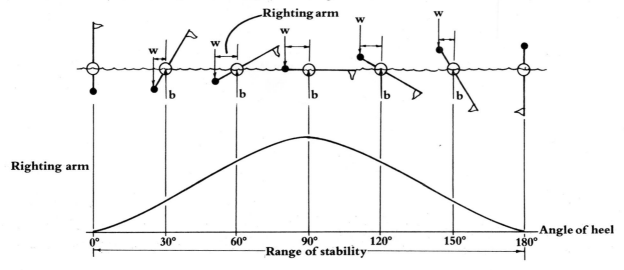

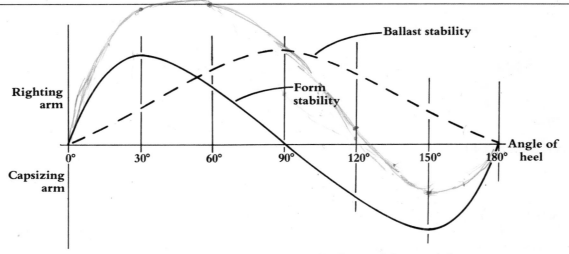

Figure 7. A comparison of the characteristic curves of ballast and form stability.

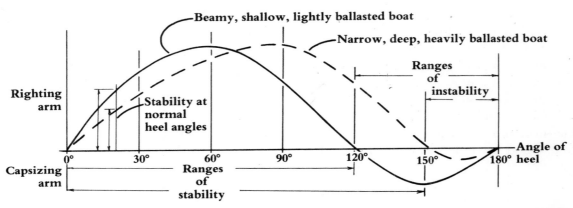

Figure 8. Typical stability curves for two different types of boat, showing the relative influences of form and ballast stability.

dependent upon the relative proportion of form to ballast stability. Figure 8 shows the stability curves of two sailboats. The beamy, shallow and lightly ballasted one more closely resembles the curve of form stability while the narrow, deep and heavily ballasted one shows the characteristics of the ballast stability curve.

In normal sailing conditions a sailboat seldom heels more than 25° or 30°. In this area of the stability curve the predominant factor is form stability. A boat relying too much on ballast stability would be less stable, or tender, at these small heel angles. The designer is able to calculate the stability of the boat for these angles of heel and use the results to determine the proper balance between sail area and stability, since another way to look at stability is the boat's ability to carry sail.

One method to calculate stability is to determine the amount of wind necessary to heel the boat to 20° and compare this with other boats of similar size. If the required wind velocity is higher, his design is more stable and he may choose to add sail area. If the required wind velocity is lower he may reduce sail area.

In another method the designer keeps wind speed constant and compares resulting angles of heel to determine how much sail can be carried.

In these calculations the heeling force of the sails is taken to act at their center of area, and the hull is assumed to rotate about its center of lateral area, as shown in Figure 9. These concepts will be discussed more in Chapter 7. The figure shows that a tall rig has a high center of area and a greater heeling force than a lower rig of equal area. The iden-

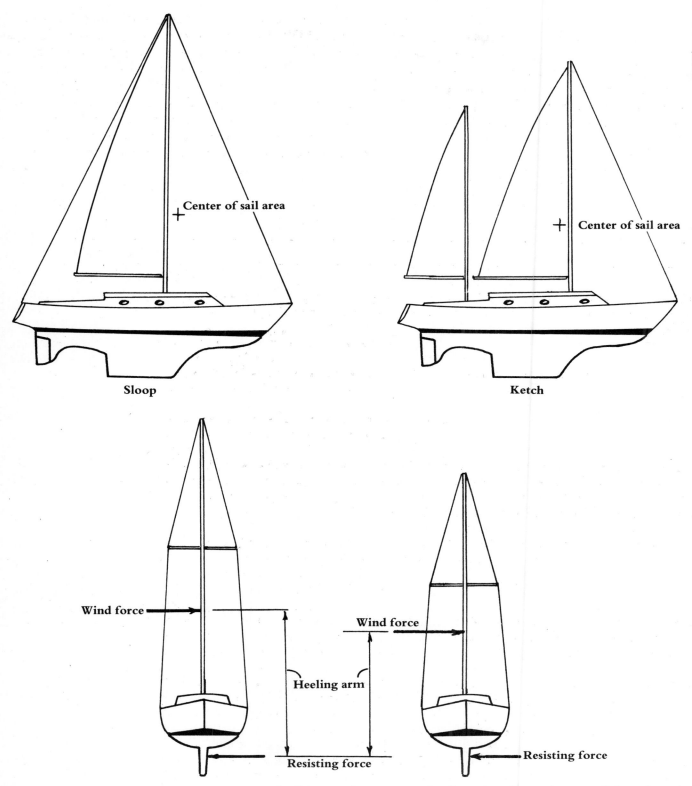

Figure 9. A tall sailplan has a higher center of sail area, and so a greater heeling arm, than a shorter sailplan of equal area.

tical hull may have low stability ("tender") as a sloop but have high stability ("stiff") as a ketch. The terms "tender" and "stiff" usually refer to a boat's stability characteristics at normal heeling angles.

Also of great concern—to the designer as well as the sailor—is the boat's stability at large angles of heel, from about 30° up to 180°. While a very strong wind can knock a boat down to 90° of heel, it usually takes the action of very large, breaking waves to heel it further. The stability of a boat beyond 90° heel, called "ultimate stability," is therefore only important for offshore cruising vessels, boats that might experience such extreme conditions. Such conditions are usually associated with ocean sailing in high latitudes but can be experienced in almost any area of open sea in extraordinary situations.

A beamy, shallow hull may be very stable in normal sailing conditions, but will lose stability quickly when heeled to 90° and become unstable if heeled much beyond that. Such a boat has poor ultimate stability. A narrow, deeper hull may be tender at normal sailing angles but may develop great stability at extreme angles of heel and show positive stability nearly up to 180° heel.

At the most extreme angles of heel, form stability is actually acting against ballast stability, tending to capsize the boat while the ballast stability is still trying to right it. So, in some conditions, the factors that contribute to form stability actually detract from ultimate stability, while the factors that enhance ballast stability enhance ultimate stability.

It is a lengthy, time-consuming calculation for the designer to determine the precise values of ultimate stability. When the boat is heeled to the point that the deck and cabin are immersed, the buoyancy characteristics of those parts become significant and must be considered. It's conducive to ultimate stability to move the center of buoyancy upward toward the deck but also to keep it as close as possible to the boat's centerline. Figure 10 shows that in a boat with high freeboard or raised deck, the center of buoyancy remains closer to the centerline than in a boat with low freeboard. In this position, it still forms a righting moment with the weight of the boat and so the boat is stable. In the lower boat, however, the center of

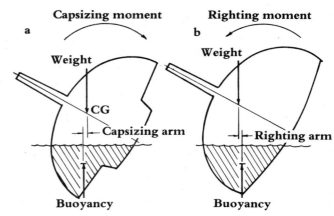

Figure 10. These two hull shapes are identical except that (b) has the side decks raised to be flush with the cabin top. Shown at an angle of heel of 120°, (a) is unstable while (b) is still stable because the buoyancy of the raised deck causes the heeled boat to float higher and moves the center of buoyancy to the right.

buoyancy is farther outboard and lower in the hull, forming a capsizing moment and making the boat unstable.

Throughout this discussion of stability, it's been assumed that the positions of all weights on a boat, and thus its center of gravity, remain fixed. This is not always the case, however. On small boats in particular the crew is shifted to move the center of gravity and thus to enhance stability. Figure 11 shows how placing crew on the windward side of the boat moves the center of gravity in that direction and helps increase stability. The greater the crew weight in comparison to the weight of the boat, the more significant the effect of crew place-

Figure 11. The effect of crew or water ballast placed to windward is to shift the center of gravity of the boat in that direction, thereby increasing the righting arm and the righting moment.

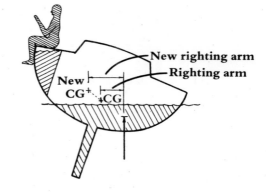

ment. The smaller and lighter and less stable the boat the more it can benefit from this movable ballast. Most sailboat racing prohibits the shifting of any weight, except crew, to increase stability. Where it is not prohibited, as in many single-handed races, competitors have installed tanks at the extreme sides of the hull to use water as ballast —achieving the same result as having crew sitting on the windward side. Philippe Jeantot demonstrated the value of such an arrangement in sailing his *Credit Agricole* to victory in the 1982-83 BOC singlehanded round-the-world race, in record time.

Achieving maximum possible stability is not the design goal of most normal cruising boats. The designer must also consider the motion of the boat. An extremely stable boat will have a quick rolling motion, and a very light boat will be tossed about to a great extent by waves. Both characteristics can cause extreme discomfort to the crew aboard.

Most boat designers agree that a boat's motion comfort is determined by how it is accelerated by waves—how quickly it is tossed about. A basic law of physics states that force is equal to mass (or weight) times acceleration. In the case of the sailboat, the weight is its displacement, and the force is the power of waves acting on the hull.

Naval architect Ted Brewer, several of whose designs appear in the design section, has derived a formula to approximate the speed at which a boat will be accelerated by waves. He considers both the vertical heaving motion and the rolling motion that a boat will experience in waves. Brewer deduced that since motion comfort is inversely proportional to acceleration, it is proportional to weight divided by force. Heaving force is a function of the waterline area, which Brewer approximates from the beam, length overall and waterline length, since the actual waterline area when sailing in waves is greater than the waterline area at rest. The heeling force that waves exert on the hull is a function of beam, and Brewer introduces a beam factor to approximate this. His formula is shown in the footnote.

Brewer's Motion Comfort Ratio[1] shows that increased displacement increases motion comfort

and that increased beam reduces it. It would appear that increased length also reduces motion comfort, but because displacement increases at a greater rate than length, longer boats generally offer increased motion comfort. We'll discuss motion comfort and other comfort factors in Chapter 6. But it's important to understand comfort considerations now as one of the critical factors the designer faces in considering stability in a cruising boat he is designing.

For most cruising and sailing in protected waters, a boat that relies more on form stability than ballast stability is superior. It is quite unlikely that survival conditions will be encountered, so the boat does not need exceptional ultimate stability. It can be beamy and light and have excellent stability characteristics in any normal sailing conditions, which can include strong winds but not large and breaking waves. Beaminess results in a spacious interior for the large crew likely to be aboard. Light weight can make the boat lively and exciting to sail, and inexpensive to build. Since the boat need not be designed to withstand capsizes or other severe situations, achieving the required strength with the light weight is not a problem. The draft of a boat that does not rely heavily on ballast stability can be reduced, a great asset in a coastal cruiser because it increases the number of suitable cruising areas.

The comfort to be expected aboard such a boat in rough conditions is not great; a coastal cruiser is likely to experience such conditions rarely, if ever. As in every other aspect of cruising boat design, judgments and sacrifices must be made.

A boat designed for offshore voyaging, on the other hand, should have more ballast stability and less form stability than a coastal cruiser. It must be designed to survive large breaking waves, knockdowns and capsizes. It requires, therefore, greater ultimate stability than the coastal cruising boat. Narrower beams, greater draft and increased displacement all contribute to ultimate stability. Accommodation space will be reduced but can be compensated for by the increased volume of the greater displacement, and by features such as increased freeboard or a flush deck, which also enhance ultimate stability.

Heavier displacement permits heavier and stronger construction, and makes it possible to

[1]Motion comfort ratio $= \dfrac{\text{Displacement (pounds)}}{.65 \times (.7\ \text{LWL} + .3\ \text{LOA}) \times \text{beam}^{1.33}}$

carry all the heavy supplies and equipment necessary for voyaging. Deep draft, which increases ballast stability and results in a deep bilge for storage, is not as serious a handicap to the offshore sailor as it is to the coastal sailor.

Sail area also can be reduced on heavily ballasted boats, increasing stability at normal sailing angles where the loss of form stability is most felt. Performance and windward ability are sacrificed, but offshore sailors in general are less interested in sparkling performance than coastal cruisers. To the offshore sailor, a comfortable and easy-to-sail boat is quite important, since he or she is likely to spend more time sailing in rough conditions.

The following table summarizes for the cruising sailor the effects of various design factors on stability.

STABILITY

factor	effect	significance
Beam	**Narrow beam** causes low form stability and thus low stability in normal sailing conditions.	Narrow boats can be uncomfortable because they will heel substantially even in moderate winds.
	Wide beam increases form stability but reduces ultimate stability.	
	Narrow-to-moderate beam results in a good compromise between form and ballast stability.	Good offshore cruising boat.
	Moderate-to-wide beam enhances initial stability but detracts from ultimate stability.	Good coastal cruiser.
	Extremely wide beam, results in high initial form stability that is lost at high angles of heel.	Wide beam combined with light displacement can cause uncomfortable sailing characteristics and a dangerous lack of stability and such boats are suitable only in moderate conditions where speed or interior volume are most important.
Draft	**Shallow draft,** if combined with moderate beam, can produce a boat with good initial and adequate ultimate stability. Increased draft increases ballast stability.	A good coastal cruiser for areas where shallow draft is important.
	Moderate draft combined with narrow beam results in a boat with adequate initial and ultimate stability and good performance potential.	This type of boat is suitable to coastal or offshore sailing in areas where severe weather is likely, and performance is more important than comfort.
	Moderate-to-deep draft combined with moderate-to-wide beam results in a boat with a good balance of initial and ultimate stability, performance and comfort.	Many coastal cruising boats and most offshore boats fall in this category. The variety of combinations of beam and draft is great.
Ballast	**Minimum** ballast combines with moderate-to-wide beam for good initial but poor ultimate stability. Performance potential is great.	High-performance boats used for racing or thrilling cruising, with substantial crew usually needed.

STABILITY

factor	effect	significance
	Moderate ballast in a hull of moderate proportions leads to good overall stability and comfort characteristics. Moderate ballast in a wider hull will sacrifice some ultimate stability but should have good performance and comfort.	Good offshore cruising boat. Suitable to coastal cruising.
	Heavy ballast may be necessary in a beamy boat to achieve adequate ultimate stability but performance and comfort may suffer.	Extremely heavy and beamy boats may be safe, but are quite slow.
Displacement	Increased displacement, in general, increases stability and comfort but decreases performance. Increasing the displacement of a boat beyond its designed displacement by raising its center of gravity through adding equipment and stores, can make it dangerously unstable.	Boats loaded down for coastal or offshore sailing should be designed for moderate to heavy displacement. Overloading any boat beyond its designed displacement should be avoided.
Sail Area	Sail area must be balanced against the stability of the boat and the level of performance desired.	
	A boat with a **large or tall sail area** for its stability will show high performance especially in light air, but will require crew weight for stability in a fresh breeze and frequent sail changes.	Can be acceptable for coastal cruising with a large and enthusiastic crew, where speed is desired.
	A boat with a **moderate sail area** in relation to its stability will be easy to handle and will perform well.	Suitable for most coastal cruisers and some offshore cruisers.
	Small sail area will reduce performance but increase comfort and handling ease.	Especially suited to shorthanded offshore cruising where speed is not critical.

Chapter

4

SPEED AND RESISTANCE EXPLAINED

Understanding the limits

UNTIL NOW, the discussion has focused on the basic mechanics of cruising boat design: why a boat floats, what makes it stable, and how a naval architect takes the largest issues of his design challenge and begins refining his plans to satisfy the demands of his client.

The next issue, then, is performance. How fast will the boat be? In what sorts of conditions? We'll take a look at the handling characteristics inherent in various cruising boat design features in the next chapter. Right now, let's look at how hulls are designed to move through water as efficiently as possible, to maximize speed by minimizing resistance.

When a boat moves through the water, its motion is resisted by the water. Picture a sailboat being towed by a tug, with a scale placed in the towline (Figure 1). At any towing speed the scale will show the force required to move the boat through the water at that speed. Another way to interpret the scale reading is that it measures hull resistance.

Resistance increases with speed. The faster the sailboat is towed the more force is required from the tug and the greater the scale reading. If the sailboat is towed at a variety of speeds, with the scale reading recorded for each, the results can be plotted graphically as in Figure 2. This is called the "resistance curve" and it shows the resistance of the hull at any speed. For instance, at two knots the resistance is equal to about 80 pounds; at four

Figure 1. The resistance of a boat at any speed is determined by measuring the force required to tow it at that speed.

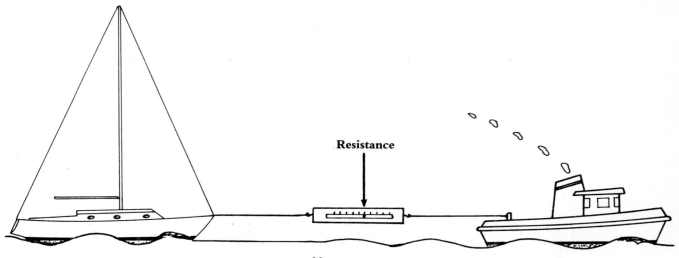

Resistance

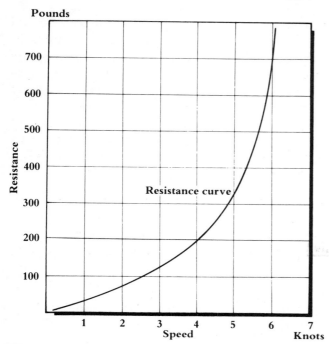

Figure 2. If a boat is towed at various speeds and the resistance at each speed is plotted on a graph, the line connecting the points is the resistance curve for that boat. It shows how much force or power is required to move the boat through the water at any given speed.

knots it is 200 pounds and at six knots 700 pounds. Notice that above a speed of six knots, the curve becomes nearly vertical; for any small increase in speed the increase in force required is very great. This is a sort of speed barrier, the maximum speed at which the hull can travel in all but extraordinary conditions.

Most sailors are familiar with this speed limit, often called "hull speed." They know it is related to the length of the boat, that longer boats have greater maximum hull speeds than shorter boats. But, comparing the speed at which two boats of different sizes sail, even in identical conditions, does not indicate the relative levels of performance of the two boats. Suppose a 30-foot boat and a 50-foot boat are sailing together, and the 30-footer is making five knots and the 50-footer seven knots. Which is performing better?

To study the characteristics of speed and resistance of cruising sailboats we must be able to eliminate the factor of length and thus be able to make significant comparisons between boats of any size.

To accomplish this, boat designers use the "speed/length ratio." Understanding this concept is absolutely essential to knowing why some boats sail well and others do not.

Speed/length ratio is just another way to say how fast a boat is moving. It is the speed (in knots) divided by the square root of the waterline length (in feet). You could cover up the numbers on the face of a boat's speedometer and replace each knot figure by that number divided by the square root of the waterline length. In the case of a boat with a 25-foot waterline (the square root of 25 is 5), a speed of three knots is a speed/length of 3/5, or 0.6. A speed of five knots is a ratio of 5/5, or 1.0, and a speed of seven knots a ratio of 7/5, or 1.4.

In Figure 3, the resistance curve of the 25-foot sailboat (boat A) of Figure 2 is plotted using a speed/length ratio scale in place of speed. Just as the conversion from speed to speed/length ratio eliminates the factor of size, the value of resistance can be divided by the displacement of the boat to make a non-dimensional ratio which is independent of boat size. With these modifications the resistance curve now represents a boat with the

Figure 3. A comparison of the resistance curves of two boats plotted on the basis of speed/length ratio and resistance/displacement.

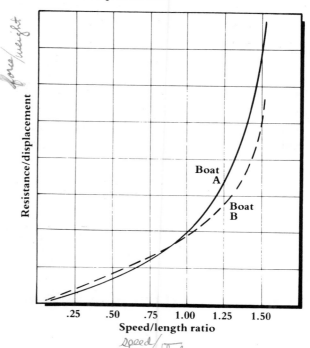

proportions of the 25-footer but of any length. It could be 125 feet long!

A second dotted line also is shown in Figure 3. This is the resistance curve for another boat (boat B) of different proportions than boat A but also of any size.

What does a comparison of these two resistance curves reveal? At lower speeds (speed/length ratio below 0.75) boat A requires less force to reach these speeds than boat B. In the lower speed range (in light winds or at low engine throttle) it is a higher performance hull. Above speed/length ratio of 0.75, boat A has a greater resistance, meaning it requires more driving force. It shows a lower level of performance at high speeds.

Note also that both boats reach maximum hull speed at nearly the same place on the graph (where the curve becomes nearly vertical). It occurs at a ratio of about 1.50. You'll see in the subsequent discussion of resistance why 1.50 is the maximum speed/length ratio a sailboat can achieve in ordinary conditions. But for now just remember that in any particular sailing situation, the closer a boat's speed/length ratio is to a value of 1.50, the higher its level of performance.

Now let's proceed to a more detailed discussion of the types of resistance and the factors that influence them. Resistance has two basic components, called frictional resistance and wave-making resistance.

FRICTIONAL RESISTANCE

Frictional resistance is due to the friction of the water flow along the hull surface. It increases with increased speed, and at any speed it is determined by the surface area of the hull in contact with the water and the roughness of that surface. Surprisingly, it has very little to do with the actual shape of the hull except where shape determines the amount of surface area.

Surface smoothness is mostly a matter of maintenance. A heavily fouled hull adds enormously to the frictional resistance. Even small areas of roughness, such as cracked or peeling paint, can have a significant effect. This is why racing sailors spend so much time painting and scrubbing the bottoms of their hulls before races.

The amount of hull area in contact with the water, called "wetted surface," is determined by the design. The naval architect can calculate the exact amount of wetted surface on a design by measuring the girth at each station, the actual length of the outline at the station below the waterline on the body plan. A hull with high girth measurements at its stations will have a high value of wetted surface, and so a high frictional resistance.

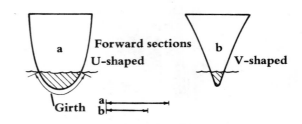

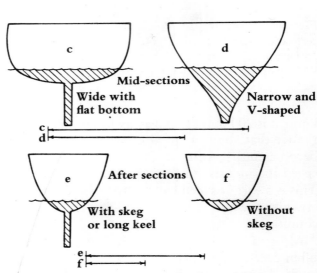

Figure 4. A comparison of the girths of various hull sections.

What factors affect girth and wetted surface? Mainly, they are the length and beam of the hull and the length and depth of the keel. Any feature that increases the girth measurement at any station increases wetted surface. Figure 4 compares six hull sections and their associated girth measurements, showing the effect of section shape on wetted surface.

WAVE-MAKING RESISTANCE

Wave-making resistance, as the name implies, is due to the waves produced by the hull as it moves through the water. Just like sound and light waves, waves in water are a form of energy transmission.

As the sailboat hull moves through the water, it pushes the water aside at the bow and draws it back together again at the stern. This action produces waves. Work, or energy, is required to produce these waves, and this work is imparted on the water by the hull. The law of conservation of energy states that energy is neither created nor destroyed, but can be transformed from one form to another. So where does the energy come from to produce these waves? From the force of the engine or the wind on the sails, whichever is providing the driving force to the hull. A portion of this energy is transformed into the waves emanating from the hull. Another basic law of physics is that the energy required to produce a wave is proportional to the square of its height.

Two other basic properties of waves need to be understood at this point. One is that the speed at which a wave travels in water is related to its wave length, the distance from one crest to the next. Theory predicts and observation confirms that the speed of a wave in knots is equal to 1.34 times the square root of the wave length in feet:

$$\text{Wave speed} = 1.34 \times \sqrt{\text{wave length}}$$
knots   *feet*

The other important characteristic is that when two or more waves meet, the resulting wave is the total of the contributing waves. Crests add to form higher crests; troughs combine to make deeper troughs; a crest and a trough subtract from each other. At any point, the height of the resulting wave is the sum or difference of the heights of the contributing waves, as shown in Figure 5.

Now let's look at a boat's wave, or wake, pattern as it moves through the water. Figure 6 shows the wake pattern consists of two major wave systems, one from the bow and one from a point just aft of the midship section, where the hull starts to taper in. Each of these systems consists of two sets of waves, one diverging from the hull with its

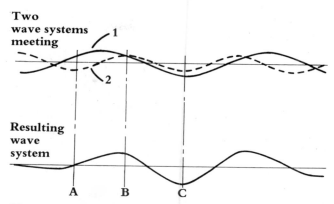

Figure 5. When two wave systems (1 and 2) meet each other, the resulting wave system (3) is the total, or combination of the two. Wave heights above or below the still waterline are added or subtracted to form the new wave system. At A, a crest and a trough cancel each other. At B, two crests combine to form a higher crest. At C, two troughs combine to form a deeper trough.

crests at an angle to the hull, and one moving along with the hull with its crests perpendicular to the hull. The four wave sets are called the diverging bow wave, the transverse bow wave, the diverging stern wave and the transverse stern wave.

In general, the two bow waves are higher than the two stern waves, and the height of the waves increases as the square of the speed. At twice the speed, wave height will be four times as great and the energy required is 16 times greater. The total amount of energy required is equal to the hull's wave-making resistance.

The transverse wave systems are the ones that appear as a series of crests and troughs along the boat's waterline. These waves move with the hull, at the same speed as the hull, and so for any constant speed the positions of the crests and troughs of the transverse bow waves are stationary along the hull. Wave speed equals boat speed, and so can be substituted in the equation previously stated:

$$\text{Boat speed} = 1.34 \times \sqrt{\text{Wave length}}$$

This is true for any boat, of any size. If you could measure the length of the transverse bow wave you could calculate the boat's exact speed.

There is a very interesting and significant relationship between boat speed, waterline length and the number of transverse waves that occur along

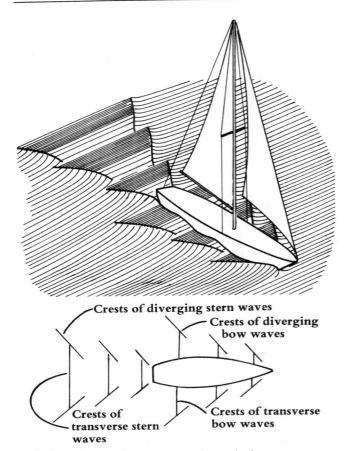

Figure 6. A boat hull moving through the water produces four sets of waves, transverse and diverging waves from the bow, and transverse and diverging waves from the stern.

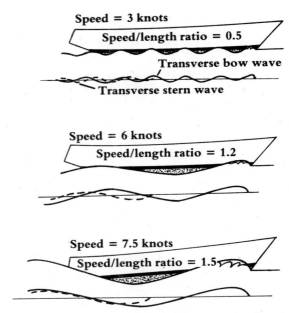

Figure 7. As a boat with a waterline length of 25 feet approaches a speed of 7.5 knots, or a speed/length ratio of 1.5, the bow and stern transverse waves coincide and cause a very deep trough aft of amidships and a high crest astern. The loss of buoyancy aft causes the boat to "squat" at the stern.

the waterline of a boat. If N is the number of waves, then:

$$\frac{\text{Boat speed}}{\sqrt{\text{waterline length}}} = \frac{1.34}{N}$$

The fraction should look familiar; it is the speed/length ratio. So, speed/length ratio = 1.34/N.

Two boats of any size, traveling at the same speed/length ratio, will show the same number of transverse wave crests along their waterline and, as I will show, the same characteristic of wave-making resistance.

Now, let me get back to the discussion of wave-making resistance and illustrate its relation to speed/length ratio. Figure 7 shows a boat with a waterline length of 25 feet. At three knots, or a speed/length ratio of 0.6, the wave length equals five feet and five transverse bow waves appear

along the length of the boat (N = 5). The transverse stern wave, which starts as a trough where the hull starts to taper in to the stern, is shown as a dotted line. It has the same length but lesser height compared to the bow transverse wave. The total of the two is shown on the hull.

At six knots, or a speed/length ratio of 1.2, the transverse bow and stern waves are longer (20 feet) and higher, N = 1.5. Also the stern wave is out of phase with the bow wave and so adds to it at some points and subtracts at others.

At seven-and-a-half knots, a speed/length ratio of 1.5, the waves are 31 feet long (N = 0.8), and coincide, creating a very deep trough aft of amidships, and a corresponding loss of buoyancy in this area. The center of buoyancy shifts forward, so the stern "squats" down.

In this squatted position, hull resistance increases dramatically and an enormous amount of force is required to increase speed. The boat has literally dug a deep hole for itself. It has reached its maximum displacement hull speed.

The significance of speed/length ratio is that

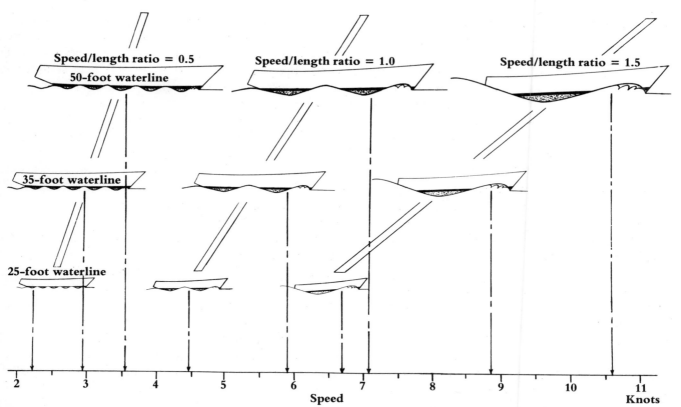

Figure 8. Shown are three boats, with waterline lengths of 20, 35 and 50 feet. Each is shown moving at three speeds corresponding to speed/length ratios of 0.5, 1.0 and 1.5. Notice that the pattern of transverse waves is the same for all three boats at any particular ratio. Dotted lines show the true speed in knots.

whatever the size of the boat, this pattern of transverse waves, and thus the maximum displacement hull speed, will always occur at a speed/length ratio of about 1.5 where the length of the transverse wave exceeds the waterline length and N goes below 1.0. Figure 8 illustrates the relationship between boat size, boat speed, and speed/length ratio.

PLANING

There are, however, situations in which boats can exceed their maximum displacement hull speed and a speed/length ratio of 1.5. To do this they must stop behaving as displacement hulls and start showing the characteristics of planing hulls. The difference is that a planing hull, such as a high-speed powerboat, develops hydrodynamic lift from moving through the water at high speed.

This lift, acting upward on the hull, takes the place of the support provided by buoyancy and lifts the hull up so that it is skimming over the surface of the water.

Figure 9 shows how a sailboat makes the transition from displacement to planing hull. In 9A it is at its maximum displacement hull speed, at a speed/length ratio of 1.5. Some lightweight and specially designed sailboats are able to exceed this speed by generating dynamic lift and rising on the back of that first transverse wave crest, as in 9B. Here the boat is in a semi-planing condition. The stern is still squatted down but the bow is lifted up out of the water. The boat is supported by a combination of buoyancy and dynamic lift. This occurs in the range of speed/length ratios between 1.5 and 3.0, corresponding to speeds of 7.5 to 15 knots for a boat with a 25-foot waterline.

Very few boats are able to reach the full planing condition shown in 9C, where dynamic lift raises

Figure 9.

A — Maximum displacement hull speed — Buoyancy — Speed/length ratio = 1.5

B — Semi-planing — Buoyancy — Dynamic lift — Speed/length ratio between 1.5 and 3.0

C — Planing — Dynamic lift — Speed/length ratio greater than 3.0

D — Surfing — Can be either semi-planing or planing — Dynamic lift

the boat up to the water surface and replaces buoyancy as the supporting force. Here the speed/length ratio exceeds 3.0, or 15 knots for the 25-foot boat. Achieving this condition requires a boat of extraordinary design and ideal sailing conditions.

However, sailboats of more ordinary design can enter the semi-planing condition by surfing as shown in 9D. In surfing, the slope of an ocean wave raises the stern of the boat from its squatted position at displacement hull speed, dramatically reducing its resistance. This, along with the added gravitational force of the boat sliding down the wave slope, allows boats otherwise incapable of planing or semi-planing to reach these conditions.

Classic surfing conditions are found in the Roaring Forties of the southern Indian and Pacific oceans where boats sailing eastward have the prevailing strong westerly winds and large seas to push them to great speeds. Boats sailing in this area reach speeds in excess of 20 or 25 knots (speed/length ratios in excess of 3.0 for even a 50-foot boat), and can average speeds of about half that.

While high-speed sailing is both exciting and essential to the racing sailor, it is often undesirable for the cruising sailor. At these high speeds a boat can become very difficult to steer. Few self-steering gears are able to safely steer a boat in planing conditions.

To get a better picture of the interplay of friction resistance, wave-making resistance and planing, let's redraw Figure 3 (the resistance curve) with a few changes. In Figure 10, an important addition is the line marked "frictional resistance." At any speed/length ratio, the vertical distance up to the frictional resistance curve is the amount of frictional resistance, and the distance from that point up to the total resistance curve is the boat's wave-making resistance.

You can see that in the lower speed range resistance is mostly due to friction. At a speed/length ratio of 0.4, total resistance is about 90 percent frictional. At a ratio of about 1.0 that percentage is about 50 percent; resistance is made up of equal parts due to friction and wave-making. Above that point, the wave-making resistance increases dramatically and becomes the predominant speed-limiting factor.

The resistance curve for a normal displacement

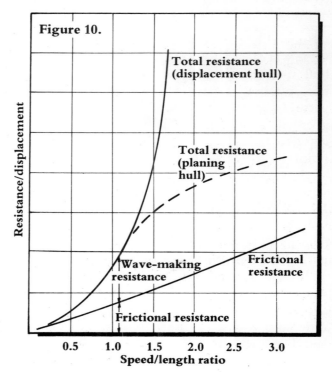

Figure 10.

Total resistance (displacement hull)

Total resistance (planing hull)

Wave-making resistance

Frictional resistance

Frictional resistance

Resistance/displacement

0.5 1.0 1.5 2.0 2.5 3.0

Speed/length ratio

hull, shown by the solid line, becomes so steep at a speed/length ratio of 1.5 that this becomes the hull's speed barrier. A boat capable of planing or semi-planing, shown in the dotted line, has a shallower resistance curve. Such a boat is less restricted by its wave-making resistance.

These are only typical curves. Every boat has its own distinct resistance curve determined by its own characteristics. A boat with minimal wetted surface, and so minimal frictional resistance (narrow beam with fine ends and a small keel) will be very fast in the lower speed ranges, in light winds. The ratio of sail area/wetted surface is an excellent indicator of speed potential at these speeds. The higher the value, the higher the speed potential in light air.

In the speed range from ratios of 1.0 to 1.5, where wave-making resistance becomes all-important, fuller ends and a higher prismatic coefficient (as defined on page 14), are called for. Displacement also is important; the lighter the displacement the smaller the size of the waves and the lower the value of wave-making resistance. A light displacement boat will usually reach its maximum displacement hull speed sooner, in lighter winds, than a heavier boat. There is a factor, similar to sail area/wetted surface ratio, that predicts a boat's speed potential at these higher speeds. The ratio is expressed as sail area/displacement$^{2/3}$. This is a non-dimensional ratio by which boats of any size can be compared.

There also are factors that affect the exact value of the maximum displacement hull speed. Any feature that can delay the point at which the bow and stern transverse waves coincide, thus reducing the squatting of the stern, will increase the boat's maximum speed.

Long hull overhangs, especially at the stern, increase the boat's effective waterline length (called "sailing length") while it is heeled and under way. This, in effect, increases the boat's length and thus the speed at which the speed/length ratio equals 1.5. Figure 11 shows two hulls of equal waterline length, one with short overhangs and one with long overhangs. Heeled and under way, the hull with long overhangs has a significantly longer waterline length.

The long stern overhang also provides what is

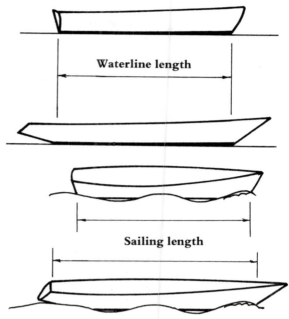

Figure 11. A boat with long overhangs, when heeled and underway, has an effectively longer sailing length than a boat with short overhangs.

called "reserve buoyancy." When the hull loses buoyancy support aft as it nears its maximum speed, the stern overhang becomes immersed, adds buoyancy and thereby reduces the amount of squat.

Another way to increase maximum displacement hull speed is to move the transverse stern wave aft. Since the stern waves originate where the hull starts tapering from its midship section toward the stern, if this section is moved aft, the stern waves' point of origin moves with it. Figure 12 shows that by moving the stern transverse wave aft, the length of transverse wave at which coincidence will occur is increased and so, too, the speed at which it will occur. Broad and flat stern sections also depress the stern transverse wave and add buoyancy as the stern starts to sink, forestalling wave coincidence and reducing squat.

A good indication of a stern's ability to reduce the size of the stern transverse wave and move it aft are the buttock lines aft. If they are straight or nearly straight near the transom, and make a fine angle with the waterline, they tend to accomplish both these objectives. If, however, they are quite rounded and hit the waterline at a large angle, they

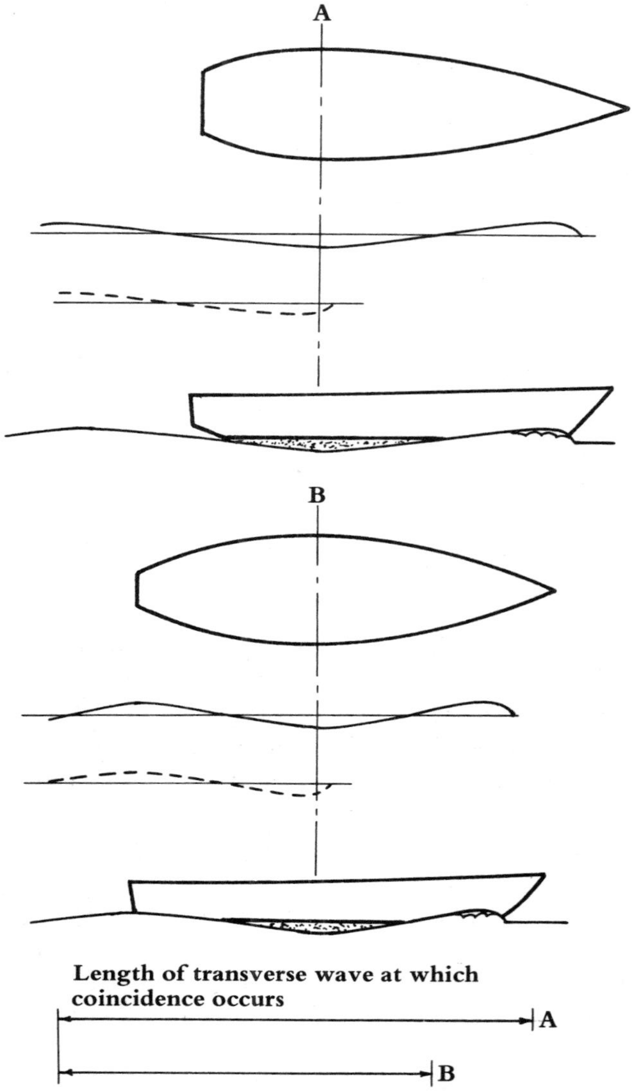

A

B

Length of transverse wave at which coincidence occurs

A

B

Figure 12. A boat with its maximum beam located far aft (A) will have its transverse stern wave also located far aft, and the length of transverse wave at which the bow and stern waves coincide is greater. The greater wave length is associated with a greater speed.

tend to raise a high stern wave just behind the boat. The water flow at the stern tends to follow the buttock lines (See Figure 13).

It is, however, difficult to achieve the straight, shallow buttock lines with a reasonably high prismatic coefficient. High C_p implies hull volume, or displacement, spread into the ends of the boat. One way to place volume in the stern while retaining the fine buttocks is with a wide stern, but then

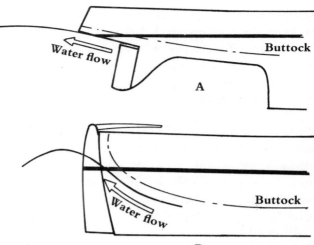

Figure 13. The flow of water at the stern of a boat tends to follow the direction of the buttock lines. The straight buttock in A, making a fine angle with the waterline, tends to flatten the stern wave and move it aft. The curved, more vertical buttock in B causes a steeper wave closer to the stern.

this increases wetted surface. It's just another example of the ever-present conflicts inherent in boat design.

When the lines plan, and so the buttock lines, are not presented with the design, you must use a little intuition to get an idea of their characteristics. Look at the line marking the shape of the hull (without skeg or rudder) near the stern, and the shape of the transom. If you do this on designs where the buttock lines are shown and see the correspondence between the shape of the stern and the shape of the buttocks, you soon will be able to make a fair guess at the buttocks even when they are not shown.

The naval architect must decide early in the design process what speed characteristics he desires and try to balance hull shape, displacement and prismatic coefficient to achieve this. Still, there are a few more types of resistance that must be considered.

The discussion of resistance so far has assumed a boat sailing in flat water, which is hardly ever the case. When a boat is sailing in waves, especially when sailing to windward, there is added resistance due to waves encountered. The magnitude of this resistance depends upon the height and wave length of the waves encountered, plus the behavior of the boat in these waves.

A boat with a sharp bow and fine entry angle at the waterline will tend to cut through the waves more easily than a boat with a bluff bow. But such a boat may also lack the reserve buoyancy necessary to prevent the bow from plunging deeply into a wave, slowing the boat and allowing water on deck. Any weights located in the bow, such as anchors or anchor chain, increase the boat's tendency to pitch excessively, and must be compensated for with full sections forward to provide the reserve buoyancy to resist this pitching. Such full sections, however, add resistance in waves.

Air resistance also is a matter of consideration, especially when sailing to windward. Low, streamlined hulls and cabins are the least affected by air resistance. But such boats also are less buoyant and have less interior volume. Dodgers or pilothouses, which are of great value to the cruising sailor, produce high wind resistance. Large mast sections, heavy rigging, radar and radar reflectors also increase air resistance.

Other contributors to overall resistance are induced drag and eddy-making. Induced drag is the added resistance due to the fact that when the boat is sailing to windward, its actual course differs from the direction in which it is pointing by an angle called the yaw angle. (See Figure 14.) The greater the yaw angle the greater the induced drag. The angle of heel also contributes to induced drag.

Eddy-making resistance is caused by appendages to the hull, such as a propeller and shaft. Discontinuities, such as the propeller aperture or any sharp edges or non-streamlined features, also cause eddies in the water flowing by them. Most of these can be reduced to a minimum by careful design and construction.

Before proceeding to a comparison of some designs in terms of their speed and resistance characteristics, it should be noted that the value of displacement quoted by some designers or builders may be what is called "light ship," which is the weight of the boat without crew, fuel, water or personal effects. They do this to make the design seem lightweight, and so have higher performance. The actual sailing displacement may be as much as 10 to 15 percent greater.

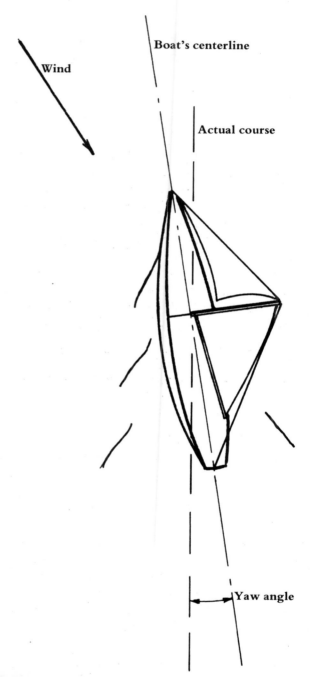

Figure 14. Induced drag is a function of yaw angle, the angle between the actual course and the direction in which the boat is pointing.

Also, in the U.S. sail area is usually calculated using the area of the foretriangle (the triangle formed by the mast, the forestay and the foredeck), whereas in some other countries the actual area of the largest headsail is used instead. This can be checked by looking on the sail plan. Caution must be used, however, when comparing the characteristic numbers and ratios for different boats.

SUMMARY

	FARR 48	PATRICE 49	VANCOUVER 50
LOA	48'4"	49'0"	50'0"
LWL	38'10"	37'6"	37'1"
BEAM	13'11"	12'0"	15'6"
DRAFT	8'0"	6'0"	4'7"
DISPL. (lbs.)	20,111	23,000	40,630
SA (sq. ft.)	1,130	1,073	1,246
WETTED SURFACE (sq. ft.)	412	437	486
DISP/L RATIO	152	195	356
SA/DISP. R	24.5	21.0	16.2
SA/WS	2.74	2.45	2.56

These three designs illustrate the way in which various naval architects deal with the factors that affect resistance, and show how boats intended for different types of cruising have widely varying speed and resistance characteristics. They are the 48-foot sloop designed by Bruce Farr (page 212), the 49-foot *Patrice* by Paul R. Kotzbue (page 214) and the Vancouver 50 by Robert Harris (page 218).

The Farr 48 was designed for racing and fast cruising, plus daysailing with a large crew, while *Patrice* was designed as a coastal cruiser with high performance potential. The Vancouver 50, on the other hand, is intended as a liveaboard, go-anywhere offshore voyaging boat.

Patrice and the Farr 48 have very similar displacement and sail areas, but quite different hull shape. The Farr 48 is almost two feet wider, has its maximum beam much further aft and shows a very broad transom. The Vancouver 50 weighs nearly twice as much as the other two boats and is

17 inches wider than the Farr, yet has a narrow, double-ended stern. The great displacement is not a choice by the designer but is necessitated by the type of boat. It must be massively strong and carry enormous amounts of water, fuel, food and other equipment.

Even with its much greater beam, the Farr 48's very small keel and absence of skeg results in the lowest wetted surface of the three. *Patrice*, with narrow sections but a long fin keel, has slightly more. The Vancouver 50, with its long, full keel and wide beam has significantly more wetted surface than the others without considering the added wetted surface of the centerboards.

Below a speed/length ratio of about 0.6 (about three-and-a-half knots for these boats), where resistance is primarily frictional, the ratio of sail area/wetted surface (SA/WS in summary table) is the best indicator of speed potential. Here the Farr 48 has the highest value, with the Vancouver 50 surprisingly second; *Patrice* is third. In these light conditions the heavy voyaging boat would, on some point of sail, be able to sail faster than *Patrice*. Without an understanding of the factors involved in resistance, this seeming contradiction would have been difficult to explain.

At speed-length ratios up to about 1.4 (about eight knots), where wave-making resistance becomes predominant, the displacement/length and sail area/displacement ratios are most significant. The displacement/length ratio indicates the ease with which the hull can be driven, and the sail area/displacement ratio the amount of driving force available in relation to the displacement.

Here the Farr 48 clearly shows greater performance potential, with *Patrice* second and the Vancouver 50 third. The Farr 48 will reach its maximum displacement hull speed in lighter winds.

At the top end of the displacement speed range, the difference in the maximum speed attainable is determined by the hull's ability to depress and move the stern transverse wave aft, increasing the boat's sailing length and postponing the coincidence of the bow and stern transverse waves.

The Farr 48's long and low stern overhang, with nearly straight buttock lines at a fine angle to the waterline will have a higher maximum displacement hull speed than the other two boats. *Patrice* also has a long stern overhang and similar buttocks, but the stern is quite narrow and will be less effective than the Farr stern in this area. *Patrice*'s stern will, however, result in better handling characteristics in certain conditions, as we'll discuss in the following chapter.

The Vancouver 50, with its pointed stern and sharply rising buttocks, will have a lower maximum displacement hull speed but, again, some handling characteristics very valuable in a voyaging boat.

The same characteristics that increase the Farr 48's displacement hull speed also enhance its semi-planing, planing and surfing potential. The designers of *Patrice* and the Vancouver 50 made little or no concession to achieving planing speeds, and would require extraordinary conditions to do so, especially in the case of the Vancouver 50.

These three boats, while showing vastly different characteristics of speed and resistance, are all very well suited to the type of cruising for which they are intended. They're excellent examples of why it's important to understand and appreciate a design's intended use in order to meaningfully evaluate the designer's success.

A PRIMER ON COURSE STABILITY

The ease of tracking and turning

ONE OF the biggest differences between cruising and racing sailboats is the relative importance of speed to steering characteristics. In a racing boat, speed (especially to windward) is of the utmost importance. Course stability, or the tendency of a boat to stay on its desired course, is secondary. On a fully crewed racing boat the helmsperson's job is to concentrate on steering the boat. When he is tired a member of the crew is always available to take his place.

On a cruising boat with a smaller crew, however, the ultimate speed of the boat is less important than its ability to maintain a course easily. The longer the distance and smaller the crew, the more important having a boat that will steer itself—with or without self-steering device—becomes.

Another quality that must be considered is maneuverability. Course stability implies a hull that wants to stay on course despite forces acting to change that course. But what about tacking, changing course, maneuvering through an anchorage or approaching a dock or mooring? Here course stability is a disadvantage.

Factors that contribute most to a boat's steering qualities and course stability are its lateral plane configuration, and its hull shape and proportions.

The lateral plane is the hull's underwater profile, showing hull, keel and rudder as viewed from the side (Figure 1). Important characteristics of the lateral plane are its area, distribution of area and position of the "center of lateral resistance" (CLR), or "center of lateral plane" (CLP), terms that can be used interchangeably.

The center of lateral plane is the geometric center of the lateral plane, or the point at which it could theoretically be pushed sideways without turning. Designers determine the longitudinal position of this point by cutting out in heavy paper the shape of the lateral plane, without the rudder, and balancing this on a straightedge perpendicular to the waterline (Figure 2). The point along the

Figure 1. Lateral plane

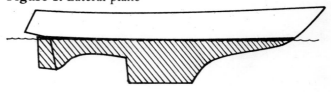

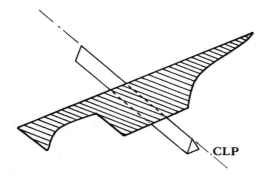

Figure 2. Balancing a paper cutout of the lateral plane (without rudder) to determine the center of lateral plane (CLP).

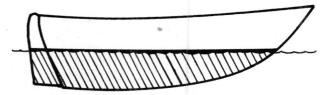

Figure 3. Full keel with attached rudder.

waterline where the shape balances is approximately the point about which the boat rotates when turning. It neglects the effect of the three-dimensional hull shape and the hydrodynamic forces acting on it, so it's only a rough approximation.

The lateral plane's area increases the boat's resistance to both sideways motion and turning motion. A boat with a large lateral area will resist the sideways force of the wind on the sails, and also resist turning about its center. Turning resistance also is affected by the distribution of lateral area. The more the lateral plane's area is located at the ends of the hull, far from the center, the more effective it is in resisting turning. The lateral area near the ends of the waterline must move through a longer arc, at a greater speed, than the area near the axis of rotation, so the ends offer a greater resistance to rotation.

Let's look at the broad spectrum of lateral plane configurations found on cruising boat hulls, and examine their advantages and disadvantages.

FULL KEEL WITH ATTACHED RUDDER

This configuration, by far the most traditional, dates back to the very first sailing yachts developed in the mid-19th century. A very large lateral area, distributed far into the ends of the boat, means course stability is very high. The long keel permits placing the ballast down low for high transverse stability.

Speed potential, especially in light winds, is di-

minished by the high wetted surface. Also, the large lateral area will detract from maneuverability, especially at slow speeds. The example shown in Figure 3 is the Passagemaker 28 designed by Thomas MacNaughton and shown on page 132.

CUTAWAY FULL KEEL WITH ATTACHED RUDDER

In an effort to both reduce wetted surface and increase maneuverability, designers eliminated some lateral area in the ends of the boat by cutting away the forefoot, and either cutting away some of the keel aft or moving its after end forward somewhat (Figure 4). Total lateral area, and thus lateral resistance, remains quite high, but the area removed, because it is far from the center of lateral plane, increases maneuverability significantly.

Racing success with boats with shortened keels and attached rudders led designers to make the keels shorter and shorter. Figure 5 shows a profile of Myth of Malham, designed in England by Laurent Giles in 1947. While she was a very successful boat, sailors found that as the keel was shortened the rudder moved closer and closer to the center of

Figure 4. Cutaway full keel with attached rudder.

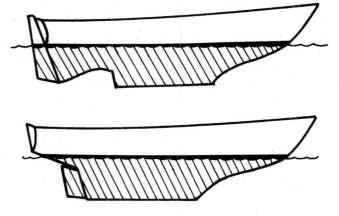

Figure 5. *Myth of Malham,* designed by Laurent Giles in 1947.

lateral plane, reducing its rudder arm and thus its steering ability. The obvious solution was to separate the rudder from the keel and move it aft.

LONG FIN KEEL WITH SEPARATE RUDDER

The separation of the rudder from the keel and the evolution of the keel into a fin were logical progressions from the cutaway full keel. The windward efficiency of the keel was improved by making it a distinctly separate part of the hull, more like a wing or appendage to the hull than the full keel, which was an extension of the hull itself.

This is associated with a factor called "aspect ratio." The aspect ratio of the keel is equal to its depth divided by its average length. A deep, narrow keel indicates a high aspect ratio. A keel with a high aspect ratio has the potential for high windward efficiency, similar to the dagger-like wings of a jet plane.

The fin keel, because the keel section is carried right up to the hull itself, has a higher aspect ratio than the full keel of similar profile, where the top part loses much of its keel-like shape in being faired into the hull (See Figure 6).

Many sailors erroneously think the fin keel is a modern development. In 1892 Nathanael Herresh-

Figure 6. The fin keel has a greater effective depth than the full keel, and thus a greater aspect ratio.

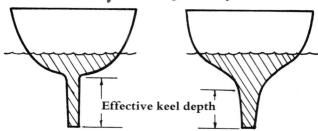

Effective keel depth

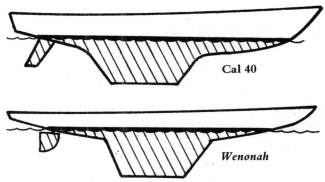

Cal 40

Wenonah

Figure 7. Compare *Wenonah,* designed by Nathanial Herreshoff in 1892, to the Cal 40, designed by Bill Tripp in 1963.

off designed the *Wenonah,* shown in comparison to the Cal 40 (which was considered a revolutionary breakthrough in 1963). See Figure 7. Denigrated as "skimming dishes" by the racing sailors at the time—who considered them unhealthy and unsafe —this design was quickly penalized by rating rules and made uncompetitive. It was not until rating rules changed, and the fin keel could compete on a more equal basis with other keel types, that its attractive qualities of windward efficiency and high maneuverability were appreciated.

Some fin keel boats, like *Wenonah* and the Cal 40, had freestanding spade rudders. Others had rudders mounted on skegs. Since the rudder itself is not considered part of the lateral area, the difference between the two types is significant (Figure 8). Even the relatively small amount of skeg area, because it is far from the center of lateral plane, contributes significantly to course stability.

Figure 8. Compare the lateral planes of the two boats, one with a spade rudder and one with a skeg-mounted rudder.

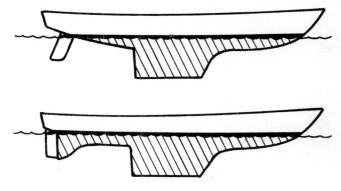

The skeg, by directing the flow of water to the leading edge of the rudder, also makes the rudder effective over a greater range of conditions than a spade rudder. When a rudder is turned at a great angle to a fast water flow, the flow can separate from the aft side of the rudder as shown in Figure 9. This is called "stalling" and is marked by an almost total loss of rudder effectiveness. The skeg in front of the rudder does not prevent stalling entirely, but it does make the rudder more resistant to stalling.

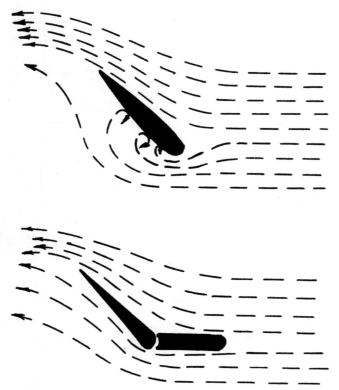

Figure 9. The spade rudder (top) is more prone to stalling and loss of effectiveness than the skeg-mounted rudder (bottom).

A case can be made for the spade rudder, however, especially on boats where high performance is more important than course stability. Not only is wetted surface reduced, but the spade rudder can be made "partially balanced" by placing the rudder axis aft of the leading edge. When it is turned the water pressure on the area forward of the axis counteracts some of the pressure on the area aft of the axis, and makes the rudder easier to turn than

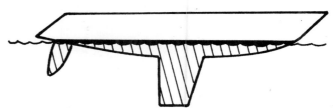

Figure 10. Short fin keel with spade rudder.

an unbalanced rudder. This gives the helmsman a more sensitive feel for the boat.

SHORT FIN KEEL

In the quest for racing boats with more speed, more windward ability and more maneuverability, naval architects designed more extreme boats, cutting both wetted surface and lateral plane to the minimum. The resulting high aspect keels had to be very deep, and their small volume often made it necessary to fill them entirely with ballast, resulting in a relatively high ballast placement.

The short fin keel/spade rudder configuration (Figure 10) has proved most successful in ocean races, but has a number of disadvantages to the cruising sailor. The high aspect keel and rudder are both very efficient but only in a narrow range of sail trim and helm position. The helm and sails require constant attention to realize their potential. If the "groove" is defined as the range of sail trim and helm position in which a boat sails at its maximum efficiency, a boat with a short fin keel and spade rudder will have a "narrow groove." A less extreme design, though possessing a lower maximum speed potential, often has a "wider groove," giving reasonably high performance with less concentration from its crew.

CENTERBOARDS

Designers often try to compromise between the course stability and shallow draft of the long keel and the windward ability of the deep, narrow keel; the keel/centerboard is a logical result. The Hinckley Bermuda 40 (Figure 11), which has been in continuous production since 1959, is a good example of this configuration. The added advantage

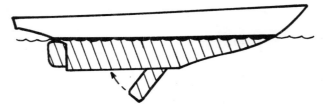

Figure 11. The Hinckley Bermuda 40 with long, shallow keel and centerboard.

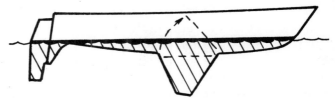

Figure 12. The Tanzer 10.5 with a swing keel.

to the centerboard is that it allows the sailor to adjust the center of lateral plane and thus the balance of the hull in various conditions.

But the centerboard also is one more item susceptible to damage or failure. As with the spade rudder, appropriate engineering and construction can reduce, but not eliminate, this potential weakness. It is an excellent arrangement, especially on larger boats where a deep fixed keel would limit coastal cruising, but a shallow draft would reduce windward ability.

A centerboard also can be arranged inside a shallow fin keel, with separate rudder. Responsiveness and maneuverability are increased over the long keel/centerboard configuration. Wetted surface, but also directional stability, are somewhat reduced.

MOVABLE KEEL

A disadvantage to a centerboard arrangement, with its relatively shallow keel, is that the ballast must also be shallow and less effective in contributing to stability. Centerboard boats usually require more ballast or beam to have the same stability as a boat with a deeper keel.

Designers have attempted to solve this problem with movable ballast keels, such as Dick Carter's Tanzer 10.5 (Figure 12). With the swing keel in the down position it performs as a fin keel, yet retains the ability to achieve shallow draft and reduced drag when desired.

Because the keel is very heavy, the forces it imparts on the hull and the strength required in its support mechanism are great. Superb engineering and construction are called for. The interior space taken up by the keel trunk also is a considerable sacrifice in interior living space.

DAGGERBOARD

Rather than a centerboard, which pivots up into a trunk in the keel or hull, a daggerboard slides up and down in a vertical trunk (Figure 13). It is used mostly in boats under 25 feet, and can be either unballasted—like a centerboard—or have lead placed at the bottom for stability. It is simple to construct, but its disadvantage is the potential for damage to board and hull should the board strike an object while the boat is moving. In the same situation the centerboard would be more likely to escape damage by swinging up into its trunk.

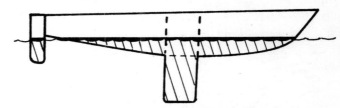

Figure 13. A daggerboard or lifting keel arrangement.

TWIN KEELS

Yet another way to achieve shallow draft is with twin keels. Both keels contribute to stability and lateral area, yet draft is reduced substantially from a single keeled hull of comparable stability or lateral place area. The moving parts—and potential weakness—of a centerboard or movable keel, are eliminated.

This configuration was first developed in England in the 1920's, and is still more popular there than anywhere else. One major reason for this is the large tidal range there, which causes many harbors and anchorages to dry out at low tide. A twin keel boat can stand on its own while other boats need some sort of support.

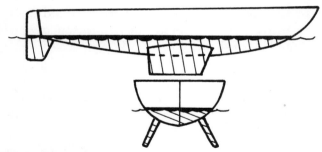

Figure 14. John Letcher's twin-keeled Aleutka.

This same quality makes twin keels very attractive for shallow-water cruising. Unlike any other hull type, a twin keel boat's draft is reduced when it reduces its angle of heel. If it goes aground while heeled, the sheets can be released and the boat will stand upright, floating free. Any single keel boat increases its draft when it reduces heel.

John S. Letcher, Jr. designed and built his 25-foot twin keel Aleutka (Figure 14), and sailed it extensively in the Pacific and Atlantic with his wife. He advocates twin keel cruising boats, pointing out the extended coastal cruising possible, the ability to run right up to the beach and step ashore, and the ease of drying out for hull maintenance. But he is also an aeronautical engineer, and freely admits that they are slower and less efficient to windward than a single keel boat.

OUTBOARD RUDDER

A rudder arrangement that is particularly attractive to the cruising sailor is the outboard, or transom-hung rudder. It can be skeg mounted or attached to a long full keel, or it can stand free with or without some balance (See Figure 15).

Since they don't require through-hull fittings, outboard rudders are simpler to construct and easier to service than inboard rudders. But they also are more exposed to damage from stern collision. They're slightly less efficient than inboard rudders because an inboard rudder's top edge is against the hull, which functions as an "end plate" to prevent the movement of water over the top of the rudder from the high pressure area on one side to the low pressure area on the other. Without this end plate effect the outboard rudder is somewhat less effi-

cient, but it is further from the center of lateral resistance and so has a greater lever arm to turn the boat. Its overall steering effect is usually comparable.

The greatest advantage to the outboard rudder from the cruiser's point of view is the ease with which it can be fitted with a trim tab and self-steering gear. Many types of self-steering are available that are suitable to inboard rudders, including units with an auxiliary rudder or devices using control lines to the tiller or wheel. A self-steerer that operates on a trim tab and outboard rudder, however, is the simplest, least expensive and most effective. Many offshore voyagers choose the outboard rudder for just this reason.

Figure 15. Possible outboard rudder arrangements—full keel (a), on a skeg (b), or freestanding (c) with or without balance.

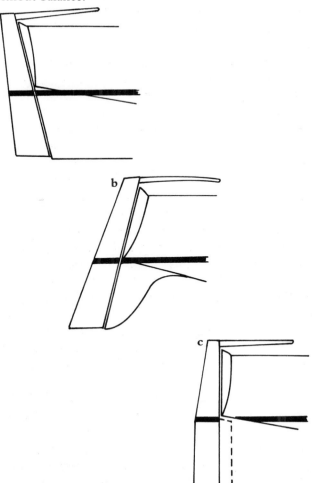

So far, we've looked at lateral plane and its effect on course stability and steering characteristics considering only length and depth, or the two-dimensional shape of the hull. Now let's progress to the actual three-dimensional shape of the hull and its effect on a cruising boat's handling.

HULL SHAPE

No matter what the hull shape, when a sailboat is upright it is symmetrical on each side of the centerline. When it heels, however, it becomes asymmetrical. The lower, or leeward side, becomes deeper, wider and fuller while the upper, or wind-ward side becomes shallower, narrower and finer. The degree of this asymmetry is a function of beam and hull shape.

Nearly all cruising hull forms will, if heeled while under way, have a tendency to turn to wind-ward. This is called "weather helm" because the tiller must be brought to the weather, or wind-ward side of the boat to maintain course.

The opposite of weather helm is "lee helm" and indicates a boat that has a tendency to turn to lee-ward, or away from the wind. In between the two is "neutral helm" meaning a hull that tends to go straight even if the tiller is left free.

Slight weather helm is desirable in a sailboat, even over neutral helm, for a number of reasons. A rudder offset slightly to leeward gives it an

Figure 16. The asymmetric shape of the heeled waterline leads to a larger bow wave on the leeward side.

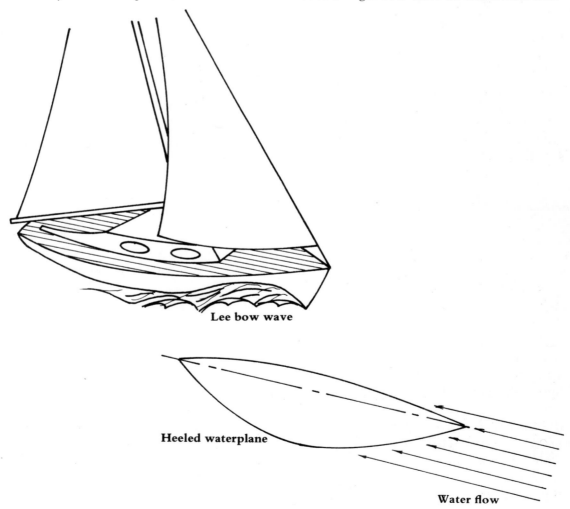

Lee bow wave

Heeled waterplane

Water flow

asymmetric, wing-like cross section and an angle of attack that optimize lift to windward. A bit of weather helm also gives some "feel" to the tiller or wheel, which allows the helmsperson to sense the boat's balance and performance. The fact that a boat with weather helm will round up into the wind if the helm is released is also a safety factor and is far preferable to a boat that will bear off away from the wind, or continue to sail straight away.

The ideal boat will have a slight weather helm that remains nearly constant over a broad range of heel angles. When the rudder must be offset more than about five degrees to maintain course, however, the weather helm is excessive. Greater rudder angles result in a large increase in rudder resistance and a corresponding reduction in speed. A helmsperson wrestling with a heavy weather helm also is soon exhausted.

Sailboat balance, the natural steering tendency of the boat, is a function of both the shape of the hull and the arrangement of the sails. The effect of the sails on this factor will be discussed in Chapter 7. For now, let's limit the discussion to hull shape.

How exactly does hull shape affect the steering characteristics of the hull? Many theories exist. The two most widely accepted explanations involve the transverse distribution of volume of the heeled hull, and the bow wave formed by a heeled boat on its leeward side.

The "lee bow wave" explanation holds that the shape of the waterline changes as the boat heels so that the leeward side of the bow pushes up a larger bow wave than the windward side (See Figure 16).

Newtonian physics, which says that for every action there is an equal and opposite reaction, predicts that the leeward bow, in pushing a bigger wave than the windward side, is also pushed harder by that wave than the windward bow. The bow, therefore, is forced to windward.

Another explanation that makes sense holds that balance is determined by the transverse distribution of underwater hull volume. Picture what happens when the various stations of a hull are heeled over. A wedge-shaped volume on the windward side comes out of the water, while a wedge-shaped volume on the leeward side is immersed. The center of area of each station moves to leeward but by

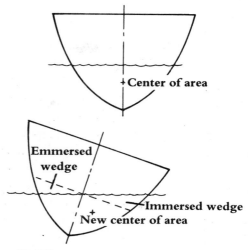

Figure 17. When a section is heeled, the emmersed and immersed wedges cause the center of area of the section to shift to leeward.

varying amounts, depending upon the beam and hull shape at that station (See Figure 18).

If you were to plot the center of area of each heeled station along the length of the boat, you'd see that the underwater shape of the hull is no longer symmetrical, but curved and convex to leeward. The water flowing over this curved shape makes the boat turn to windward.

To minimize the effect of heeling on course stability, a hull's heeled waterline should be as symmetrical as possible. Increased beam usually increases the asymmetry when heeled. Many mod-

Figure 18. When the boat is heeled, the shift in underwater areas makes the hull assume an asymmetric shape, which forces the boat to windward.

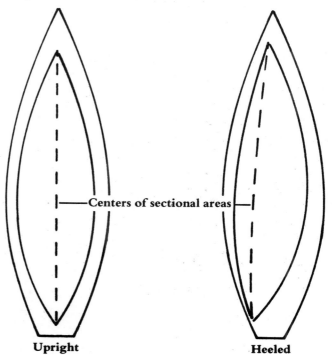

Upright   Heeled

ern boats are designed with a very wide beam, and in order to keep the forward waterline fine designers move the position of maximum beam aft. This wedge shape gives excellent performance at low to moderate angles of heel but at extreme angles the broad stern sections develop much more buoyancy than the fine forward sections, causing the stern to rise and the bow to sink. This shifts the center of lateral plane forward and increases the weather helm even more.

Throughout the history of sailboat design, naval architects have attempted to create boats with ideal balance. They've tried hulls with identical forward and aft sections and hulls fuller forward than aft (called "fish shape" or "cod's head and mackerel tail"). And they've designed boats with fuller sections aft than forward.

Because so many other factors are involved in hull shape, both the fish shape and the hull with symmetrical fore and after bodies have proved undesirable. It is generally accepted now that characteristics that contribute to good balance and steering in a heeled hull—and to good all-around performance—are moderate beam with its maximum width slightly aft of amidships, coupled with fairly fine stern sections with some similarity to the bow sections. These must be balanced, however, against other considerations, such as stability, speed and the position of the center of buoyancy. The double-ended hull form shows merit here.

Cruising boats designed for long distance, shorthanded sailing should possess a moderate weather helm through a wide range of heel angles. They can be driven hard with fewer sail changes or reefs taken, and require less work for the helmsperson or self-steering device. Being fairly narrow and with a narrow stern, such a boat will have less stability and less interior living space than a beamier hull. Its potential to plane or reach high speeds also is reduced.

Cruising boat owners who intend to use their boats for shorter distances with larger crew—and who demand greater performance—will find the beamier, full-sterned hull form attractive. It must be kept at moderate angles of heel so will probably require more frequent sail changes. But on the plus side, such boats are faster, roomier and lighter (and thus less expensive to build).

ONE OF cruising's greatest attractions is the freedom it allows, freedom from schedules, restrictions and outside control. It's also a unique form of self-expression.

Today, cruising sailors can choose from an almost limitless variety of shapes and types of boats.

Before boats were mass-produced, early cruisers and voyagers used fishing dories, sailing canoes, converted lifeboats, sailing pilot boats, often whatever was available or suited their fancy. The history of cruising shows that almost any type of boat, with proper preparation and handling—and perhaps a bit of luck—can sail along coasts and across oceans.

Naval architects and cruising sailors are always seeking to design boats that are faster, more comfortable, stronger, easier to handle, and easier or less expensive to build. They're also stretching their creative imagination for more beautiful boats, or sometimes just a boat that's different from all the rest. Nothing helped more in this quest than the introduction of fiberglass as a boatbuilding material in the early 1960's. It made boats more affordable and easier to maintain, and thus attracted many new people to sailing and cruising. Fiberglass construction also gave boat designers much greater freedom in shaping hulls; no longer were they restricted to using wooden planks, which resisted formation into complex shapes.

Fiberglass could be molded into any shape imaginable, although building a mold is an expensive and time-consuming job, and so is most suited to building boats in large numbers.

But in the last decade or so many new materials and building techniques have made practical the construction of a single boat or a limited number of boats. Most of these same techniques have made it possible for the amateur builder, with little or no previous boatbuilding experience, to construct excellent quality boats.

We'll look at these building techniques—including cored fiberglass, C-Flex fiberglass, laminated wood and epoxy, and steel—in Chapter 10.

The combination of new building techniques and so many new cruising sailors have encouraged an even greater diversity of cruising boat types, rigs, sail handling equipment and sailing techniques. Nowhere is this diversity more apparent

Chapter

6

A LOOK AT CRUISING HULL TYPES

Different boats for different folks

than in the designs naval architects have created for custom or amateur construction in the past 10 years. These designs have explored the extremes of possibilities in size and shape and weight, and blazed new paths for production boats to follow.

In the past decade, *Cruising World*'s design section has presented many of these new and interesting designs to cruising sailors. The second half of this book showcases some of the best of these designs and illustrates to the cruising sailor the incredible variety of boats available to suit almost any set of requirements—esthetic, financial or practical.

Having studied the basic elements of cruising boat design, our challenge now is to learn how to use this knowledge to compare the potential performance, comfort and cost of the myriad boats in existence. Let's start with the most important aspect of any cruising boat design, the shape, or form of the hull. It is here, more than in any other aspect of boat design, that diversity is greatest and thus the proper choice most important to the cruising sailor.

Hull forms can be categorized in a number of ways—by length, displacement, hull proportions, type of bow, type of stern or historical derivation. The most definitive single basis of comparison is the "displacement/length ratio."[1]

This is the displacement in long tons (2,240 lbs.) divided by one hundredth of the waterline length (in feet), raised to the third power, or cubed. It is a non-dimensional ratio that can be used to compare hulls of any size and is a precise measure of the "heaviness" or "density" of a hull. It's the volume of the hole a boat makes in the water in comparison to its length. Since a greater displacement/length ratio means a bigger hole, it also means that the stations or cross sections of the hull have greater underwater area.

To illustrate the significance of the displacement/length ratio in cruising boat design, I have chosen five designs, between 30 and 34 feet long, which represent not only five quite varied values of this ratio but also five distinctly different types of cruising boat hull forms.

[1] $\text{Displacement/Length Ratio} = \dfrac{\text{Displacement (in long tons)}}{(.01 \times \text{LWL})^3}$

Boat	Olson 30	Tiffany Jane	Wylie 31	Sarah 31	Vancouver 32
LOA	30'0"	34'0"	30'7"	31'4"	32'0"
LWL	27'6"	25'0"	25'3"	25'10"	27'6"
Beam	9'4"	8'0"	9'3"	10'3"	11'8"
Draft	5'1"	5'6"	6'0"	4'9"	4'6"
Ballast	1800 lbs.	3010 lbs.	3400 lbs.	4800 lbs.	6500 lbs.
Displacement	3600 lbs.	5790 lbs.	7910 lbs.	10750 lbs.	14513 lbs.
Sail Area	380 sq. ft.	451 sq. ft.	434 sq. ft.	500 sq. ft.	579 sq. ft.
Disp/Length Ratio	77	165	221	278	312

Olson 30–With a displacement/length ratio of under 100, the Olson 30 is classified as an "ultralight displacement boat" (ULDB). The design was developed in the Santa Cruz, California area in the late 1960's and early 1970's. Pioneering designers George Olson and Bill Lee designed and built the boats for maximum speed and excitement in the prevailing reaching conditions of that area. The boats, which are designed to plane as easily as possible, have reached speeds in excess of 20 knots. They are intended for speed and racing, but with some limited cruising potential.

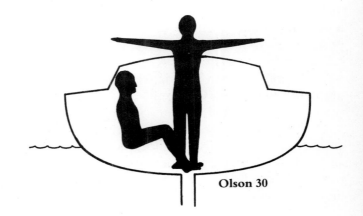

Olson 30

Tiffany Jane—"Light displacement" is the term used to describe boats with displacement/length ratios between 100 and 200. Unlike the Olson 30, Tiffany Jane is not designed to plane, but rather to be a very fast and easily handled displacement hull. The emphasis in the design of Tiffany Jane, and most light displacement cruisers, is a sparkling but predictable performance, with accommodation space taking a subordinate role. Tiffany Jane also is an extraordinarily graceful looking boat.

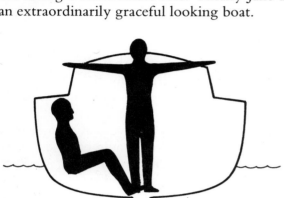

Tiffany Jane

Sarah 31—Sarah's moderately heavy displacement/length ratio (between 250 and 300) classifies her as a traditional cruiser. This does not imply that she is a reproduction of a traditional design, only that she has the same sort of proportions and weight as the older cruising boat designs. Designer Chuck Paine, one of the leading designers of cruising boats in the world, specializes in drawing boats with classic esthetics combined with more modern levels of performance.

Sarah 31

Wylie 31—This is an excellent example of what has come to be called the "performance cruiser." This type is characterized by moderately low displacement (ratios between 200 and 250) and performance approaching very closely that of racing designs. Robert Perry's Valiant 40, introduced in 1974, is considered by many to be the first performance cruiser and is still the standard to which others are compared.

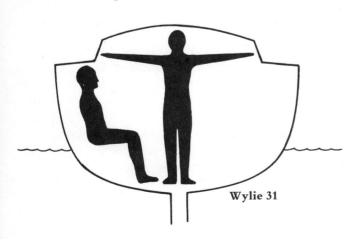

Wylie 31

Vancouver 32—Boats with displacement/length ratios larger than 300 usually are considered heavy displacement. An excellent example in this category is this Robert Harris design, intended for long-distance voyaging with a small crew. The Vancouver 32's heavy displacement gives it the comfort, carrying capacity and general seaworthiness. Performance is a somewhat less significant consideration.

Look at the sections of the five boats shown here. The Olson 30 has only sitting headroom. The limited interior volume provides room for the very basics, such as berths, stove, sink, chart table and head, but little additional stowage space. Anyone using the boat for extended cruising would have to be satisfied with a "backpacker" or "camper" level of existence.

A deeper hull and higher cabin enables Tiffany Jane to achieve sitting headroom under the side deck and about 5′6″ headroom elsewhere. Many believe that "almost standing headroom" isn't much better than just sitting headroom, or that

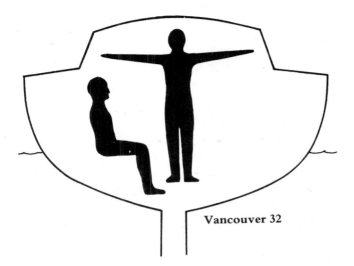

Vancouver 32

"almost standing" is a rather uncomfortable position. Still, the amount of increased interior space in Tiffany Jane over the Olson 30 does make her quite a bit more habitable. Tiffany Jane's stowage space is minimal, not much more than the Olson 30.

The Wylie 31 has full standing headroom. The deeper hull also results in a significant amount of storage space under the settees, certainly enough to classify this boat as a coastal cruiser. As in the Olson 30 and Tiffany Jane, the bilge area under the cabin sole is very shallow and could not hold much bilge water before some would slop over.

The Sarah 31, a traditional cruiser, has traditional levels of comfort and stowage. Her increased beam and depth permit the settees to be kept under the cabin, with a pilot berth or huge stowage area outboard. She also has a much larger keel, which contains a sump for collecting bilge water, so a greater amount can be accumulated before it finds its way into stowage areas or the cabin sole.

Finally, the Vancouver 32's greatly increased beam and depth allow the volume of accommodation and stowage necessary in a liveaboard, voyaging boat. Headroom is so great that the cabin sole can be raised up, allowing additional tankage for water or fuel to be placed below—where they will help lower the boat's center of gravity. The only better place to add tankage is in the keel itself, and the Vancouver 32 also is able to accommodate that. Spacious pilot berths or cavernous lockers can be placed outboard of the settees.

There is also an interesting relationship between displacement/length ratio, comfort and size. As mentioned in Chapter 3, Ted Brewer derived a motion comfort ratio to approximate the severity of motion a boat will exhibit at sea.[2]

I calculated the motion comfort formula for all the designs that appear in this book, and plotted their values as a function of boat length. The result is shown in Figure 2. It shows that in general, motion comfort increases as length increases, a fact known to anyone who has spent time at sea in small and large boats. There is, however, another less obvious conclusion to be drawn: As a boat becomes larger, its displacement/length ratio can be reduced and its level of motion comfort will remain constant.

As an example, to achieve a motion comfort ratio of 22, a 20-foot boat would have to possess a very high displacement/length ratio, a 30-foot boat could have a moderate displacement, a 40-foot boat could be of light displacement and a 50-foot boat of ultra-light displacement. Looked at another way, a light displacement 30-footer would have a motion comfort ratio of about 16, perhaps less than acceptable to many sailors. A light displacement 60-footer, on the other hand, could have a motion comfort ratio higher than 30, comparable to that of a moderate displacement 45-footer.

Accommodation and stowage space on the larger light displacement boat, though still small compared to other boats of the same length, becomes more and more acceptable to the cruising sailor as the size increases.

Now let's talk about speed potential. As displacement/length ratio increases, so does wave-making resistance. Thus, performance decreases in the upper speed ranges. This is due to the fact that moving a larger size and weight of boat through the water produces larger waves. As shown in Chapter 4, wave-making resistance varies as the square of the wave height of the wake.

Frictional resistance also tends to be lower for the light displacement boat, because its small sections and small keel reduce wetted surface. The voyaging boat, with greater beam and longer keel, has more wetted surface. Light-air performance,

[2]Motion comfort ratio = $\dfrac{\text{Displacement}}{.65\,(.7\,\text{LWL} + .3\,\text{LOA}) \times \text{beam}^{1.33}}$

Figure 2. Motion comfort ratios.

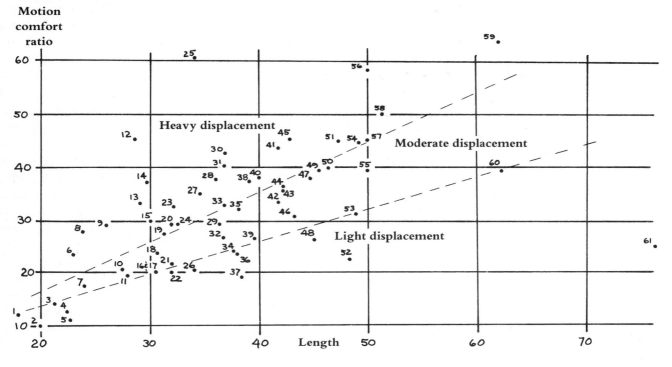

1—Webb 18	16—Coast 30	31—Mason 37
2—Antrim 20	17—R 9–30	32—Scheel 37
3—Solo 21	18–Wylie 31	33—Tanton 37
4—Seaboat 225	19—Sarah	34—Marshall 37
5—Plyboy	20—Vancouver 32	35—Benford 38
6—Sourdough	21—CW 9.75	36—Concordia 38
7—Bahama Sandpiper	22—32′ Dory	37—Maxi-Trailerable
8—Allegra	23—Sail Ho	38—Spirit 39
9—Frances	24—Brewer 32	39—Ambra
10—Shearwater	25—*Sunrise*	40—Benford 40
11—Sassy	26—Tiffany Jane	41—Vancouver 42
12—Passage Maker 28	27—Integrity	42—*Nightrunner*
13—Annie	28—Vancouver 36	43—Fidelity
14—Falmouth Cutter	29—Morris 36	44—*Harry Tabbard*
15—Bulldog	30—Spray 36	45—Alaska 43

46—Cartwright 43

47—Sandpiper 44

48—'apenny Dip

49—Inscrutable

50—*Galaxie*

51—Northeast 47

52—Farr 48

53—Patrice

54—49' Steel Ketch

55—Vancouver 50

56—50' D.E. Ketch

57—*Palawan*

58—*Kay*

59—*Falcon II*

60—Deerfoot 62

61—Academy 76

too, tends to decrease with increased displacement/length ratio.

Other areas of importance to the cruising sailor in the choice of a boat are strength and cost. While increased displacement is no guarantee of stronger construction, the greater the amount of weight permitted for the hull and deck, the greater the potential for high strength. With careful design and construction, using modern materials and techniques, even ultra-light displacement boats can be built with more than enough strength to withstand the stresses experienced in ordinary sailing. Greater hull weight permits building hulls that can withstand some extraordinary forces, such as hitting floating objects, encountering breaking waves, or grounding. Quality of construction, however, cannot be overlooked. A well built light displacement boat can certainly be stronger than a poorly built, heavier boat.

Cost of construction also is a major consideration to someone considering a custom or self-built boat. But this can be misleading. The actual cost

Type	ULDB	Light displacement Cruiser	Performance Cruiser	Traditional	Voyager
Displacement/ Length Ratio	50-100	100-200	200-250	250-300	300-350
Accommodation and Stowage	Poor in the smaller boats, fair in the larger boats.		Fair, becoming good with increased size.	Good to excellent	Excellent
Performance	Fast and exciting in all normal conditions. Frequent planing.	Fast and exciting	Relatively fast and fun to sail.	Fair to good all around performance.	Fair to good, slow in light winds
Strength	Sufficient for all ordinary sailing conditions.		More able to survive severe conditions.	Most able to survive punishment.	
Stability	Low but suitable, may require crew weight in strong winds.	Low to moderate	Moderate	Moderate to high	High
Cost per Pound	Slightly above average		Average	Average to above average depending on the cost of hardware and equipment.	
Motion Comfort	Acceptable in moderate weather but uncomfortable in rough conditions. Comfort increases significantly with size.		Fair to good	Good to excellent	Good to excellent

of constructing the hull and deck is a small part of the total cost of the finished boat, often only 25 to 30 percent. This figure, however, can vary widely depending upon the amount of money spent for expensive items like spars, winches, sails, hardware and interior furnishings. The owner/builder who makes his own spars or sails or does without expensive hardware can enjoy substantial savings.

The fact remains, however, that the best indicator of hull construction cost is displacement. Every pound of material that must be purchased and then assembled, costs money. Does this mean that a boat that weighs half as much as another will cost half as much to build? Not exactly, but close.

In the early days of the ultra and light displacement boats, the more sophisticated construction materials and techniques necessary to build them were relatively expensive. The cost per pound for building a light displacement boat was significantly higher than the cost per pound for a heavier boat. Now the price difference between lightweight construction materials and ordinary building materials has narrowed to the point that the cost per pound for a lightweight boat is only slightly more than the cost per pound for a heavier boat. Developments in techniques and instructional texts also have made it possible for the skilled amateur to use the more sophisticated materials.

This discussion of building cost concerns only the construction of hull and deck. Since a heavier boat requires larger and heavier sails, larger spars, heavier rigging, larger winches, etc., the final cost of a boat is directly related to final displacement. There are so many variables, it is impossible to place a dollar-per-pound figure on boat construction, but if all other factors are held constant, the cost of a hull and deck or completed boat is almost directly proportional to its displacement.

The preceding table gives the general characteristics of the five types of boats used in this chapter to illustrate the significance of displacement/length ratio. Remember, however, that the variety of cruising boat hull types is enormous. Many do not fit easily into one category but may be a mixture of different types.

Chapter
7

SAIL PLAN FUNDAMENTALS

Transforming wind into power

THE RIGS used today on cruising sailboats are no less diverse than the hull shapes on which they stand. In fact, a strong argument can be made that more truly revolutionary development has occurred in the last decade in the field of sails, rigs and sail handling than in hull design and boatbuilding. New sail and spar materials have emerged, along with new gear for handling and supporting sailboat rigs. Dramatic developments continue to take place every year, and many believe it is in this arena that the most significant near-term changes will take place, particularly for the cruising sailor.

BALANCE

Whatever rig a designer selects for a particular design, he must consider the important relationship between sail plan and hull shape, or balance. Let's look at some of the forces involved.

Figure 1 is a view from directly above a sailboat beating to windward. The total driving force produced by the wind acting on the sails can be divided into two components. One drives the boat forward and the other pushes it sideways. These forces act at a single point, called the "center of effort," or CE, of the sail plan.

The resisting forces caused by the water on the hull likewise can be divided into two components. The first is longitudinal force or the hull resistance as it moves straight ahead. The second is the perpendicular force, or the resistance of the hull to sideways motion.

We saw in Chapter 5 that when a hull is heeled over its asymmetry results in a tendency to turn toward the wind. Figure 1 shows that the forward driving force of the sails and longitudinal resisting force of the hull—because they are not acting along the same line—form a couple that also tends to turn the boat to windward.

The lateral driving force on the sails and lateral resistance force on the hull, however, form a couple that tends to turn the boat away from the wind. To balance a boat, these conflicting forces must cancel each other out. The factor that determines the effect of the lateral forces, and thus the balance of the boat, is the distance between the center of effort of the sails and the center of lateral resistance of the hull.

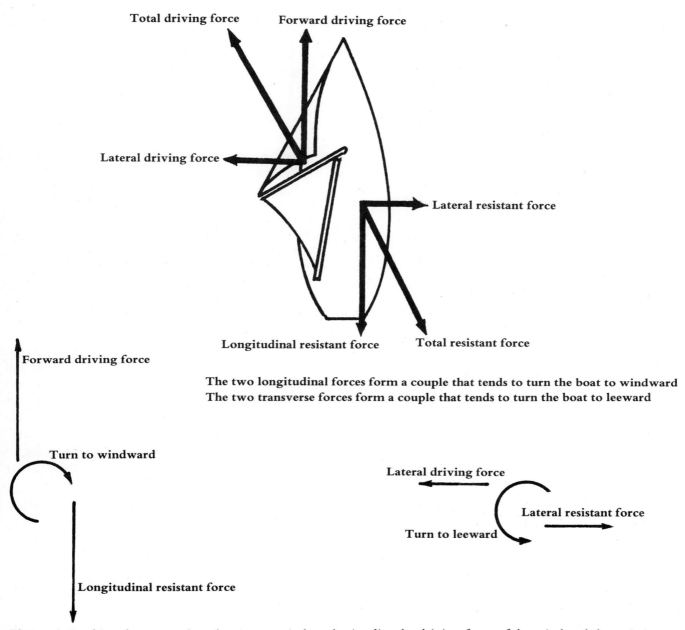

Figure 1. Looking down on a boat beating to windward, visualize the driving force of the wind and the resisting force of the water, each divided into their longitudinal and transverse components.

CENTER OF EFFORT

The center of effort is the geometric center of the sail plan. Just as the center of lateral resistance approximates the point at which the hydrodynamic forces of the water act on the hull, the center of effort approximates where the aerodynamic forces of the wind act on the sails.

Figure 2 illustrates how the center of effort is determined. The centers of the individual sails are found by treating them as triangles, and the center of a triangle is the intersection of the lines from the corners to the midpoints of the opposite sides. It is normal practice to compute the center of effort for the foretriangle (the triangle formed by the mast, headstay and deck) rather than for the actual headsail.

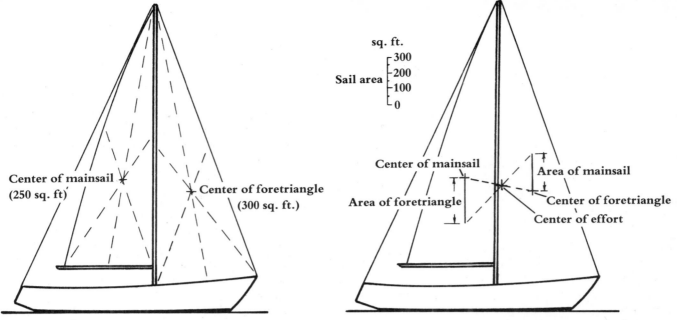

Figure 2. The centers of the mainsail and foretriangle are determined by drawing lines from the corners to the midpoints of the opposite sides. The point of intersection is the center.

The combined center of effort is found by first drawing a line connecting the individual centers. Then, at the center of the mainsail a vertical line is drawn equal in length to the foretriangle area taken from the scale. At the center of the foretriangle a vertical line is drawn in the opposite direction and a scaled mainsail area marked. The intersection of the line connecting these points and the line connecting the centers is the combined center of effort (CE).

The total center of effort is on a line connecting the individual centers. Its exact location on that line is determined by the exercise shown in Figure 2. For a ketch or yawl, the combined center of effort of the main and foretriangle is determined as for a sloop, and then a line drawn from that center to the center of the mizzen sail. The total center of effort is on that line and its location determined by the exercise shown in Figure 3. Because mizzen sails operate in disturbed air left by the main and jib, they have a reduced effect on helm balance, so only half its sail area is used for this calculation.

LEAD

With the center of effort of the sail plan and the center of lateral resistance of the hull determined, the naval architect plots their positions and measures the longitudinal distance between them, or lead (See Figure 4). Experience shows that the center of effort should lead the center of lateral resistance by a distance of between 5 and 15 percent of the waterline length. Experience also shows that there are certain factors, such as narrow beam, high aspect keels and low rigs, which call for leads near the lower end of the range. Beamy hulls, tall rigs and long keels call for leads near the maximum.

Boats should be designed to balance under full sail at moderate angles of heel; when the wind and angle of heel increase weather helm also increases because of the greater hull asymmetry and the fact that the sails' center of effort heels further outboard. By reefing the mainsail and/or changing to a smaller headsail, the sailor can move the center

Figure 3. To determine the center of effort for a ketch or yawl, first find the combined center of effort of the mainsail and foretriangle as in Figure 2, then repeat the procedure using that center and the center of effort of the mizzen. Only half the mizzen area is used for this calculation.

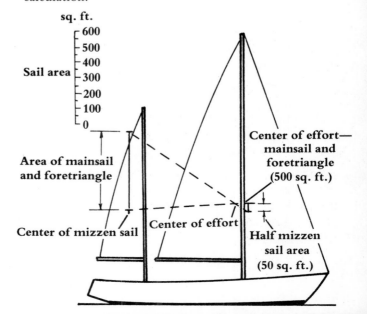

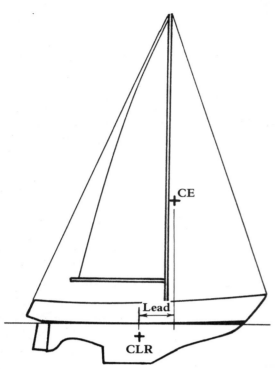

Figure 4. The "lead" is the distance between the center of effort and the center of lateral resistance, usually expressed as a percentage of the waterline length.

of effort forward and lower, reducing heel and increasing the lead as in Figure 5.

Understanding the balance between the center of effort and the center of lateral resistance makes it possible for the sailor to reef and change sails as conditions require and to maintain a balanced helm.

ASPECT RATIO

Just as aspect ratio, or the proportion of height to average width of the keel, affects the windward efficiency of the hull, so the aspect ratio of the sails affects their performance to windward. The very tall and narrow mainsails found on racing sloops have high potential for speed and weatherliness, but do not have great power. They are suited to light, easily driven hulls but would be unsatisfactory on a heavy cruising boat.

Low aspect ratio mainsails, lower in height and longer on the foot, have a lower speed and weatherliness potential but have much more power. They can drive a heavy boat, even in seas that

would stop a lighter boat with a less powerful sail plan.

CHOOSING SAIL PLANS

What are the qualities, besides balance, power and speed, that are important in selecting sail plans for cruising boats? Speed and efficiency on the various points of sail, ease of handling, versatility; strength, weight and cost. Let's look at the variety of rigs and evaluate them on these qualities.

GAFF RIG

As recently as 50 years ago the gaff rig was still considered the only practical rig for an oceangoing sailboat. It is unquestionably strong and reliable, and requires fewer pieces of expensive rigging or hardware than most modern rigs.

While it is not as weatherly as the modern Bermudan rig, it can surpass these rigs when reaching or running without having to resort to spinnakers or other large, specialized headsails.

Figure 5. When the mainsail is reefed and when a smaller headsail is substituted for a larger one, the center of effort shifts forward and down, increasing the lead and reducing the heeling arm.

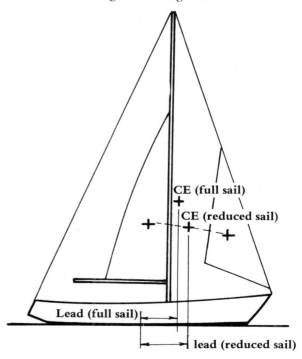

Few cruising sailors today have any experience with the gaff rig. With aluminum spars and perhaps some other concessions to modern technology, however, the gaff rig's performance could probably approach that of the Bermudan rig to a point where it is worth considering for some offshore voyaging boats. Figure 6 shows a gaff ketch rig.

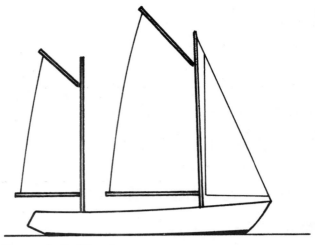

Figure 6. Gaff ketch

BERMUDAN RIG

By far the most popular rig today for sailboats is the Bermudan or Marconi rig. Because this is the rig dictated by the rules for nearly all racing sailboats, it has received the greatest attention in terms of development and refinement. Aluminum masts, Dacron sails and modern rigging hardware all were produced first for racing boats and then put into use on cruising boats.

SLOOP

The Bermudan sloop (Figure 7) has, as a result of modern racing impetus, reached a very high level of development, with the greatest emphasis on windward ability because that is what wins races. Many cruising sailors have accepted the racers' standards of performance and so also consider the Bermudan sloop the best cruising rig.

The standards by which rigs for cruising and racing boats should be measured, however, are quite different. To the racer, speed to windward is far and away the most important consideration. It does not matter to him if large crew and sail inventories are needed to sail efficiently on all points of sail. Cost and long-term reliability also are secondary considerations.

The cruising sailor, especially one who wants to sail with a small crew, should not be too ready to accept the racers' ideas of performance. Performance in a cruising boat implies the combination of a reasonably high level of sailing efficiency with versatility and ease of handling. While the racing skipper has a large crew whose job it is to change sails frequently and in any conditions, the cruising sailor with a small crew should be willing to trade a small reduction in speed for reduced crew work. He is, after all, sailing for enjoyment.

CUTTER

The cutter rig (Figure 8), with two headsails and a slightly smaller mainsail than a sloop of similar size, has become a popular cruising compromise. The variety of possible sail combinations results in greater versatility. Sail area can be reduced quickly by dropping the headsail while retaining a balanced combination of mainsail and staysail. It is also convenient to be able to slow down the boat when entering harbors, or eating or navigating at sea. A large headsail, and perhaps a removable inner forestay, permits the cutter to be sailed as a sloop, with sloop-like performance.

Many cruising sailors say the cutter is the ideal rig in boat sizes up to 35 or 40 feet, at which point the sails become rather large for one or two people to handle. With modern sail materials, however, sails are both lighter and stronger. Developments in reefing and furling equipment for both mainsails and jibs also have made handling larger sails easier. Singlehanded racing sailors are now routinely sailing 60-foot sloops across oceans and around the

Figure 7. Bermudan sloop

world. Production cruising boats of this size also are appearing with enormous sloop and cutter rigs and sophisticated sail-handling equipment.

KETCH AND YAWL

The cruising sailor who values ultimate performance less than sailing ease, and who does not want to depend on sophisticated mechanical systems for sail handling, will prefer multi-masted rigs even in smaller boats. The 30-foot Seawind ketch was the first fiberglass boat to sail around the world and still is a classic cruising boat.

Perhaps more important than reducing sail size is the increased versatility, the great variety of possible balanced sail combinations. In a sudden squall the mainsail on a ketch or a yawl can be dropped very quickly and the boat has a quite small but balanced jib and mizzen combination. The mizzen sail also is of great value in maneuvering the boat in tight quarters, moving forward or in reverse, under sail or power.

As the mizzenmast and sail become larger in comparison to the main, windward ability gradually is reduced but speed on other points of sail is much less affected. Cost and complexity, however, are high for ketches and yawls.

The distinction between a ketch and a yawl is that the ketch mizzenmast is forward of the rudderpost while the yawl's mizzen is aft. Traditionally ketches have relatively larger mizzens and smaller mains than yawls. But with more rudders now located further aft, many boats that are technically ketches have the sail proportions and performance

characteristics of yawls. Look more at these proportions than at mast placement.

SCHOONER

In larger cruising boats, over about 50 feet, the "modern schooner" has become increasingly popular. Dick Carter's 128-foot *Vendredi 13* (Figure 10) built for the 1972 Singlehanded Transatlantic Race, had what he calls the Luna Rig. It had three masts of equal height carrying three jib-like sails. Carter has since placed a two-masted version on smaller boats, down to 35 feet.

Other designers had tried the arrangement of two or three masts of equal height with a headsail forward and mainsail-type sails set on the masts. These, too, proved both fast and easy to handle.

UNSTAYED RIGS

Garry Hoyt's Freedom 40 and Mark Ellis' Nonsuch 30, shown in Figure 11 were breakthrough designs in modern unstayed rigs. The technology and development of unstayed spars is changing rapidly at this time and certainly there is much more progress to be made. This is, I am sure, the area where the greatest advances in cruising boat rigs will be made in the near future.

The new technology—constructing spars with carbon fibers and epoxy resins and other high-strength materials—is resulting in incredibly strong and lightweight self-supporting masts.

Eliminating all the rigging and its associated hardware reduces both the wind drag and the pos-

Figure 8. Bermudan cutter

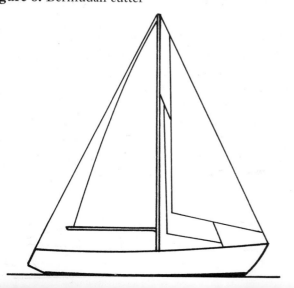

Figure 9. Bermudan ketch

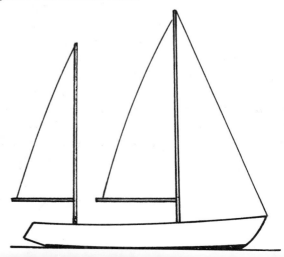

sibility of gear failure. Current development of elliptical section and wing masts will certainly lead to increased sailing efficiency. Indications are that there is also promise in the area of partially stayed spars.

The backstay on a stayed mast restricts the mainsail to a triangular shape with little roach (area outside of the straight line from the head to the clew). On an unstayed mast, however, the sail can have full-length battens, a huge roach and a much more efficient wing-like shape and a lower center of area.

JUNK RIG

The ancestor of today's unstayed rigs is the Chinese junk or lug rig. Naval architect Tom Colvin argues that the two or three-masted lug rig is without doubt the ideal rig for cruising boats. He and other advocates of this rig point out its low cost and ease of handling. Sails can be raised, reefed and lowered from a remote location, even from the protection of the cockpit or belowdecks.

Blondie Hasler's 26-foot junk-rigged *Jester* competed in the first singlehanded transatlantic race in 1964 and every race since then except one. In 1976 Jock McLeod sailed his 46-foot junk-rigged *Ron Glas* in the race and said he never had to go on deck, or even remove his carpet slippers.

The choice of rig must be made considering both the hull and the type of cruising. A heavy displacement hull with moderate performance po-

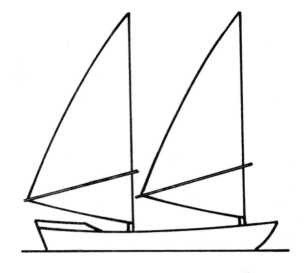

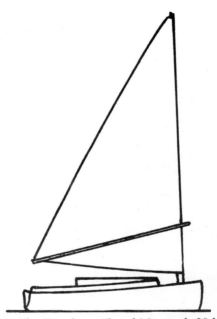

Figure 11. The Freedom 40 and Nonsuch 30 have unstayed rigs.

Figure 10. The 128-foot *Vendredi 13*, a modern schooner.

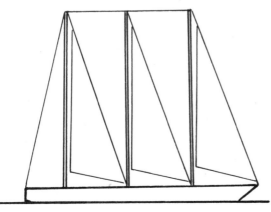

tential calls for a rig with more power than speed potential, while a lightweight performance cruiser should have a rig with high speed potential and windward efficiency.

On an offshore voyaging boat, strength, reliability and ease of handling versatility are necessary. For a coastal cruiser, speed and windward performance assume increased importance. Low cost also is a factor.

There certainly is flexibility and much room for

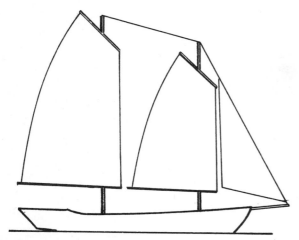

Figure 12. Thomas Colvin's junk-rigged Gazelle.

personal preference in the choice of a suitable rig. Many boats have been rigged in a variety of ways with satisfactory results. The 26-foot *Frolic* (in which I sailed 40,000 miles, mostly singlehanded) was rigged as a Bermudan cutter, while other hulls from the same mold were rigged as a gaff cutter, gaff sloop and gaff schooner.

The following table outlines some of the major advantages and disadvantages of the different rigs to the cruising sailor.

Rig	Advantages	Disadvantages
Gaff Rig	Strong, reliable, and inexpensive; fast reaching and running with working sails.	Heavy, with poor windward efficiency.
Unstayed Rigs	While the unstayed or partially stayed rig is still in its infancy, elliptical mast sections, wing spars and large, fully battened sails show great potential for advantages in speed and efficiency. Can be very simple and reliable.	Cost for the spars, built of sophisticated materials in limited numbers, is high.
Junk	Very inexpensive. Easy to handle and adjust sail area.	Very low windward efficiency.
Marconi or Bermudan sloop	Simple and efficient to windward.	Requires changing headsails for changing wind conditions and points of sail.
cutter	Added versatility of two headsails. Easy to reduce sail and retain balanced sail plan without changing headsails.	Slightly less windward efficiency than sloop, and more difficult to tack a large headsail.
yawl	Reduces individual sail size and increases variety of sail combinations, including mizzen staysail; mizzen sail useful for maneuvering under sail and at anchor can be used as a riding sail.	A further reduction in windward efficiency and increase in complexity and expense.
ketch	Sail sizes further reduced and versatility increased.	Less windward efficiency but greater reaching performance. Greater expense.
modern schooner	Smallest possible sail sizes and mast heights; greatest versatility.	Lowest windward efficiency of the Bermudan rigs.

8

THE RUDIMENTS OF INTERIOR ARRANGEMENT

Balancing comfort, security and utility

UP TO now, it has been possible to measure or assign numerical value to every cruising boat design factor. Weight can be measured with a scale, stability can be accurately measured or mathematically approximated, speed can be both predicted and measured—even the sea-kindliness of the hull can be given a relative numerical value.

The level of interior accommodation, however, which together with motion comfort determines the ultimate comfort of a boat, cannot be measured or even given an approximate numerical value. Evaluating a boat's interior accommodations is an entirely subjective activity. What one considers ideal another may judge intolerable.

Designers and cruising sailors, through clever and efficient use of space and materials, are challenged to create within the tiny and unusually shaped volume of the cruising boat a comfortable living area. This challenge is complicated by extremes of weather, temperature, moisture and heeling angles. The satisfaction experienced when living comfort is achieved inspires serious designers and sailors to experiment with new ideas and to recognize the traditional ones that work better.

Just as the introduction of fiberglass construction and other innovative building materials and techniques gave the naval architect much greater freedom in designing hull shape, so they permitted innovation in interior arrangement and construction. Traditional wood construction, with planking, ribs and interior ceiling, resulted in a hull structure three or four inches thick compared to less than a half-inch in the same size boat built in fiberglass. Even laminated wood, steel or aluminum construction produces boats with more usable interior volume. Molded and laminated interior parts also have made possible lighter, more varied, more efficient and more easily maintained interior furnishings.

Despite the advances made in other areas of cruising boat design, and the wonderful new materials recently arrived on the scene, the design and construction of truly practical and comfortable cruising boat interiors has not received adequate attention. Perhaps it's fortunate for designers that interior arrangements cannot be quantitatively graded. Many marks would be low. A recent personal experience illustrates this point.

In designing my latest boat, *Integrity,* I was determined to have settees as comfortable as my favorite couch, in a friend's house in Newport. I went to two major boat shows and sat on settees in hundreds of boats of every size, and did not find one that elicited the "ahh" of relief that my favorite couch provoked.

Some did not have adequate headroom (and I had bumps on the back of my head to prove it), some were too wide for me to sit back, some were too high for me to reach the cabin sole, and most had backrests that were too low and too vertical. Who would put an uncomfortable bench instead of a sumptuous couch in their house? Why have one in your boat?

I'm a little ashamed to admit that I devoted quite a lot of energy to this search before realizing the obvious: Copy the couch!

No matter what size cruising boat the designer is creating, or its intended use, there is one extremely important factor he cannot forget or ignore: the size and shape of the human body. Whether he is working on a small coastal cruiser or a liveaboard voyaging boat, he must design the interior around the human dimensions. To make the interior suitable for the majority of men and women he should consider the dimensions of bodies from about 5'0" to 6'2". In general he has to make sure there is room for the 6'2" person to stand, sit, move about and lie down, while also making sure that the shorter person can also sit and reach everything comfortably. Windows should provide visibility for both short and tall people.

Figure 1 illustrates a 6'1" figure in a variety of views and positions with dimensions indicated. The dimensions in parentheses are for a 5'3" person. Remember that these are body dimensions; clearances of varying sizes must be allowed for in determining the dimensions of the interior features.

To better apportion living space, I have constructed ½-inch-to-the-foot scale figures complete with jointed limbs. Together with a 12-inch-high mannequin with realistic proportions and joints, they live on my drawing table and are often called upon to determine appropriate dimensions.

It is important for anyone evaluating a design to be able to measure various dimensions on that de-

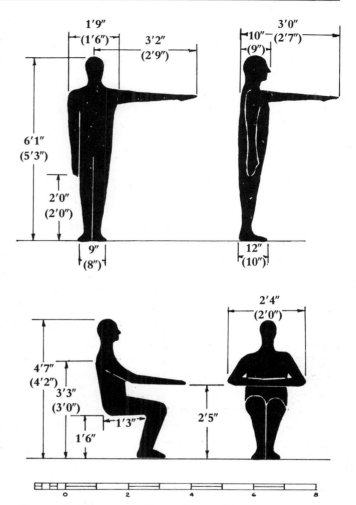

Figure 1. Shown are dimensions of the average 6'1" person, with dimensions for a 5'3" person in parentheses.

sign. With the designs in this book I have included a scale of feet with each. To measure a dimension take a pair of dividers and set them to the length to be measured. Then move the dividers to the scale with that drawing, set one point on the "O" mark and read the length at the other point.

If a scale of feet is not given with a design it is possible to calculate it. It's convenient to have a millimeter ruler (rather than inches) and a calculator. Because the metric ruler is divided into 10ths (rather than the 16ths of an inch ruler) it is far easier to make calculations.

To determine the scale, first measure the greatest beam as shown on the accommodation plan. With the calculator, divide the known value of the

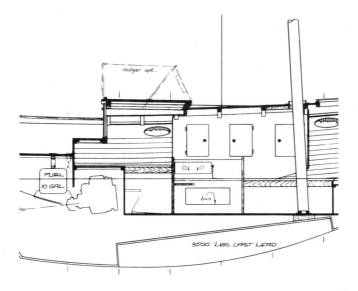

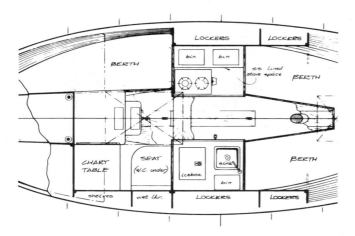

Figure 2. Chuck Paine's flush-decked Frances is well arranged for having only sitting headroom. There is standing headroom under the dodger for standing and looking out. To starboard is a chart table and seat (with toilet under), and forward is a seat on centerline to use when cooking.

beam (in feet and 10ths of feet) by the measured beam in centimeters. The resulting value is the scale factor, the number of feet per centimeter measured. For example, if the actual beam of a boat is 12′3″ (12.25′) and you measure the beam of the drawing as 10.2 cm, then the scale factor is 12.25/10.2, or 1.20 feet per centimeter.

Check the scale factor by measuring the overall length of the boat and multiplying it by the scale factor determined. The product should agree with the given length of the boat.

If your calculator has a memory, store the scale factor there. If not, write it down. Then, to make any measurements on the drawing, measure with the centimeter ruler, multiply by the scale factor, and the result is the true length in feet.

HEADROOM

The dimension that contributes most to the feeling of spaciousness belowdecks is headroom. It might appear from Figure 1 that 6′1″ headroom is sufficient, but there should be some clearance there. Also remember that the transverse curvature, or crown, of most decks reduces headroom away from the centerline of the boat, and that many decks slant downward toward the bow, reducing headroom as you move forward. Thus, the maximum headroom should be at least 6′3″, and 6′6″ if possible. If sufficient drawings are provided you can check the headroom in various locations.

Standing headroom is not an absolute requirement in a cruising boat. Many well-known, well-traveled and popular cruising boats had only sitting headroom, such as L. Francis Herreshoff's 28-foot *Rozinante,* John Letcher's 25-foot *Aleutka,* John Guzzwell's 21-foot *Trekka* and the Crocker-designed Stone Horse 23. Boats designed with sufficient sitting headroom above the seats, especially if they are flush-decked so that the headroom is carried out to the hull sides, can be surprisingly spacious and practical. If they are arranged with seats well positioned for performing the various tasks (such as cooking and navigating), and if there can be standing headroom in the companionway (perhaps under a dodger), the inconvenience of less-than-standing headroom can be minimized.

WIDTH

Boats with wide beams obviously have more interior volume than narrow boats, but the arrangement also can have a major effect on the feeling of width. If the settees and other furnishings can be moved outboard, resulting in a wider cabin sole

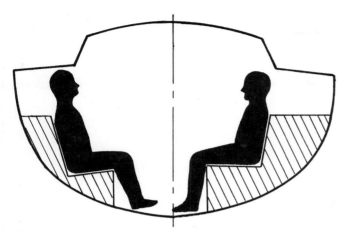

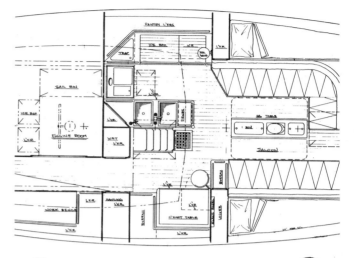

Figure 3. On the left, with the settee placed far outboard, the spaciousness of the cabin is increased but stowage is reduced. On the right, with the settee well inboard, spaciousness is decreased but stowage is greater.

and more open space at shoulder and head level, there will be more room. Storage and pilot berth space below and outboard of the settees, however, will be sacrificed, as shown in Figure 3. To the coastal cruiser the feeling of spaciousness may be more important while to the liveaboard or voyaging sailor increased storage may be crucial.

Yves Tanton's 37-footer, shown on page 174, is an excellent example of the roomy and innovative arrangement possible with a beamy, flush-decked boat.

GALLEY

The most difficult activity performed on a boat probably is cooking, especially at sea. Storage and working space is a very small fraction of what people are accustomed to ashore. Cramped quarters often are complicated by extreme angles of heel and violent motion. A good seagoing galley is difficult to achieve.

The best location for the galley is amidships or aft. If it is too far forward the motion experienced will often make work there impossible. A galley adjacent to the cockpit makes communication and the passage of food between cook and crew easy. Proximity to the companionway also improves ventilation.

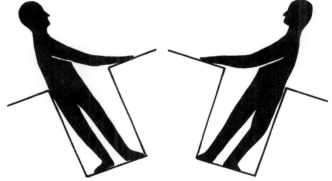

Figure 4. With the galley U-shaped in the fore and aft direction, and properly proportioned, the cook can brace easily on either tack.

When the boat is under way the cook must be able to brace him or herself and still have two hands free. If the galley is U-shaped in the fore and aft direction as shown in Figure 4, the cook can lean on either tack. I would argue this is the best configuration. If the galley is U-shaped in the athwartships direction, or L-shaped, provision must be made for a sling, which the cook can clip to rings for security as in Figure 5. The disadvantage of this is that it requires time and effort to clip and unclip. And the cook is less able to dodge a spilling pot or dropped knife.

Speaking of time and energy, the effort required to perform even the simplest task on a boat at sea is many times that required in port or on land. Simply standing up or sitting down, or opening and closing a cupboard, can be a difficult operation. Any design features that reduce the number and extent of movements will be greatly appreciated by the cruising sailor.

Thus the placement of sink, counter, storage, stove and icebox are also important. All should be as easily reached as possible.

Whether single or double sinks are chosen, they

Figure 5. With a galley U-shaped in the athwartships direction the cook needs a strap for security when heeled to one side.

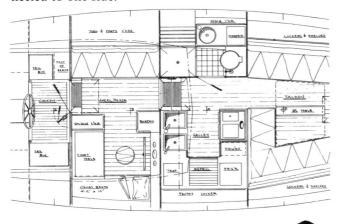

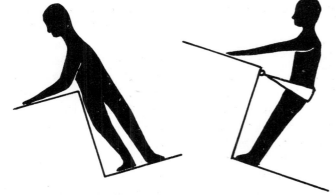

should not be located far outboard. Figure 6 shows that a sink placed outboard can be below water level when heeled to that side, allowing seawater to flow up the drain unless a valve is closed. Such a sink would be unusable on that tack and a potentially dangerous feature.

A simple two-burner stove can be quite compact, but a larger stove with oven, given adequate swinging room, takes up much more space. Many cruising sailors can be satisfied without an oven. It is, however, an important decision because if space is not allowed initially for a large stove, it will be difficult to install one later.

Look at the size and location of the icebox. A large box allows the fitting of thick insulation (four to six inches) while a smaller box may only permit insulation two inches thick. Don't skimp on insulation; it is probably better to reduce the inside dimension of the icebox to achieve good insulation.

Many galley arrangements place the icebox next to the stove and use the top of the box as counter space. The use of the icebox top as a counter means that crumbs and spills will get into the box, and that food under preparation must be moved to access the box. I prefer a counter adjacent to the sink, either stainless steel or epoxy coated to make it watertight and easy to clean. Polyester fiberglass resin is not recommended for a food preparation surface.

If the icebox is next to the stove (or engine) heat will accelerate ice melting unless special precautions are taken. Thicker than normal insulation and a reflective barrier can minimize the effect.

Stowage space for food and cooking utensils

Figure 6. A sink placed too far outboard risks water entering the boat through the sink drain when heeled to that side.

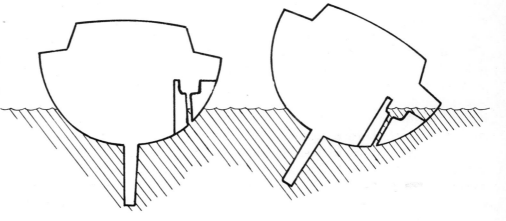

also must be handy. Safety in a knockdown, which is something any cruising boat may encounter, demands that all locker and stowage compartments, plus the icebox lid and stove, have strong catches or bolts to prevent flying objects.

Safety in the galley, and throughout the boat, demands that all corners be rounded as much as possible and that handholds be strategically placed so there is always something strong to grab. Probably more injuries occur down below in rough weather than on deck.

NAVIGATOR'S STATION

After cooking the next most difficult job on a boat at sea is navigating. Here, too, good design makes the job easier. The table can be arranged facing forward or aft, inboard or outboard, with the navigator standing or sitting. Each of these arrangements is favored by some sailors. As in the galley, the navigator should be able to brace himself or herself on either tack with both hands free, and be able to communicate easily with the cockpit.

If the navigator is facing either forward or aft, a deep U-shaped seat as shown in Figure 7 gives comfortable sitting at any angle of heel. If he is standing, foot braces are necessary. If he is facing outboard or inboard, a high-backed seat or some structure to lean back against is required. Seats that are actually the ends of berths are inconvenient and should be avoided if possible.

Chart table size is determined by chart size. The largest common charts are approximately 3′0″ by 4′0″, so a table to store and work with them unfolded must be slightly larger than those dimensions. This usually is not possible, however, especially on boats less than 40 feet in length. A table to accommodate charts folded once would be just over 2′0″ by 3′0″ but might require the chart to be placed sideways on the table. A table 3′0″ square, however, could display a once-folded chart either horizontally or vertically. Smaller tables require charts to be folded twice.

A chart table that slants downward toward the navigator makes chart work a little handier, but makes the table unsuitable for most other uses, such as for eating or as a work table. A glass can-

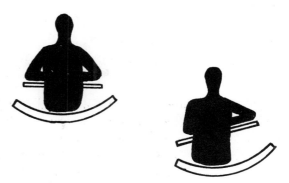

Figure 7. If the chart table faces forward or aft, a large saddle seat allows comfortable seating at any angle of heel.

not be placed on it without spilling. A flat table is more versatile.

A navigator's station is more than just a chart table. Radios, navigation equipment, wind instruments, books and drawing tools should also be handy and securely stowed. For offshore sailing, locating the sextant box close to the chart table is convenient.

SETTEES AND BERTHS

Not only must the cook and navigator be able to perform their tasks with ease and safety, they and the rest of the crew need sleep when they are off watch. They also must be comfortable when they're not in their berths, or cruising will not be pleasant.

At sea, only berths in the middle and after portion of the boat are suitable. Berths further forward will experience much more motion in any sort of sea and are unacceptable for most sailors. Quarter berths and pilot berths are the most useful. Settees also can be used, but have certain drawbacks. If they're narrow enough for sitting they are too narrow for sleeping. Anyone sleeping on a settee is more likely to be disturbed by, or be in the way of, those off watch.

The minimum width for a sea berth is 1′8″, and such a narrow berth would most likely be too warm in hot climates, where the minimum width is 1′10″ to 2′0″. Berths between 2′0″ and 2′4″ can be used both at sea and in port, while those wider than 2′6″ are too wide for security at sea. All should be at least 6′4″ long, with 7′0″ better (most beds are 7′2″ long). Figure 8 shows a variety of berth proportions.

Sea berths should be as nearly parallel to the centerline of the boat as possible, and with vertical sides inboard and outboard. Attention must be paid to the ventilation of each berth, especially quarter berths tucked under the cockpit. A reading light and bookshelf for each berth aids in rest and relaxation.

While a berth has a minimum width of about 1'8", a settee has a maximum width of about 1'5". If it is wider than that, the back of the person's knee hits the front edge of the settee before his back reaches the backrest. Some settees are designed so they can be made wider for sleeping. But they must be set-up to be used for sleeping. Especially for use at sea, berths should be ready to use, and provide some privacy, if maximum restfulness is to be achieved.

In port there's no better sleeping spot than the forward cabin. A large double berth there, with

Figure 8. Proportions of berths.

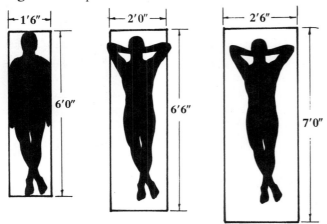

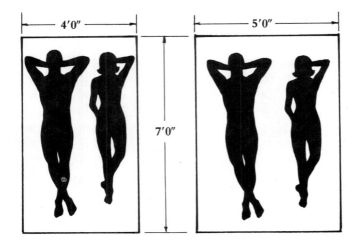

sitting headroom and an overhead hatch, is my idea of luxury. The hatch makes possible quick access to the deck, and permits use of a windscoop for ventilation in hot weather.

It's not just berth width, but also headroom over the berth that determines its comfort and usefulness. While 1'6" to 1'8" of clearance allows room for sleeping it also can lead to claustrophobia. If a berth has 3'0" to 3'2" headroom, at least at the head, it can be used for lounging and relaxing—in addition to sleeping—increasing the boat's liveable space.

New construction methods allow much more use of the area under and aft of the cockpit. Without the old networks of ribs and beams, designers have been able to fit large berths under cockpits and frequently have designed boats with cabins aft of the cockpit.

Aft cabin boats have become very popular with both families and charter groups because of the privacy and isolation they provide. After cabins have been designed into boats as small as about 26 feet, where they usually consist of a berth or two and little else. On larger boats they can be true staterooms, with standing headroom and their own head/shower and perhaps a desk or settee. Some designers have made the area into a "great after cabin" and located the galley and living area here.

An important feature of after cabins is the means of access. On smaller boats the access usually is through a forward-facing companionway into the cockpit, which is fine in port or in good weather. In rain or rough conditions, however, it can be awkward, inconvenient or even dangerous to use this unprotected companionway.

Larger aft-cabin boats can have inside passageways from the forward cabin. This usually is under the cockpit seat and most often lacks standing headroom. It is difficult to judge the ease with which such a passage can be used, especially at sea, without actually trying it.

Many designers also tuck quarter cabins under the cockpit of an aft-cockpit boat. This is an attractive feature, but some such cabins, which appear to be sumptuous in the accommodation plan, actually lack clearance above the berth and convenient access to the berth.

STOWAGE

In theory, due to today's boatbuilding materials, modern boats have more stowage space. But with the trends toward roomier accommodations and reduced displacement, stowage space on many boats actually is very limited. For the short-distance coastal cruiser, this may not be of great concern. But for anyone considering extended cruising, the importance of abundant stowage space can't be overemphasized.

Most light or moderate displacement fin keel boats do not have room in the bilge for water or fuel tanks. So they use the area under the settees for tankage. This isn't a bad location for tanks, but it does eliminate using this area for other stowage.

The weight of liquids carried in tanks is significant. Water weighs about eight pounds/gallon, diesel fuel seven pounds/gallon and gasoline six pounds/gallon. If tanks can be positioned low in the boat, in the bilge or keel, they can contribute to ballast. Also, the closer they can be to the center of the boat, the less effect they'll have on the boat's trim. A tank in the extreme bow or stern will cause a large change in trim when it is filled or emptied.

In boats constructed of welded metal, either aluminum or steel, it is possible to make tanks an integral part of the keel. Ted Brewer's 32-foot aluminum cutter (page 156) shows a keel divided in half, with the forward half containing 4,500 pounds of ballast and the aft half 40 gallons of water. The tank also acts as a sort of double bottom for the boat. If the keel is holed, such as in a grounding, the water in the tank would be contaminated by saltwater, but no water would enter the hull.

Bob Harris' Vancouver 42 (page 190) has all its tankage under the cabin sole. In addition to 200 gallons of water, there are two 60-gallon fuel tanks, a 50-gallon holding tank and a sump. The weight of the full fuel and water tanks is more than a ton!

On my last boat, *Frolic*, a 26-foot fiberglass cutter, I removed the cockpit footwell. Not only was I able to locate the head there, but also to stow an inflatable dinghy, a portable generator, dinghy oars and spars, sails and many cases of food and supplies. In designing *Integrity*, my next boat (page 162), I set aside an area to hold 12 plastic crates similar to those used by dairies (these are, I think, ideal for storing most things on a boat).

Consideration was also given to the stowage of long items, such as awning poles and long pieces of lumber, plus oars and dinghy spars. On many boats that are claimed to be suitable for offshore cruising, all this gear must be lashed on deck where it can get in the way, tangle sheets, and be lost or damaged in rough weather.

Another feature handy on a cruising boat is a

Figure 9. A large wet locker, placed adjacent to the companionway, is a valuable feature on an ocean-going boat.

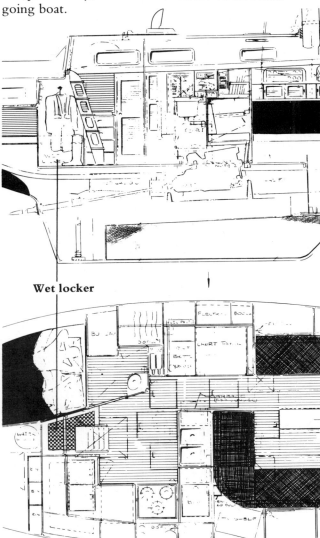

Wet locker

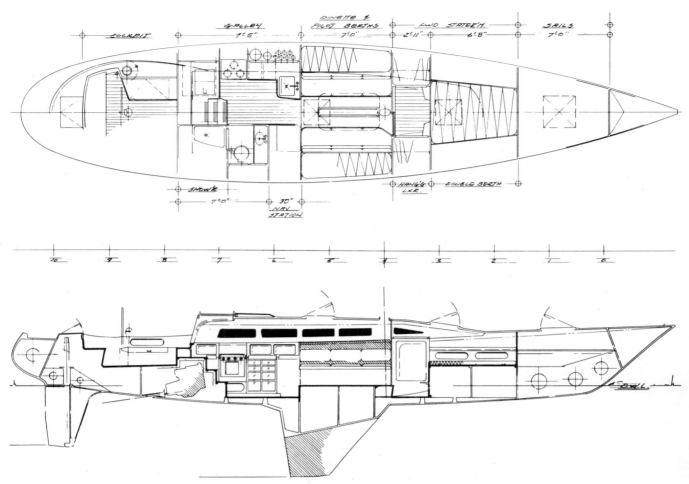

Figure 10. In designing his own ideal cruising boat, naval architect Robert Perry listed his interior arrangement requirements: a large galley, a separate shower stall, large chart table, two pilot berths, high visibility dinette, large double berth and sail locker. He fit them masterfully into a long, narrow hull. The galley is 9′5″ long, and the head 7′0″, but the cook would have to be strapped in at sea. To achieve his "high visibility dinette", Perry raised the cabin sole 10″ in this area. Those sitting at the dinette have their eyes at window level. He says that to move to the forward stateroom, you "simply sit on a dinette seat and scoot along in a sitting position until you reach the headroom area forward." The starboard settee also acts as a seat for the navigator. Steps are provided for climbing into the 6′8″ berth forward. At 7′0″ in length, the sail locker forward could also serve as a sleeping cabin accessible from the deck. It is an arrangement intended more for coastal than offshore cruising.

wet locker, a place to hang foul weather gear near the companionway. Figure 9 shows the arrangement on the Vancouver 42, which also has a drying tray for boots behind the companionway ladder.

"A place for everything, and everything in its place," is a good motto to remember. If stowage can be planned for every item, from the crews' toiletries to food stores, it's easier to keep the boat orderly and uncluttered.

ENGINES

Subordinate attention often is given to engines in the space arrangement of boats. At a recent boat show I inspected a 40-foot production fiberglass boat built by a major manufacturer. It had pitiful access to the engine. Just to check the oil, the sailor would have to empty a cockpit or hanging locker, remove a panel and then perform the contortions

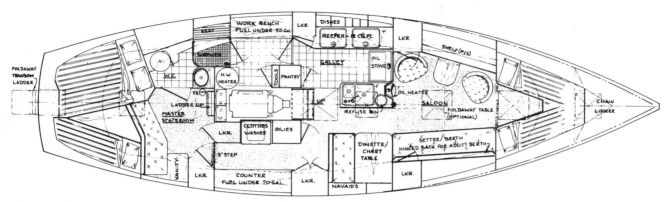

Figure 11. Fidelity was designed by C. John Simpson as a liveaboard retirement boat and shows a high level of comfort. The master stateroom aft, with double and single berths, head and seating, is connected to the main cabin by a passageway to port, which also contains a washing machine and counter space. Opposite is a large workroom. Headroom in these areas is under the wide cockpit coamings. The galley appears spacious, yet secure for use at sea. The dinette/chart table is a useful feature. Lounge chairs give the saloon a true living room feel and the V-berths forward have good overhead clearance.

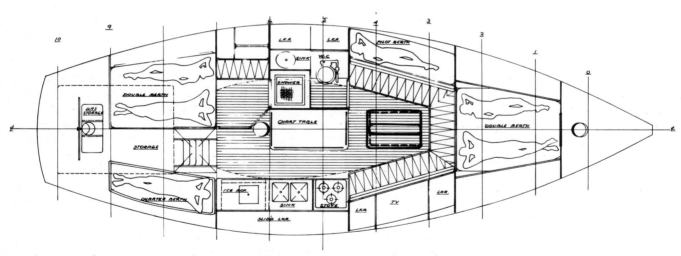

Figure 12. Yves Tanton's arrangement for his 37-footer is unusual and imaginative. With wide beam and a flush deck, he had a large interior volume with which to work. To port of the off-center companionway is a private quarter cabin with large double berth and good headroom and clearance above the berth. To starboard is a single quarter berth. There is excellent stowage under the cockpit. The chart table amidships covers the easily accessed engine and gives the cook a place to lean on a starboard tack. A large head, accessible from both cabins, is opposite the galley. In the main cabin is a huge dining area, pilot berth and locker space. Forward is another king-size double berth with access over its head. It is a spacious layout that appears to be suitable for living aboard at sea or in port.

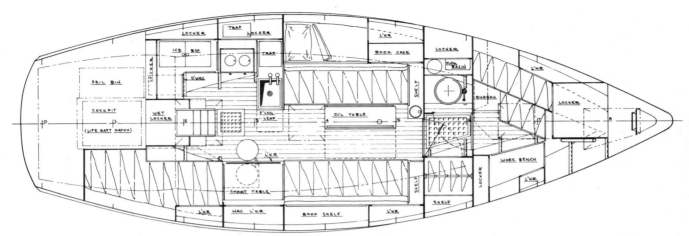

Figure 13. Bulldog, at only 30 feet in length, possesses an extraordinary amount of accommodation space. The galley is compact and secure for use at sea. Behind the ladder is a wet locker, and to starboard is a large quarter berth and outboard-facing chart table with swing-out stool. The pilot berth to port provides a second good sea berth without having to use the settees, and features shelves and lockers over its foot. A bulkhead-mounted cabin heater is shown. The head with hanging locker opposite separates the main cabin from the forepeak, which contains a very useful workbench, numerous drawers and lockers, a single berth and a large seat. A 75-gallon fresh water tank is fitted into the keel.

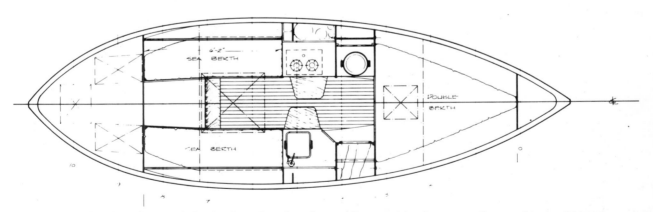

Figure 14. Chuck Paine designed the 24-foot Carol as the smallest cruiser that can sail anywhere safely. Her interior arrangement is a model of simplicity and usefulness in a boat without standing headroom. The raised flush deck results in a surprisingly spacious living area. Standing headroom in the companionway, under a dodger, gives the sailor a place to stand for dressing or looking out. The two quarter berths will be comfortable at sea or in port, while the full width double V-berth is a bit narrow at the foot and requires users to climb over the head of the berth. Both these problems are necessary and acceptable compromises in such a small craft. Amidships are a stove and head to port with sink and hanging locker to starboard. Fold-down seats on each side provide convenient seating for work at the galley. Without an engine, there is stowage space under the cockpit in addition to beneath all berths.

of a gymnast. Servicing it would be extremely difficult and removing it practically impossible.

For convenience and safety, engines must be accessible. Modern sound-deadening materials make placing the engine in the living area of the boat, rather than under the cockpit, much more practical. They are often found today under a galley counter or a table in the main cabin, where removing side panels gives excellent all-around access.

Batteries, too, should be easily accessible. They must be securely tied down so they'll remain in place at extreme angles of heel or even in a capsize.

CONCLUSION

When studying the accommodation plan of a cruising boat, try to picture it in use, at sea and in port, with a varying number of crew and in varying conditions. Check important dimensions. Look for stowage for all necessary gear.

Chapter

9

DECK ARRANGEMENT PRINCIPLES

Casting a cautious eye for safety

AS IN the design of comfortable, practical and safe living accommodations, the design of the cockpit, deck and cabin on a cruising sailboat must be done with the dimensions of the human body in mind. The entire deck structure, as well as its various components, must allow the crew to perform hundreds of different tasks easily and safely in widely—and often wildly—varying conditions.

The most important consideration, at least on a boat intended for offshore cruising, is the structural and watertight integrity of the boat. The deck is a cover over the hull and its interior, like a roof on a house, and should be able to keep water out in all conceivable conditions. A strong, tight deck can even make up for a less-than-ideal hull or some mistakes in seamanship, while a weak deck can mean disaster for the best of hulls and sailors.

In 1981 the 55-foot *Blue Jacket* was smashed by a large breaking wave off Bermuda. The cockpit of this well-built boat was broken loose from the deck and pushed down into the hull, leaving a gaping hole in the deck. In addition, the one-inch-thick wood cabin sides were split completely around the cabin. Only the valiant efforts of the crew kept her afloat.

Perhaps few boats would have survived the wave that struck *Blue Jacket*. But the design and construction of the deck often is the weakest part of a cruising boat. A strong, well-engineered, watertight deck and hull/deck joint is a requisite on a coastal or offshore cruiser.

Deck and cabin structures also are the most visible parts of a boat, either on a drawing or in reality and probably contribute more than any other feature to someone's first impression. Few deck and cabin arrangements actually enhance the appearance of the boat, and many detract significantly, especially on smaller boats where achieving standing headroom below necessitates a high cabin. The designer is again challenged to create a deck design that is strong, comfortable, easy to work on, watertight and good-looking.

COCKPIT

The cockpit consists basically of seats, footwell and backrests. No matter what size boat, or overall size of the cockpit itself, the size of bodies to be

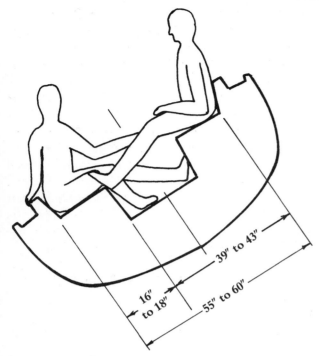

Figure 1. A section view of a cockpit shows the dimensions necessary for sitting to windward and to leeward. Backrests should be high (12 to 14 inches if possible) and angled back.

accommodated is the same. Figure 1 shows a typical cockpit cross section with appropriate dimensions. For short coastal cruising it is usually desirable to have a large cockpit with seating for four to six people. This requires a seating length of four to six feet. In this type of sailing the crew spends most of its time in the cockpit.

In longer distance and offshore sailing the number of crew usually is smaller and less time is spent sitting in the cockpit, as there are (or should be) more comfortable places for those off watch. With the widespread use of wind vanes and autopilots, even those on watch don't have to sit at the helm. Cockpits and cockpit footwells can be made smaller.

On an offshore cruiser, a smaller cockpit will hold less water if a wave breaks onto the boat. This smaller volume adds less weight to the stern and drains more quickly than a larger volume. Often a raised bridgedeck placed at the forward end of the cockpit reduces the possibility of cockpit water spilling down the companionway. A bridgedeck also adds useful volume below.

On my 26-foot *Frolic* I eliminated the cockpit footwell almost completely, leaving only a four-inch deep well. A teak grate made the area flush with the seats or could be inverted to provide sunken foot holds when sailing. The same grate could be elevated to form a table.

I found the comfort and versatility of this arrangement very attractive. I don't think that any fixed cockpit seating arrangement can be comfortable for long periods and at all angles of heel. With a flush—or partially flush—arrangement and a few cockpit cushions, the variety of possible positions can make a great difference.

Protection from the wind, spray, cold and rain is an asset in any cockpit design, whether for coastal or offshore sailing. A large, ruggedly built fabric dodger is a relatively inexpensive and valuable addition to any cruising boat. For a simple and effective dodger installation the deck should be designed with a dodger in mind. A continuous, spray deflecting lip from one cockpit coaming, up over the cabin top forward of the companionway, and down to the opposite coaming (Figure 2) is ideal. A hatch box, over the companionway sliding hatch, is also necessary to keep water from running aft along the deck, under the hatch and down the companionway.

A well built dodger can take quite a beating from wind and spray. A breaking wave or falling object, however, can damage it just when you need it the most. Boats built for offshore sailing in extreme conditions are often seen with rigid, structural dodgers made of wood, fiberglass or aluminum. With Plexiglas or Lexan windows they provide better visibility than the flexible plastic windows in fabric dodgers.

Figure 2. A spray-deflecting lip around the companionway, and a hatch box, make the installation of a dodger simple and effective.

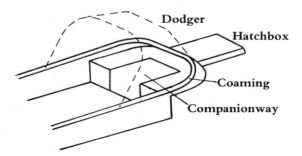

On a cruising boat of about 40 feet or larger, a fully enclosed cockpit or inside pilothouse is possible. The difference between the two is that an enclosed cockpit is still a cockpit, so is outside the watertight integrity of the boat. If a window is broken or water somehow finds its way inside, it will drain overboard and not enter the boat.

A pilothouse, however, is usually inside the boat, so care must be taken in its design to build in greater strength and protection—a difficult task with the large windows and high structure required in pilothouses.

While on the subject of cockpits I would like to discuss cockpit lockers. On most cruising boats there are one or two of these lockers, under the cockpit seats. They usually are very deep, leading to the bilge area of the boat.

In addition to being a poor and inefficient means of stowage they are one of the most dangerous features found on cruising sailboats. It is very difficult to make them watertight, so water on the seats often finds its way into the locker and gets everything wet. The seldom used items at the bottom of the locker (storm sails or life jackets, perhaps) may thus stay wet all the time and be mildewed or rotten when needed.

The real danger, however, is the enormous volume of water that can enter the boat through a broken or open locker lid in rough weather. It is the weakest link in the watertight protection of most boats.

Figure 3. On the left, a cockpit locker that leads to the bilge offers inefficient stowage space and can be dangerous by allowing water to enter the boat. The small cockpit locker on the right is self-bailing, more convenient and safer. The stowage space beneath is dry and is accessible from the boat's interior.

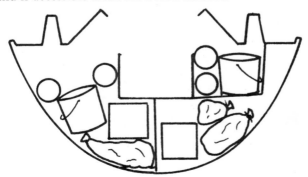

It is important though to have stowage for certain items handy to the cockpit. The solution, I think, is to have shallow cockpit lockers that drain naturally into the cockpit footwell and to use the space beneath them as stowage accessible only from inside the boat. These smaller cockpit lockers could hold propane tanks, spare lines, buckets and life jackets, as in Figure 3.

More thought also is being given to life raft stowage in the cockpit. Designers have located them under helmsman's seats, in lockers in the transom and in various other locations. A life raft is a large, heavy and extremely valuable item. Its placement should receive consideration during the design.

DECKS

When it is necessary for the sailor to leave the cockpit and walk forward to perform some sail-handling chore, this movement should be unobstructed and secure. Look for side decks at least 18 inches wide. This might seem unnecessarily wide,

Figure 4. A side deck 18 inches wide is just wide enough for convenient use when the boat is heeled.

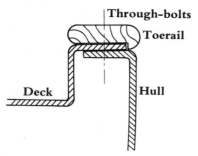

Figure 5. This hull-to-deck joint, common on fiberglass boats, forms a raised bulwark around the deck and reduces the possibility of leaks by elevating the joint.

but consider what happens when the boat is heeled sharply as in Figure 4. When the designer does not present a deck plan, or arrangement, he should show the outline of the cabin and cockpit as dotted lines on the general interior arrangement plan.

High toe rails or bulwarks all around enhance security on deck; five or six inches is very effective. In fiberglass construction a hull-to-deck joint

Figure 6. When chainplates are at the deck edge, as on the left, the lower shrouds can severely inhibit passage on the side deck. If the lower shrouds are moved inboard (dotted line) this problem is avoided. When shrouds are inboard, as on the right, passage can be severely restricted.

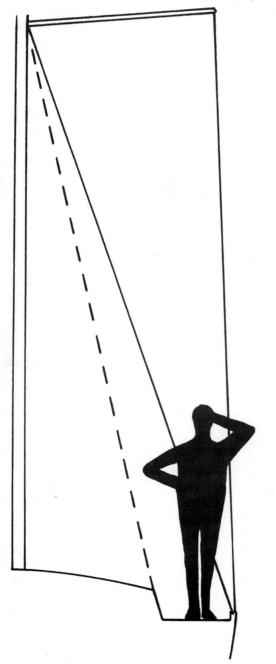

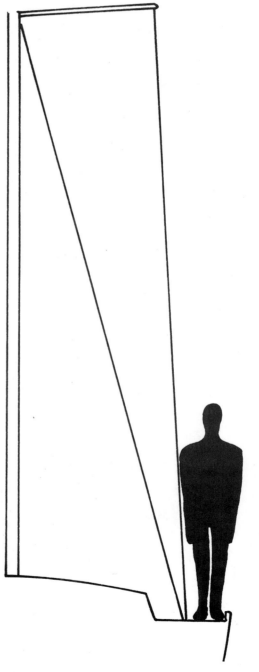

has become popular that combines a toe rail with a waterproof overlap of the hull and deck (Figure 5). Adding a bulwark to an existing boat also is quite possible.

Shrouds supporting the mast can severely restrict passage forward. On many modern sailboats chain plates are well inboard for close headsail sheeting, and so are right in the middle of the side deck. Even if the chain plates are at the deck edge, the lower shrouds can obstruct passage forward and aft. Figure 6 illustrates both situations and possible solutions.

Foredecks also should be as clear as possible, free of things that will stub toes and snag sheets. Many boats feature covered wells in the bow for anchors, anchor windlass and cleats. These make foredeck work easier and safer. Short anchoring bowsprits,

Figure 7. A high railing on each side of the mast adds great security to anyone working there.

which keep the anchors off the foredeck and out of the way, also are popular and useful.

Since quite a few jobs must be performed at the mast, security in this area also should be considered. Railings designed to provide a bracing point for someone at the mast (Figure 7) are a valuable addition.

HATCHES AND VENTILATION

One of the primary roles of the deck is to keep water out of the boat. This would be much easier if it were not necessary to make so many holes in the deck. For both comfort and safety every one of these holes should be capable of being sealed watertight, or nearly so.

Modern aluminum frame hatches are watertight, come in a variety of sizes from small ventilation hatches to large foredeck hatches, are light in weight, low in profile and reasonably priced. Some models can be made to open in two different directions, aiming forward for maximum ventilation or aft to keep spray out. A large hatch with a fabric windscoop is a must in tropical climates.

The companionway is the most difficult opening to make watertight. The common combination of a sliding hatch and hatchboards has a number of drawbacks. In foul weather when the hatch must be kept closed, entering or leaving the cabin is a difficult operation, requiring the hatch to be slid open and the boards removed. If one of the boards is lost, the resultant hole makes the boat very vulnerable. Swinging doors in place of the hatchboards is not much of an improvement.

Racing boats often use an aluminum frame hatch for the companionway, either hinged or sliding. A dodger over such a flush hatch, unless very high, demands bodily contortions from those using the hatch.

A reasonable compromise is a sliding watertight aluminum hatch with shallow hatchboard, as in Figure 8. In moderate weather both can be left open for easy access. In foul weather the board can be secured in place and only the hatch opened and closed.

Just when the designer has achieved a completely watertight deck, he has to cut holes for

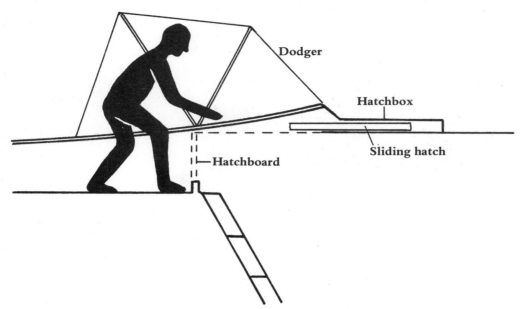

Figure 8. A good companionway arrangement with a sliding hatch and a single hatchboard allows the hatchboard to be secured in place and only the sliding hatch opened and closed in severe weather.

ventilation. Sailing in a poorly ventilated boat, especially when hatches must be kept closed, can make a cruise or passage hellishly uncomfortable.

A large, waterproof dodger will allow the companionway to be left open in fairly rough weather, and aft-facing deck hatches with small fabric dodgers also are very effective. The time will come, however, when all must be closed and secured.

Traditional Dorade ventilators (Figure 9) with large cowls are effective in admitting air without admitting water. They, too, should have covering plates that can be screwed in to make them watertight in survival conditions.

There also are a number of low-profile deck ventilators on the market, some with electric fans for forced draft and others that work on natural circulation. One even has a solar-powered fan.

Although it is more a matter of construction than design, the subject of non-skid deck surfaces should be mentioned. There are a variety of surfaces possible: molded-in non-skid fiberglass, substances added to deck paint, teak or rubber matting glued to the deck. All can be effective. What is very important is that any possible area that may be stepped on be finished in non-skid material.

Many boats use very attractive patterns of non-skid on the deck, leaving large areas in between, especially the cabin sides and cabin top, slick and shiny. When the boat is heeled and you need traction the most, you should not have to look carefully where to step. Slanting cabin sides and deck hatches are prime accident areas.

With the excellent hatches, ventilators, epoxy adhesives, bedding compounds that retain their adhesion and flexibility indefinitely, and other modern materials and techniques, there is no excuse for leaky decks. With proper design and construction the cruising boat deck can be made to withstand severe conditions, keep the boat afloat, and keep the crew dry and comfortable.

Figure 9. In a Dorade ventilator, the baffle prevents water from entering the cabin but allows air to flow.

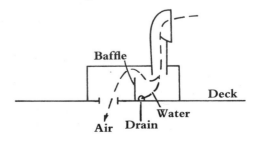

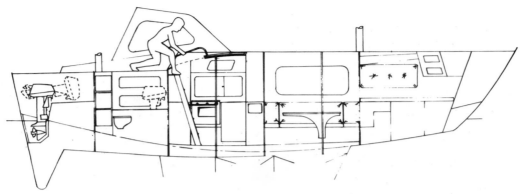

Figure 10. The raised, flush–deck arrangement of my own Integrity is easy to construct, inherently strong and offers an uncluttered deck for dinghy stowage and sail handling. The cockpit, too, is mostly flush with just a small footwell aft. A large, rigid dodger with Lexan windows provides great protection.

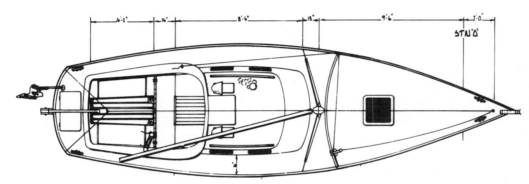

Figure 11. The deck on Graham Shannon's Coast 30 is mostly flush with a small cabin aft of the mast, thus retaining many of the attractions of a flush deck while adding cabin windows for visibility and light below. The cockpit is small, well protected and comfortable. Notice the cockpit coaming carried right around the companionway for installing a dodger.

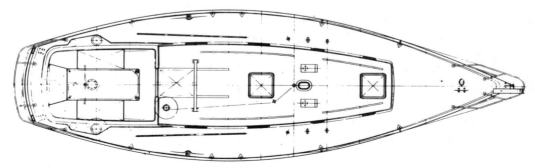

Figure 12. Chuck Paine's Morris 36 has a very traditional trunk cabin, with wide side decks and spacious foredeck. Ports in the cabin sides add light and visibility and can open for ventilation. There is room on the cabin top between the mast and the main sheet for dinghy stowage. Note the fitting to hold the anchor out over the bow, where it is handy but out of the way.

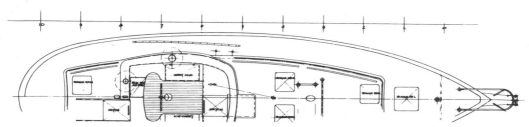

Figure 13. The center cockpit of Seaton-Neville's Sandpiper 44 is deep and well protected. A permanent framework of pipes supports a fabric Bimini top to keep out sun and rain, also protecting the forward-facing companionway to the after cabin. Railings are provided for working at the mast and there are handrails all around the cabin top. The short bowsprit increases sail area and permits stowage of two anchors. There are five opening deck hatches, and an ice chest in the starboard cockpit locker.

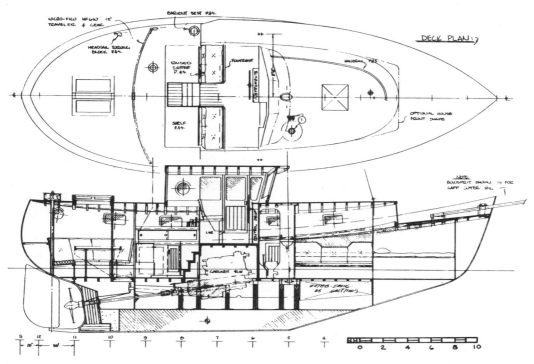

Figure 14. Jay Benford's 40-foot motorsailer has a true pilothouse, with a chart table and seating for three or four people. It is designed more for coastal cruising in areas where protection from the weather is important. Offshore, its large windows could be vulnerable to damage and the boat is not self bailing. Having such a cozy place from which to run the boat would greatly increase the range of areas and length of sailing season for coastal cruising.

CABINS

Closely related to the deck configuration is the type of cabin, or deckhouse. This feature, in turn, is a function of boat size and interior arrangement. Modern building techniques have allowed the designer to experiment with shapes that would have been difficult to achieve in traditional wood construction.

Figures 10 through 15 illustrate a variety of cabin types, from flush deck to pilothouse. Among other things, a cabin gives protection to the cockpit, makes using the companionway easier and permits a varying quantity of windows to light the interior. The higher the cabin, however, the more susceptible it is to damage under severe conditions. This becomes a major consideration in a boat intended for extended offshore sailing.

The cabin top aft of the mast often is the best location for dinghy stowage. Look for a space eight feet long, four feet wide and about 18 inches high. If this is impossible, consider the foredeck.

Will a dinghy fit there and still allow easy passage to the bow? For extended cruising a boat should be able to carry both an inflatable and a rigid dinghy. Both have their attractive qualities, and if there is more than one person aboard or if one dinghy is lost, stolen or damaged, there is always transportation ashore.

AS RECENTLY as 25 years ago nearly all sailing yachts were constructed of wood, mostly in the traditional carvel planking technique. Since that time entirely new materials, many new ways of putting materials together and new coatings to protect them from the ravaging elements have revolutionized the design, construction and maintenance of pleasure boats.

Any one of more than a dozen basic construction methods can be used to produce an excellent cruising boat. Some are more suited to specific categories of boats, such as by size or intended use, and some are more suited to certain types of production, such as custom or amateur building. The range of choices for the designer, builder and sailor is enormous.

Comparing and evaluating all these possibilities is difficult because there are so many ways in which to judge them. They can be compared by cost, strength, weight, maintenance, ease of repair, suitability to amateur construction, insulative qualities and resale value. None of these considerations is a simple one; quantitative values are often impossible to assign.

The most suitable choice for the cruising sailor, especially if the boat is intended for living aboard or long-term offshore sailing, is a very personal one. If the sailor is to feel comfortable and safe, both vital in the true enjoyment of cruising, he or she must have an affinity for the material. This, I think, should be the ultimate consideration. But it also is the most subjective and difficult decision to make without a great deal of experience.

After reading about the many possible construction techniques presented in this chapter, try to "get a feel" for each material. Use this new-found knowledge along with any previous experience to form opinions on the appeal and suitability of the various techniques.

Before proceeding to descriptions of the materials and techniques, let's briefly review the trade-offs of cost, strength and weight in evaluating the different choices.

The matter of cost in selecting a hull material often is overemphasized. With a few exceptions, a comparison of the cost per square foot of materials for hull construction reveals there is surprisingly little difference between them. More important is

Chapter
10

A SURVEY OF CONSTRUCTION MATERIALS AND TECHNIQUES

Cost, weight, strength

the amount and cost of labor required to put the material together into a finished hull.

The actual cost of the material for the hull and deck is generally only about 10 to 15 percent of the total cost of the finished boat. Thus, a choice that saves the builder even 50 percent in materials expense probably affects the final cost by less than 10 percent. The other material costs, such as mast, rigging, sails, hardware, engine, winches, anchors, etc. are the same no matter what the hull material and cost many times more.

However, if the boat is professionally built, labor cost must be considered. The amount of labor required varies significantly among the various building techniques. Still, the cost of the hull and deck, including labor, usually amounts to only about 25 percent of the complete boat. So, while it is a necessary consideration, it should not be an overriding one.

For the amateur builder, who is not placing a price on his own labor, material cost is somewhat more important. The amateur, however, must still consider how much labor and time will be required to complete the project.

Sailboats are subject to, and must withstand, three types of structural punishment. These are flexural stress, impact stress and abrasion.

Flexural stress is imposed primarily by the mast and rigging but also from waves and water. In an effort to make sailboats, especially racing boats, sail very close to the wind, designers have called for a great deal of tension in headstays to keep the luff of the jib straight, and narrow staying bases for the shrouds to allow close headsail sheeting. Both of these features result in high loads imposed on the hull by the stays and the mast, loads which tend to flex the hull and distort its shape. Unstayed spars also impose flexural loads on the hull. Did you ever hear creaking noises or notice a door or cupboard which would not open easily when a boat is being sailed in strong winds? These are signs of flexure or distortion of the hull.

Impact stress is the result of a severe and concentrated blow, such as from striking a rock, a pier or a large floating object. Abrasion to the boat is the result of a scraping or grinding to the hull from an unfendered dock, another boat or a grounding situation.

The many different construction materials and

Figure 1. A single-skin fiberglass hull can be stiffened and strengthened by bonding internal structures to the hull.

techniques for building have widely varying resistances to these structural loadings. Some can be engineered to withstand all or most of the stresses but perhaps only with great weight or expense, and some have insurmountable weaknesses in certain areas.

Basic factors in the choice of building a system should be the amount and type of strength called for, and the associated weight and cost required to achieve it.

FIBERGLASS

The introduction of fiberglass as a boatbuilding material in the late 1950s and early 1960s marked the beginning of a revolutionary change in cruising boat design, cruising boat construction and cruising in general. No longer were designers and builders restricted to hull shapes that could be formed from planks of wood or panels of steel, and no longer were boat owners subjected to the tedious maintenance required by most wood boats. For the first time boats could be mass produced, which reduced boat prices and made boat ownership possible and attractive to a greater number of people.

Fiberglass construction, also known as fiberglass

reinforced plastic (FRP) and glass reinforced plastic (GRP), is basically a laminated structure consisting of a plastic polyester resin and fabrics or materials made from glass. The material is built up in layers and saturated with the resin to bond the layers together. By using different types of resin and material, built up to varying thicknesses, the naval architect can design a hull structure that suits each particular area of the hull, making it stronger in areas of high stress and lighter in areas of lower stress. Used correctly, it is strong and efficient construction material.

Fiberglass has a few significant structural weaknesses. It exhibits relatively low resistance to both impact and abrasion. These weaknesses can be reduced by various design and construction details, such as strategic placement of reinforcements and wood or metal rubbing strakes.

Another occasional problem, which has been occurring with increased frequency, is the absorption of water into the outer fiberglass laminate by a process called osmosis. Polyester resin does not form an absolutely waterproof barrier, and neither does anti-fouling bottom paint. If certain conditions (which are not fully understood at this time) exist, water can migrate through the outer fiberglass layer and form blisters just below the surface. In most cases it is not a structural problem, but a troublesome cosmetic one. The blisters must be ground out, filled and faired, and this may be necessary every year. This "boatpox" has occurred on even the highest quality production fiberglass boats. A number of remedies have been proposed and tried, such as coating the underbody with a waterproof epoxy paint. Results are still inconclusive.

On the plus side, the skills required to build, maintain and repair fiberglass boats are well within the capabilities of the average boat owner. Most find it a somewhat unpleasant material to work with, especially if much grinding and sanding must be done. With proper protection, such as ventilation and a breathing mask, it can be tolerated. Some find fiberglass work more unpleasant than others.

The first fiberglass boats were constructed of solid, or single skin, lamination, with the hull built up entirely of layers of material and resin. Overall strength is achieved by adding and bonding internal structure in the form of bulkheads, longitudinal stringers and other reinforcing members, inside of the hull as shown in Figure 1. Often all the interior parts of the boat, including the "furniture," are bonded to the hull to increase strength. The designer and builder must work out a balance between hull thickness and internal reinforcement. The hull can be made thick, with reduced internal structure, or thin, with greater internal structure, for the same overall strength.

A popular later development was cored construction—two thinner fiberglass skins separated by a lightweight core material. A cored hull is much stiffer than a single-skin hull and a more effective use of materials. However, the bond between the core material and the skins must be very strong. If this bond fails the structure can become dangerously weak. Coring also adds valuable insulating qualities to a fiberglass hull.

Here are descriptions of the various fiberglass construction techniques.

SINGLE SKIN—FEMALE MOLDED

Single skin, or solid, fiberglass construction is the most basic method of construction, and the one used for the first boats produced. The usual technique employs a female mold, a concave mold whose inside surface matches the outside surface of the hull to be produced.

Female molding is basically a three-step process. First a "plug" or full-size model of the hull is built. The plug can be made of any material and need only be strong enough to maintain its desired shape. The plug is then used to build the mold, usually by applying layers of fiberglass cloth and resin to the plug's surface, building up thickness and strength until the mold is strong enough that the plug can be removed. The inside shape and surface finish of the mold matches the outside shape and finish of the plug.

The final step is the laminating, or laying up of the hull inside the mold. The mold is first coated with a substance to prevent the hull from sticking to it, then a specially formulated resin called "gel coat" is sprayed to cover the inside of the mold. This gel coat will be the outside surface of the finished hull. The gel coat is followed by layers of

Figure 2. Workers at C. E. Ryder Co. lay up fiberglass in one half of the female mold for the Sea Sprite 34.

material and resin built up to the desired hull thickness as in Figure 2.

When the hull laminate is complete, the hull is pulled from the mold. Its outside surface is as smooth and fair as the inside surface of the mold. If care was taken in the building of the plug and then the mold, the molded hull is virtually finished, ready for fitting the internal structure.

The great attraction of the female molding technique is that once the mold has been constructed, many hulls can be built in it quite quickly and easily with little or no finish work required. This makes it extremely attractive for volume or production building, where the time and expense of building the plug and mold can be spread out over perhaps hundreds of hulls. Virtually all production boats are built by the female molding technique. It is not usually appropriate for amateur or one-off construction.

SINGLE SKIN—MALE MOLDED

Single-skin fiberglass construction is not limited to female molding. Materials developed in the 1970s have also made it attractive for custom or amateur construction on a male mold. A male mold is a convex mold over which a hull can be layed up, with the first layer applied to the mold being the inside of the final hull, rather than the outside as with a female mold.

With these materials, it is not necessary to have a mold with a complete, continuous surface as with the female mold. It is only necessary to have the hull shape defined with a series of building stations, similar to the stations of the lines plan, and perhaps some longitudinal members attached to these stations but with spaces between them.

It is not possible to lay the fiberglass over the stations or longitudinals because it would sag in the spaces in between where it is not supported. One method of dealing with this problem was developed by William Seemann. He calls his product C-Flex, and it is a sort of fiberglass planking consisting of a 12-inch-wide strip of fiberglass cloth with lengthwise bundles of fiberglass fibers attached to it. Alternating bundles have already been saturated with resin and cured, so that they are quite stiff. C-Flex is produced in rolls, 250 feet long.

Figure 3 shows the rigid fiberglass C-Flex rods being layed longitudinally on a male mold to form a fair surface over which normal fiberglass material and resin can be layed up to the desired hull thickness. After the outside laminate is complete, it is lifted off the male mold and additional laminate applied to the inside over the C-Flex.

The disadvantage to this, and any other male mold technique, is that the outside of the hull does not automatically have the smooth, shiny surface produced by a female mold. Such a surface can be achieved, but only by the builder filling, sanding and fairing the outside hull surface. Careful building can minimize the amount of work necessary to achieve a high-quality finish, but it is still a time-consuming operation.

Another material developed to allow single-skin fiberglass construction on a male mold is called Str-r-etch Mesh, developed by Platt Monfort of Alladin Products, Inc. It is a woven wire material somewhat similar in appearance to ½-inch hardware screening, but with the wires neither welded nor galvanized to each other. It is designed and engineered so that it can be layed over a male mold bending fair in all directions. Just as with the C-Flex, it forms a fair shape over which a fiberglass hull can be laminated. When the hull is removed from the mold, the wire can be torn out from the inside of the fiberglass or left in place. In either case, additional fiberglass laminations are added to the inside.

The attraction of the male mold technique to the amateur or custom builder is that it is only a two-step operation. The male mold is much easier to construct than the female mold because it does not have to possess a continuous surface. Single-skin fiberglass can be designed to be very strong but does have several disadvantages, its poor insulative qualities and its poor impact and abrasion resistance.

CORED FIBERGLASS

Including a core material between two fiberglass skins increases a fiberglass hull's stiffness and its insulative qualities. On a racing boat, or a cruiser where extremely light weight is desired, the outer skin can be about 40 percent as thick as a single fiberglass skin, and the inner skin 30 percent, reducing the required fiberglass and resin about 30 percent. While the core material can increase the impact strength of fiberglass, it does nothing for its abrasion strength.

On a cruising boat, where weight is not so critical, the outer skin can be made thicker, perhaps as thick as an ordinary single fiberglass skin. The core and the inner skin then add significantly to the hull's flexural and impact strengths.

Core materials are usually weak in compression, so in highly stressed areas or where through-hull fittings are placed it is necessary to substitute a block of wood or other strong material in that area. Wherever a fitting is placed, or a hole drilled through the fiberglass, it is critically important to seal the exposed surface of the core and bed the fitting with a waterproof compound to ensure that water cannot find its way in between the fiberglass skins.

One solution to these problems is to core the hull only above the waterline. In this way, the strength and insulation qualities of the topsides are improved, and the potential coring problems in these areas are eliminated.

END-GRAIN BALSA

The first application of balsa wood cores was in the British DeHavilland Attack Bombers of World War II. The balsa used was in sheet form, similar

Figure 3. At left, the male mold is prepared for the application of C-Flex, completed at right.

to the balsa sold in hobby shops, with the grain running lengthwise in the sheets. It could not be formed to complex shapes and had some structural disadvantages.

In the early 1960's a product called Contourcore was developed by the Baltek Corp. It consists of small blocks of balsa wood, about two inches square and ½-inch thick, fitted closely together and bonded together in sheet form by a lightweight fiberglass material on one side. The blocks of balsa are cut so the grain runs in the ½-inch direction and so the exposed surfaces on both sides are end grain.

Because the balsa blocks are not attached to each other but only to the backing material, the sheets are very flexible and can be draped over complex shapes. It is so flexible, in fact, that it is not suited to open male mold construction, where it would form hollows in the spaces in the mold. It is, however, well suited to female mold fiberglass construction, and is probably used in a majority of today's production fiberglass boats. Baltek estimates that it has been used in the construction of more than three million boats.

In the female molding process, the gel coat and fiberglass laminate is applied to the hull until the desired outside skin thickness is achieved. While the last layer of resin is still curing, sheets of the balsa are layed into the hull. It is absolutely essential that the surface of the balsa be totally bonded to the uncured resin. One of the biggest criticisms of all cored construction is the structural problems that can occur if the core material is not completely and permanently bonded to the fiberglass laminate. Not only is the strength of the hull severely diminished if this bond fails, but water can get in between the skin and rot the core. Critics of cored fiberglass construction use this as their primary objection, and it is a valid one. With the proper materials, and care and attention to detail during construction, however, a complete and long-lasting bond can be achieved.

After the balsa core has been applied to the inside of the hull as in Figure 4 the fiberglass lamination is continued to form the inside skin. The core is usually omitted in certain high-stress areas, such as around the keel and at the upper edge of the hull where the deck will be attached. In these areas the inside skin and the outside skin combine to form a single, thicker skin. Contourcore balsa also is used extensively in molded deck construction.

Figure 4. Workers smooth the inner surface of the balsa core before applying the inner skin for this J-24.

Figure 5. Foam core material, in solid sheet form at left and scored for bending over tight curves at right.

FOAM CORE

The other popular material for cored construction is closed cell structural foam. This foam consists of small, hollow spheres, or balloons, which will not absorb water. There are three brands of foam used for boatbuilding, Airex, Klegecell and Divinicell. They are produced in various thickness, usually ⅜ inch or ½ inch but sometimes up to one inch or more, in varying densities, and with somewhat different structural characteristics.

Airex foam is called a "non-cross-linked, rigid-elastic" foam. It is quite stiff, but can be bent and also compressed somewhat and still return to its original shape. Klegecell and Divinicell are stiffer and less compressable "cross-linked, rigid" foams. All are available in continuous sheets, or come cut into small squares and attached to a fabric backing similar to end-grain balsa. See Figure 5.

Unlike balsa core, foam core is particularly suited to one-off construction on a male mold. Its major popularity is with amateur and custom builders.

Sheets of the foam are attached to the open male mold, either with screws from the inside or by stitching it to the mold with thread or wire. For fitting tight curves, the foam can be heated (in a special oven or with a heat lamp) and will become quite flexible. The contoured cut foam can be used over especially tight curves.

After the foam is attached to the mold, fiberglass material and resin are laid up on top of it to form the outer skin. Then, after the fastenings holding the foam to the mold are removed or cut, the foam and outer skin are removed from the mold. Finally, the inner skin is applied.

Proponents of Airex foam core material point out that, unlike balsa core, the foam can be compressed significantly without crushing, and still return to its original shape. They argue this quality gives the hull a greater ability to absorb shock or impact without fracturing. In the infamous storm that struck Cabo San Lucas, Mexico, in December of 1982, driving a fleet of anchored cruising boats onto the beach in pounding surf, a Ted Brewer-designed Cabot 36 of Airex core construction was one of only four fiberglass boats to remain intact and salvageable. Also, a small but significant number of high quality manufacturers of fiberglass production boats in this country use only Airex foam for their hull construction.

HI-TECH FIBERGLASS

A number of new, high-technology products and building procedures have been developed to achieve extraordinarily lightweight, high-strength laminates. Due to high cost, these have been used almost exclusively for racing boats, where the advantage of light weight and high performance is critical.

These materials consist of specially woven fiberglass cloths, using carbon and kevlar (used to make bulletproof clothing) fibers, plus new high-strength resins. The costs of these materials and the skill and care necessary to use them successfully make them suitable for use only by skilled builders.

CARVEL-PLANKED

Carvel, or plank on frame, construction is the most traditional boatbuilding technique. The hull consists of a skeleton structure of sawn, steam bent or laminated wood frames to which wood planks are fastened. See Figure 7. Since the wood planks expand and contract as they absorb and lose water, a space must be left between them to allow for this

Figure 6. Sheets of foam are attached to a male mold by nailing through temporary blocks of wood.

movement, and the gap filled with flexible caulking material.

Carvel-planked hulls require not only high-quality wood, but also quite specialized building skills. Regular maintenance is also greater than for most other hull materials. Maintenance is particularly difficult in tropical waters, due to teredo worms below the waterline and the increased effect of the sun in drying the wood above the waterline.

STRIP-PLANKED

In a strip-planked hull, Figure 8, the planks are much narrower than in carvel planking and are glued and fastened to each other rather than to frames. Because the planks are glued together the hull is much stronger, even without internal framing. A lower quality of wood can be used than for carvel planking, and although the greater number of planks makes the construction slower than carvel, the skills required are more within the range of the amateur builder.

The weakness of the strip-planked hull is the glue joint between the planks. Modern glues and variations on the building technique (see cold-molded construction) reduce this vulnerability.

COLD-MOLDED CONSTRUCTION

Cold molding is a method of laminating thin layers of wood together to form a plywood-like hull structure. Molded plywood hulls were first built in the 1940s, and the glues used at that time required that the hull be baked at high temperature and under pressure to achieve adequate adhesion and strength. For this reason only rather small boats, such as Luders 16s, Thistles and outboard motor runabouts, were built using this technique.

Epoxy glues now permit hulls to be laminated at room temperature—hence the term "cold"—as compared to oven curing. Epoxy glues also result in a more total sealing and a stronger bond between the laminations, improving strength and reducing the possibility of delamination or rot.

Pioneers in the development of the epoxy resins

Figure 7. Larry Pardey works inside the framed hull of his Falmouth Cutter, before the planking was applied.

and techniques for cold-molded hull construction were Meade, Joe and Jan Gougeon of Bay City, Michigan. In 1968 they started using epoxy resins as both an adhesive and a sealer, mostly to build ice boats and high-speed multihull sailboats. They formulated their own resins and associated materials, calling them WEST System products, for Wood Epoxy Saturation Technique.

Because most wood hull problems are moisture related, and in cold-molded construction every piece of wood is encapsulated or sealed with epoxy, maintaining these hulls is more akin to laminated fiberglass than carvel planking.

Epoxy resin costs three to four times as much as polyester resin, but the woods normally used (western red cedar, Douglas fir and mahogany) are quite reasonable. The cost of materials for a cold-molded hull are, in fact, only slightly greater than the cost for a single skin, female-molded fiberglass hull and less than for any other fiberglass method.

Cold molding is a labor-intensive method, requiring more man-hours than any of the fiberglass techniques. For this reason it is more appropriate for amateur than professional construction. The Gougeons estimate that of the approximately 60,000 customers for their products in the past 10 years, 60 percent are amateurs and most of those built (or are building) cruising sailboats.

There are basically two cold-molded construction methods. One is a variation on strip planking,

Figure 8. A strip-planked hull under construction. Note the plastic covering the edges of the building mold to prevent the hull from sticking to the temporary mold.

where the hull is first planked, using epoxy glue in between the strips. Then two or three layers of thin (usually ⅛-inch) veneers are laminated in diagonal directions on top of the strip planking.

The veneers add enormous strength and rigidity, greatly improving upon conventional strip-planked construction. It is the least expensive and labor intensive of the two cold-molding methods, and the one most suited to the amateur boatbuilder.

The other cold-molding method is called the Stringer-Frame system. Figure 9 shows widely spaced transverse frames that remain as a permanent hull structure, set up instead of the more closely spaced, temporary frames used for strip planking. Then full-length wood stringers are laid longitudinally over the frames, spaced approximately five to eight inches apart. The hull is then covered with a thin layer of veneer, epoxy glued and fastened to the stringers. This is followed by more layers, each positioned at an angle to the preceding layer. Five or six layers are usually applied, with their thicknesses varying from about ⅛ inch on boats up to about 30 feet, up to as much as ½ inch on some 100-foot boats.

Stringer-Frame construction requires more skill, labor and epoxy resin than the strip-plank method, but results in a lighter hull. It is used more for racing boats than cruising boats. With the many stringers, the inside of the hull is more cluttered and difficult to finish than with strip planking, but the warmth and attractiveness of the wood interior from either method is preferred by many sailors over the interior of fiberglass boats.

Figure 9. The racing boat *Hot Flash* under construction in the stringer-frame system of cold-molded wood.

PLYWOOD

Yet another method of wood hull construction uses sheets of plywood. The fact that plywood cannot be formed into complex, three-dimensional shapes, but is limited to cylindrical forms, restricts the possible hull shapes. The simplest shape is Jay Benford's single-chined, flat-bottomed 32-foot dory on page 152. As the number of chines increases, the hull shape more nearly approaches a rounded form.

In plywood construction, frames are set up and chine pieces laid longitudinally. Plywood panels are then fastened to the chine pieces and frames. To protect the outside surface of the plywood and make it easier to maintain, it is usually covered with some type of resin, polyester or epoxy, and a thin layer of reinforced fiberglass material.

Plywood construction is relatively quick and less expensive than most other techniques. One of the best known and most popular designs intended specifically for plywood construction by amateurs is the 26-foot Thunderbird.

STEEL

Steel sailboats, always more popular in European countries than in the U.S., have recently begun catching on in America. A number of recent developments is making this material much more attractive to the cruising sailor.

The traditional objection to steel boats is the amount of work required to maintain a rust-free hull. New zinc and aluminum primers and application techniques, plus new polyurethane and epoxy paint systems, have reduced this problem. Today, a properly designed, constructed and painted steel boat is just as easy to maintain as a boat built of any other material.

Steel undoubtedly is the strongest hull construction material. Not only is the material itself able to withstand unbelievable punishment, but the bond formed when steel is welded is 100 percent as strong as the material itself. Many steel hulls have survived groundings and collisions that would have destroyed hulls of any other materials. It is

no coincidence that the only sailboats to transmit the northwest passage across northern Canada and circumnavigate Antarctica, *Williwaw* and *Ice Bird,* were steel boats.

Another significant objection to steel is its weight. The thinnest plate that can be conveniently formed and welded is about ⅛-inch thick, and weighs a little over five pounds a square foot. In a hull of about 30 feet in length, it is about twice the weight of the various fiberglass materials and about three times the weight of cold-molded wood. This would probably result in the overall displacement of a 30-foot steel boat about 25 percent heavier than fiberglass and 35 percent heavier than cold-molded wood.

As the size of the boat increases, however, the thickness of the steel plating need not be increased as much as for other materials, and the difference in weight becomes less and less significant.

Steel boats can be built in either chined hull forms, from flat steel plates, or in rounded forms with bent plates. The former is the quickest and most appropriate to amateur construction but limits the hull shape to developable surfaces, surfaces that can be formed from flat plate. Rounded hull forms require bending and forming the plates, necessitating greater skill and time to build, but resulting in hulls indiscernable from fiberglass.

Traditionally, steel hulls have been built over closely spaced transverse frames with some longitudinal stringers as in Figure 10. This is usually a heavy building method, and the distortion in the hull caused by welding often gives the hull a rippled surface. In an effort to reduce weight and improve hull smoothness, builders have been constructing hulls with fewer and more widely spaced transverse frames and more closely spaced longitudinals as in Figure 11, often welding the hull plating only to the longitudinals. The results have been lighter, fairer hulls with no significant loss of strength. Some builders have eliminated the frames entirely.

An increasing number of designers and cruising sailors, attracted to steel but desiring as light a boat as possible, have chosen to combine a steel hull with lighter deck and cabin materials. Plywood, aluminum and cored fiberglass have all been used successfully. The greatest potential for problems

Figure 10. A steel hull under construction in the traditional transverse framing system.

Figure 11. Longitudinally framed steel construction is shown on my Integrity design.

with this composite construction is the joint between the steel hull and the deck. It must be well designed and constructed to avoid leaks.

Steel has very low insulative qualities, and is not particularly attractive on the inside of the hull. The interior must be both insulated and finished with wood or some other material to make it attractive.

For voyaging sailors in particular, who must decide whether to pay exorbitant premiums to remain insured or go without insurance altogether, a steel hull's great strength and durability offers the kind of insurance no company on earth can offer.

ALUMINUM

Aluminum construction is also experiencing an increase in popularity, due to attempts to produce very large, very lightweight racing boats using new aluminum alloys and welding techniques that recently have been developed.

Aluminum is quite expensive, and the welding procedures required are more sophisticated than steel. Unlike steel, the welded aluminum joint is not quite as strong as the material itself, so every weld is a potential weak spot. The aluminum alloys used for boats—and the painting systems—are quite resistant to corrosion, but are still very vulnerable to electrolytic deterioration. Even with extreme care in the installation of the boat's electrical system, some sort of active protection system is necessary to protect the hull from attack by stray electrical currents in the water. When electrolysis does occur, it can damage aluminum plate alarmingly fast with little of the warning shown by steel.

In racing boats, aluminum achieves very lightweight hulls. But the thinness of this type of construction is not as tough as steel. It is possible, however, to increase plating thicknesses to achieve nearly the strength of steel and at a lighter weight, but the cost of the material becomes three or four times that of steel.

For cruising sailors to whom high performance and strength are more important than cost, and for those who are prepared to deal with the possible problems, aluminum is worth considering.

COPPER/NICKEL

An extremely interesting material for hull construction, but probably the most prohibitively expensive, is an alloy consisting of 90 percent copper and 10 percent nickel. It is about 15 percent heavier than steel and has welding and strength character-istics similar to steel. Its most unusual feature is that the presence of the copper makes the hull self-anti-fouling and non-corrosive, even in saltwater. If any material is "forever," it is copper/nickel.

Only a handful of yachts have been built of copper/nickel, and some fishing boats in the Gulf of Mexico. One 52-foot ketch, *Asperida,* built in Holland 15 years ago, is still in excellent condition. The copper/nickel alloy costs about 10 times as much as steel. While this added cost can be recouped in eliminating haulouts and expensive anti-fouling paint, if the increased expense of building in this material were invested and a less expensive material chosen, the interest earned would probably cover the haulouts and paint.

FERRO-CEMENT

In the late 1960s and early 1970s, this building technique enjoyed a rather brief period of popularity. In this system, metal rods are bent to form the building stations, and layers of wire mesh are fastened over the rods to form the hull surface. Concrete is then plastered through the mesh and smoothed off on the inner and outer surfaces to form the hull skin. See Figure 12.

While a satisfactory hull can be produced, and I have seen some excellent ones, extreme care must be taken in every step of the operation. Expert

Figure 12. At left is the hull for a 53-foot ferrocement boat ready for plastering. At right, workers trowel on the cement.

plastering skill is an absolute necessity. Many people were attracted to ferro-cement construction by the promise of very low material costs and the lack of corrosion. The number of terribly built hulls (many had to be buried) of this material is certainly greater than for any other technique. A few professional builders produced some very fair and strong hulls, but they were often quite heavy. Repair or modification is very difficult.

KEY

VL = Very Low   **H** = High
L = Low   **VH** = Very High
M = Medium

Construction Technique	Material Cost	Labor Required	Strength Flexural	Strength Impact	Strength Abrasion	Weight	Insulation	Formability	Maintenance	Suitability to Amateur Construction
Fiberglass										
Single Skin										
Female Mold	VL	VL	L to M	L to M	L	M	L	H	L	L
Single Skin										
Male Mold C-Flex	M	M	M	L to M	L	M	L	H	L	H
Stretch Mesh	L	M	L to M	L to M	L	M	L	H	L	H
Cored										
Female Mold, Balsa	M	L	H	M	L	L	H	H	L	L
Female Mold, Foam	M	L	H	M	L	L	H	H	L	L
Male Mold, Foam	M	M	H	M	L	L	H	H	L	H
High-Technology Cored materials	H	M	H to VH	H	M	VL	H	H	L	L
Wood										
Carvel planked	M	H	H	M	L	M	M	M	H	L
Strip planked	L	H	H	M	L	M	M	H	M	M
Cold molded, strip planked	L	H	H	M	L	M	M	H	L to M	M
Cold molded, Stringer-Frame	L	H	H	M	L	L	M	H	L to M	M
Plywood, sheathed	L	L	M to H	M	L	M	M	L	L to M	M
Steel	L	M	H*	VH	H	H	L	L	M	M
Aluminum	H	M	H*	H	H	L	L	M	L	L
Copper/Nickel	VH	M	H*	VH	H	H	L	L	L	L
Ferro-Cement	VL	H	L to M	M	M	H	M	H	L	H

* Will bend, but high ultimate strength

TOWARD DEVELOPING A CRITICAL EYE

Does form follow function?

TO MOST sailors, looking at cruising sailboat designs is a thoroughly delightful way to brighten even the dreariest winter day. But it's a practical exercise as well.

On the one hand, understanding the physical restraints and design limitations of your own boat helps develop more realistic expectations about its performance. And knowing the trade-offs inherent in cruising boat design, on the other hand, makes us wiser consumers when we start shopping around for a new boat. Knowing how a boat works and also how that knowledge is expressed and transmitted into a two-dimensional design, helps us more fully enjoy our time afloat.

Design presentations, as they usually appear in magazines, books and advertisements, do not contain all the information necessary for the reader to fully appreciate and evaluate the design. This may be due to the naval architect's reluctance to publish design features that he feels might be "pirated," or to the limited space available in the publication. Whatever the reason, the result is that the reader is challenged to use intuition and a bit of detective work to fill in the missing information.

Obviously, the more knowledgeable the reader is about boat design and the greater the person's experience, both in sailing and in looking at designs, the better equipped he or she is in evaluating a design.

The second part of this book contains 62 of the best designs that have appeared during the past 10 years in the *Cruising World* "Design" column. They illustrate the many types of possible cruising boats and the variety of results achieved by naval architects when they successfully combined the art with the science of cruising boat design. Studying these designs and the comments that accompany them should help you develop your own critical eye for designs.

With experience you will probably develop your own strategy for studying a design and deriving as much information as possible. But at this stage, it may be helpful to many readers to see how one naval architect evaluates the work of another. As an illustration of how I critique a design, let's take a close look at the 30-foot sloop, R9-30, designed by Rolf Eliasson and presented on page 142.

When I first look at this, or any design, I am

immediately attracted to the profile and sail plan. I try, however, not to form conclusions too quickly. First impressions, and the architect's artistic skills, can be misleading.

My first positive reaction to the R9-30 is to its sleek, handsomely proportioned hull. The sheer is traditional and pleasing to the eye, and the bow and stern overhangs are quite graceful. The deck appears to be very streamlined in shape and the sloop rig is moderately tall and simply stayed.

INTENDED USE

When I am able to shift my eyes away from the drawings, I look in the accompanying text for a statement or indication of the type of cruising for which the boat is intended. It is elemental in any

evaluation to judge a design on the basis of how well it is suited to its intended use—rather than how well it suits the reader's own cruising needs. To do otherwise is a disservice to the designer and limits the understanding to be gained by the reader.

The R9-30 was designed for *Cruising World*'s 1976 Design Competition, which called for a cruising boat for a family of four. It had to be handled easily by two and be able to carry supplies for a week without replenishment. Moderate cost and the ability to make an occasional short offshore passage also were specified.

My own experience tells me that to fulfill these requirements, the boat should be relatively small and lightweight, making it inexpensive and easy to handle. To accommodate four people and be capable of an offshore passage there should ob-

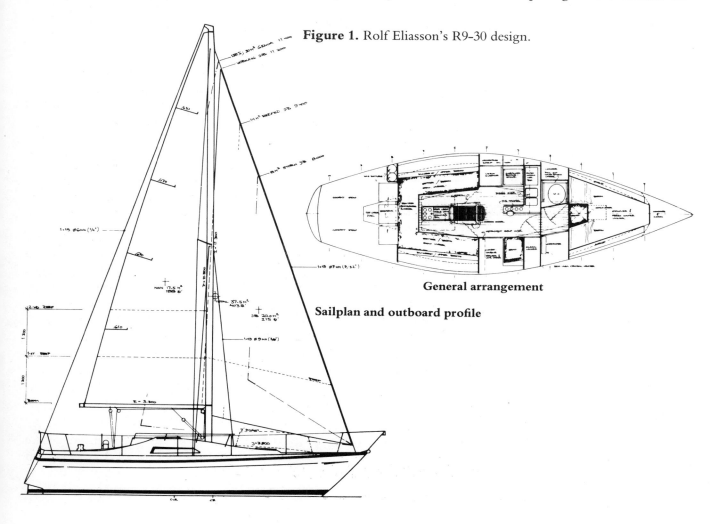

Figure 1. Rolf Eliasson's R9-30 design.

General arrangement

Sailplan and outboard profile

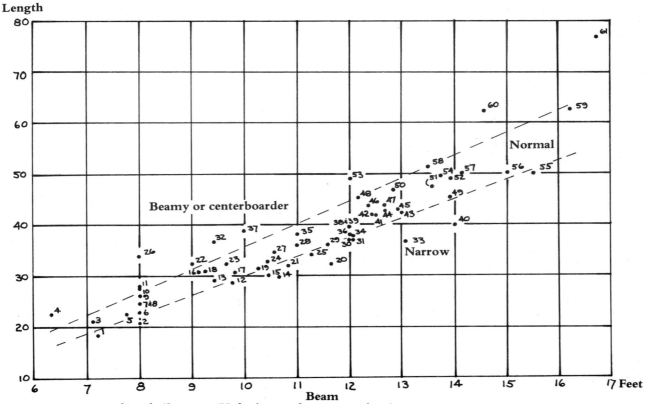

Figure 2. Beam vs. length (See page 55 for boat reference numbers)

Figure 3. Draft vs. waterline length

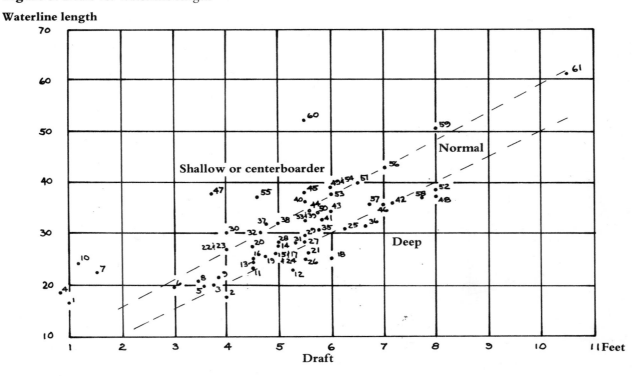

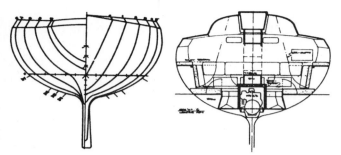

Figure 4. Body plan and hull section

viously be at least four berths, two of which must be suited to use at sea. For family cruising, some degree of privacy—achieved by separating the sleeping areas—is also a necessity. The R9-30 appears to meet all these requirements, including the requirement for good stowage space. I will consider most of these matters in greater detail later.

HULL SHAPE

My next—and usually most difficult—task is to try to form a picture in my mind of the three-dimensional shape of the hull. In this case, because the complete lines plan is shown, the task is made easy. In most design presentations, however, this is not the case. Then I must use other clues as to the actual shape.

The plan and profile views show the overall dimensions and proportions of the hull. These dimensions also are given in the table of specifications. But their relative proportions are more evident in the drawings. To help the reader

more easily determine a design's relative beaminess or depth I have plotted in Figures 2 and 3 the relationship between overall length and beam, and waterline length and draft, for the designs shown in this book and a few other well-known designs.

Entering these graphs with the dimensions of the R9-30 shows an average beam in relation to overall length, with a draft just slightly on the deep side of average in comparison to waterline length.

Next, I try to determine the sectional shape of the hull. In this case, with the body plan shown, it is easy. When the body plan is not included, often a representative section or two, such as in Figure 4, are illustrated and can be used to figure out sectional shapes. When no sections are shown I must use a combination of other factors.

One of the most helpful clues is the displacement/length ratio. This indicates the fullness of the sections below the waterline. A high value of this ratio means a boat with great underwater volume and large sectional areas.

Other useful clues are the height and width of the cabin sole shown in the inboard profile (Figure 5) and general arrangement plans, respectively. Picture the outline of the cabin sole in the arrangement plan as one of the waterlines shown in the lines plan. The rather narrow sole of the R9-30 indicates V-shaped rather than U-shaped, sections.

The outboard edges of berths and other interior parts that extend out to the hull reveal some of the hull shape above the waterline. I look at their height and width in comparison to the sheer line to get an idea of the amount of flare in the sections. The outboard edge of the forward berth, which

Figure 5. Inboard profile

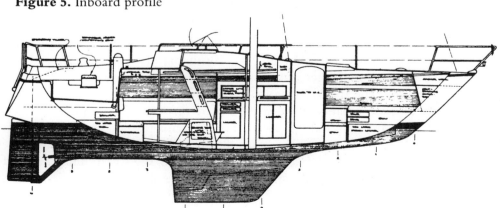

comes quite close in plan view to the sheer line, indicates only moderate flare in the forward sections, while the greater distance between the outboard edge of the settees and the sheer line aft show greater flare there. Referring to the body plans confirms these conclusions.

The degree to which I am able to determine hull shape varies greatly with the amount of information provided in the design presentation. When I am satisfied that I have used all available data, I combine my impression of hull shape with the configuration of keel and rudder to try to visualize the many qualities of the boat, again keeping in mind its intended use.

STABILITY

Next, I try to determine some of the boat's performance and seakeeping characteristics. With her relatively narrow waterline beam, and relatively high ballast/displacement ratio, the R9-30 will show stability characteristics tending toward those of ballast stability. Stability at small angles of heel will not be great, but as heel increases the flared sections will increase the waterline beam significantly and the ballast will also contribute greatly to increase stability. Stability at normal sailing angles will probably be more than satisfactory. While ultimate stability is not a great consideration in a coastal cruiser, this boat is intended for an occasional offshore passage. Its moderate beam and healthy ballast should give it a wide range of stability.

RESISTANCE

Next, I want to know how fast the boat will be in varying conditions. The narrow waterline beam, short fin keel and small skeg give the R9-30 a small amount of wetted surface. Performance in the lower speed ranges, in light winds, should be excellent.

To evaluate the boat's wave-making characteristics, I look at the displacement/length ratio and the underbody shape, particularly in the stern. The displacement/length ratio for the R9-30 is quite low, indicating low wave-making resistance. The moderate stern overhang and the nearly straight and relatively shallow buttock lines reinforce this conclusion. While the hull shape is not that of a planing-oriented boat, it should have a long sailing length and be capable of reaching its maximum speed easily. That maximum speed will be approximately $1.5 \times \sqrt{26.4}$, or 7.7 knots.

STEERING AND COURSE STABILITY

The next question I want to answer is how will the boat handle under way? With her fin keel and large skeg-mounted rudder, the R9-30 has a lateral plane with a good compromise between performance, maneuverability and course stability. The relatively fine stern and nearly symmetrical waterlines will result in an easily steered boat, even at high angles of heel. It will not develop the heavy weather helm of broad sterned boats at these heel angles. These qualities are all appropriate to the intended use of the boat. The location of the propeller in an aperture in the skeg reduces the chances of fouling or damage.

RIG

The sloop rig is moderate in size and simply, but strongly, stayed. Swept-back lower and upper shrouds, plus the "baby stay" just forward of the mast, give good support to the middle section of the spar. With a luff/foot ratio of over three, the sail plan will have high speed and weatherliness potential, complementing the easily driven and hydrodynamically efficient hull form.

Both mainsail and jib sheets are convenient to the helmsperson—handy on a boat which may be sailed shorthanded. Sails are small, about 200 square feet each in the main and working jib, and so are manageable even by children in most conditions. With the 130 percent genoa, reefable working jib and storm jib, good performance over the entire range of wind strengths is assured with a small sail inventory.

DECK AND INTERIOR ARRANGEMENT

In considering the arrangement of a cruising boat I try to picture myself in all the different areas, performing the many activities in all possible conditions. I imagine myself steering, changing sails, cooking, navigating, relaxing and sleeping, alone, with crew, at sea and in port, in various conditions and climates. I look at comfort and security on deck and below, stowage space, ventilation, visibility, and the engine installation. Capacities and locations of tanks also are important.

Eliasson's R9-30 has a well protected and comfortable-looking cockpit. With the pedestal for the wheel steering at the forward end of the cockpit and an arched seat, the helmsperson could be comfortable and well protected by a dodger and close to both the sheets and the halyards and reefing lines, which are led aft on the cabin top.

The sleek deck and cabin arrangement appears to result in a foredeck well suited to sail handling and the stowage of a dinghy, often not possible on a 30-foot boat. The railing on the cabin top at the same height as the lifelines is a noteworthy feature for the security it provides. The two deep cockpit lockers are, I think, a potential hazard on any cruising boat.

The wide bridgedeck leading to the companionway results in a number of desirable features. It is an excellent area for lounging both under way and in port; it reduces the possibility of water in the cockpit finding its way down below; and it results in adding very useful interior volume.

Eliasson has made very good use of the relatively small interior volume of a boat this size. Aft of the companionway ladder is a large, U-shaped settee arrangement with a drop-leaf table. It appears to be a very liveable area, and the seat backs fold up to form pilot berths, which are most useful at sea. With the seat back up there are four berths aft, as widely separated as possible from the double V-berths forward. Curtains can be used to close off the forward sleeping area.

The galley is U-shaped in the fore and aft direction and thus well suited to use at sea. Opposite are the aft-facing chart table and hanging locker.

Conveniently located under the table is the inboard diesel engine. Batteries are under the after section of the settee, and a 26-gallon fuel tank is aft.

Eliasson designed the R9-30 to be built of fiberglass in a female mold. Her light weight and simplicity should allow her to be constructed on a production basis at a reasonable price.

CONCLUSION

Having filtered Eliasson's design for the R9-30 through my own sensibilities, I've concluded he has done quite well reaching his objectives, even though this isn't what I'd want for my own boat. In many respects, making an honest appraisal of any boat design requires some soul-searching. At every step we must confront our own prejudices and determine whether they are valid—particularly seeing whether they should be applied to the design, given the design specifications within which the designer was forced to operate. We learn that our prejudices do not apply in all cases, and certainly not to all people. The more we are able to set aside our own prejudices the easier it will be to form sound conclusions about any design. At the same time we should leave ourselves open to considering new ideas that can enhance our cruising experience. And that is the magic of cruising boat design.

CELEBRATING THE BEST OF A DECADE OF CRUISING BOAT DESIGN

WEBB 18

David Webb submitted this design to the 1982 *Cruising World* Design Competition, which called for a lightweight trailerable cruiser. A maximum trailering weight of 1,000 pounds and a maximum trailering draft of 12 inches were specified. Webb has incorporated some innovative and interesting features to meet these requirements.

The total of 690 pounds of ballast is made up of a lead bulb at the bottom of the drop keel, and water ballast in tanks on each side of the keel trunk. The .42 cubic-foot bulb weighs 300 pounds and the water ballast 390 pounds.

There is an inspection port in the top of each tank and a thru-hull fill/drain plug in the bottom. After the boat is launched, the plug can be opened by reaching through the port and the water will flow into the tank until it is even with the water level outside. The water could be pumped from the tanks before hauling out or allowed to drain out after the boat is on the trailer. The tank tops are just above the design water-line (DWL), so there is no danger of flooding the boat through the tanks and inspection port.

While some valuable storage space is lost to the tanks, it does permit a heavier boat with more stability than would otherwise be possible given the trailering weight.

The triple-chine plywood hull is beamy and high to achieve form stability and adequate interior volume, but still has a stout and racy look to it. High sheer is somewhat disguised by the wide stripe and ports in the hull.

WEBB 18

LOA
18'0" (5.48 m.)

LWL
16'4½" (4.98 m.)

Beam
7'3½" (2.22 m.)

Draft
1'0"/3'5" (.30/1.07 m.)

Ballast
690 lbs. (313 kg.)

Displacement
(trailering) 999 lbs. (453 kg.)
(sailing) 1,813 lbs. (822 kg.)

Sail Area
182 sq. ft. (17.8 sq. m.)

Construction
Plywood

Disp./Length Ratio
184

Sail Area/Disp. Ratio
19.7

DAVID I. WEBB
1943 South Holt Ave.
Los Angeles, CA 90034

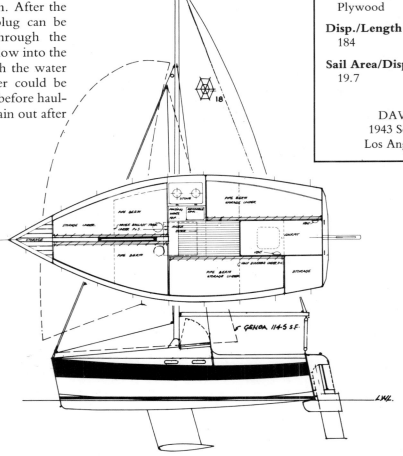

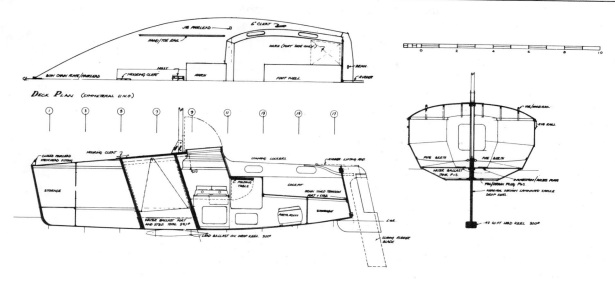

The keel is constructed of laminated spruce with the lump of lead attached at the bottom. When it is drawn up into the hull only a bulb protrudes, and draft is 12 inches.

To match the drop keel, the rudder blade also is retractable. The sliding blade is housed within a trunk in the rudder, which has area forward of its turning axis to achieve a degree of balance and have adequate area with the blade raised. Sailing with raised keel and rudder would be possible, but with diminished performance.

The very simple fractional sloop rig has only a forestay and two shrouds, no spreaders and is stepped on deck. A genoa, reefable working jib and spinnaker are shown in addition to the main.

Accommodations appear quite comfortable for an 18-footer. There are two pipe berths forward separated by the keel trunk, another pipe berth to port for seating in the cabin and a pipe quarter berth under the starboard cockpit seat. A two-burner stove, folding counter top and portable sink make up the galley. A folding table stows under the bridge deck and the chemical toilet slides under the cockpit sole. The hinged hatch over the small cabin sole permits standing in that area.

With her plywood construction, lightweight and high performance potential, the Webb 18 may find popularity in these days of small cars, expensive gasoline and overcrowded marinas.

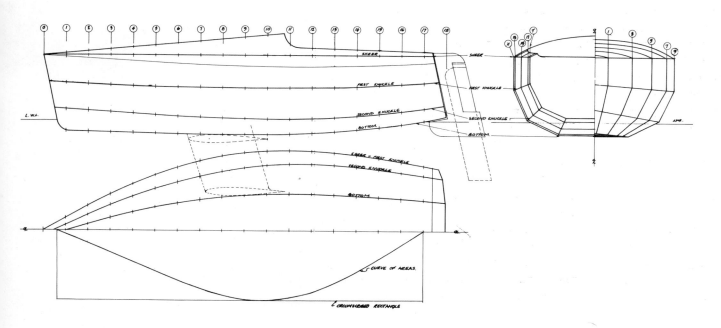

ANTRIM 20

The Antrim 20 is designer Jim Antrim's idea of a minimum cruising boat—a boat for these times of expensive or unavailable dock space, high prices for materials and fuel, and soaring interest rates. His goal was, "to draw the smallest boat with a workable interior, attractive appearance and eight-foot trailerable beam, and within this framework to provide the performance and feeling of spaciousness one might expect in a larger boat."

With its short overhangs, shallow hull and beam carried well aft, the Antrim 20 resembles a large dinghy with a keel. The enormous rig reinforces this impression. Sailing performance should be nothing short of exciting.

The broad stern and cockpit offer a number of advantages in a small cruiser. Cockpit seats can be made wide enough for lounging or sleeping with width left for substantial side decks. The added weight of three or four persons in the cockpit causes much less trim by the stern than it would in a fine-sterned boat. In stronger winds crew can sit on the side decks and act as effective live ballast. Early surfing ability also is enhanced. Down below, there is room for two full-size quarter berths.

Stability is assured by the broad waterplane aft. Also, all the ballast is placed in the lower half of the keel, where it is most effective.

A very large, slightly balanced rudder is hung on the transom. There is a cutout in the transom for the tiller and to drain the footwell. The crossbeam across the top of the transom is an alternative location for

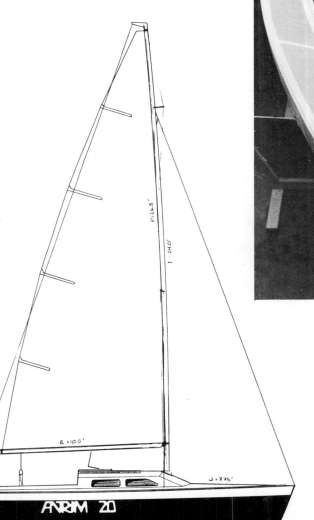

the mainsheet traveler for those who prefer an unobstructed cockpit.

Light displacement and the tall sail plan should give this boat dinghy-like acceleration and performance. With so much sail area, the value of crew weight as ballast is great. When sailing shorthanded, it may be necessary to reef early. As long as an easy and efficient reefing system is fitted, this is not really a problem.

In addition to the quarter berths and the double V-berth down below, there is seating for four on seats with comfortable, padded backrests. There is a pull-out stove in a drawer under the port counter, with a sink opposite. A portable ice box is located under the companionway and a portable head under the V-berth.

Large stowage bins are found outboard of the seats. Some sailors might also want to sacrifice one of the quarter berths to serve as a cockpit locker for sails or outboard motor.

This is a handsome, exciting little cruiser, which should be relatively inexpensive to buy and maintain. This may be the shape of things to come.

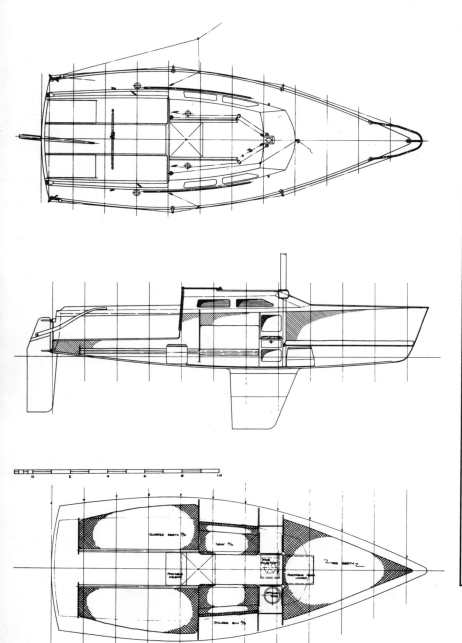

ANTRIM 20

LOA
  20'5" (6.22 m.)

LWL
  17'6" (5.33 m.)

Beam
  8'0" (2.44 m.)

Draft
  4'0" (1.22 m.)

Ballast
  750 lbs. (340 kg.)

Displacement
  1,850 lbs. (839 kg.)

Sail Area
  279 sq. ft. (25.9 sq. m.)

Construction
  Fiberglass

Disp./Length Ratio
  186

Sail Area/Disp. Ratio
  28.6

ANTRIM ASSOCIATES
4018 Archery Way
El Sobrante, CA 94803

SOLO 21

The first Singlehanded Mini-Transatlantic Race was run from England to Antigua via the Canary Islands in September of 1977. It has become a biennial event. Boats in the race are restricted to a maximum overall length of 6.50 meters, or 21'4". Steven Callahan designed Solo to fit the rules of this race and also to be a strong, lightweight cruiser capable of lake, coastal or offshore sailing.

The hull features a long waterline, moderate beam and external lead fin keel. Displacement is quite light. By avoiding the extreme beam found on many modern boats and by choosing a rather narrow, nicely shaped stern, Callahan created a boat that should be easy to steer and forgiving even when it is overpowered. A dagger-type rudder can be fully extended when maximum steering control is necessary and partially retracted in less demanding conditions.

Although foam-cored fiberglass construction is possible, the designer prefers the WEST system with three layers of ⅛-inch cedar laminated with epoxy and covered with fiberglass cloth set in epoxy. Interior furniture and bulkheads are of marine plywood, joined to the hull with large-radius epoxy fillets to form a strong structural unit.

With two sets of reef points in the jib and three in the mainsail, Solo can handle light and heavy winds without a sail change.

Notice the flush cockpit with foot braces and sliding companionway hatch with inside viewing position.

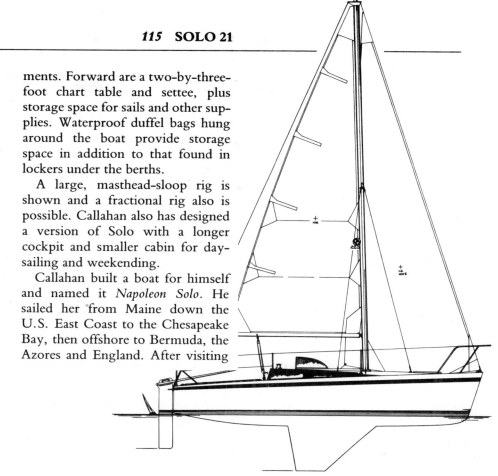

The deck and cabin are constructed of ⅜-inch plywood on ash framing, covered with fiberglass cloth and epoxy. The small and shallow cockpit will not hold much water and leaves a great deal of accommodation space below. On the negative side, it offers little protection in rough weather. It is possible, however, to have an inside steering position for these conditions.

Accommodations appear to be simple and practical, providing what Callahan calls "Spartan comfort." The double berth aft has sitting headroom under the extended cabin and good lighting from cabin portlights. A lee canvas on centerline can be used at sea to keep crew weight to windward. Its position should make this berth comfortable at sea.

To starboard of the companionway is a small galley with single-burner stove and a bucket instead of a sink. To port is a hanging locker with room for electronic instru-

ments. Forward are a two-by-three-foot chart table and settee, plus storage space for sails and other supplies. Waterproof duffel bags hung around the boat provide storage space in addition to that found in lockers under the berths.

A large, masthead-sloop rig is shown and a fractional rig also is possible. Callahan also has designed a version of Solo with a longer cockpit and smaller cabin for daysailing and weekending.

Callahan built a boat for himself and named it *Napoleon Solo*. He sailed her from Maine down the U.S. East Coast to the Chesapeake Bay, then offshore to Bermuda, the Azores and England. After visiting

Spain, Portugal, Madeira and the Canary Islands he set out for the Caribbean.

On February 4, 1982, 800 miles from the Canaries and 1,800 miles from the Caribbean, *Solo* was suddenly and violently struck amidships. She filled with water in 30 seconds. Flotation material prevented *Solo* from sinking, so Callahan was able to recover survival equipment from the boat. Rough conditions prevented him from

staying near the swamped boat and forced him to his life raft. After 76 days in his raft, Callahan was rescued by fishermen off Marie Galante, near Guadeloupe.

Scantlings have since been beefed up in the hull, with a 70 percent increase in strength and only a 10 percent increase in displacement. Keel and rig modifications also have been made. Two other Solos are under construction.

SOLO 21

LOA
21'4" (6.50 m.)

LWL
20'0" (6.10 m.)

Beam
7'1" (2.16 m.)

Draft
3'9" (1.14 m.)

Displacement
2,500 lbs. (1,134 kg.)

Sail Area
220 sq. ft. (20.4 sq. m.)

Construction
See text

Disp./Length Ratio
140

Sail Area/Disp. Ratio
18.4

S. P. CALLAHAN & ASSOCIATES
Box 277–RFD 2
Ellsworth, ME 04605

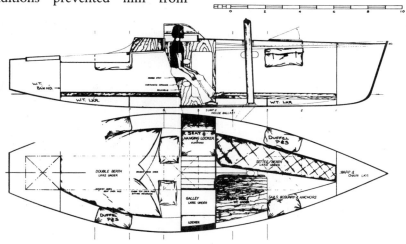

SEABOAT 225

John Westell is a British architect, little known in this country, whose most famous design is the 5-0-5 high performance racing dinghy. He also worked for many years as production director for a major English production builder of small fiberglass boats.

Now semi-retired, he has created a family of four Seaboats, similar in type and graduated in size. They are intended for the amateur or small professional builder. The Seaboat 150, 175 and 200 are sloop-rigged boats 15, 17½ and 20 feet in length. The Seaboat 225, shown here, is a ketch-rigged 22½-footer.

Westell describes the boats as "seaworthy, adaptable, maids-of-all-work." Indeed, they can be trailered, rowed, motored and sailed with relative ease.

Except for the ⅝-inch steel centerboard, which must weigh about 100 pounds, the craft is unballasted and relies on crew weight for stability. The hull is long, light and easily driven. The displacement figure given must be for the fully loaded boat including crew.

The capabilities of the Seaboat 225 probably are best described by Westell. He says, "Please bear in mind that the rig is designed to be handled by a full crew and the stability would not be adequate to carry that much sail in a breeze if shorthanded. On the other hand, she could do a trans-ocean passage with a smaller rig. With the closed centerboard trunk and extensive buoyancy spaces, a tough man would have a chance of bailing her out after being swamped. I hope I have profited from Webb Chiles!" Chiles has sailed a similar fiberglass craft across the Pacific and Indian Oceans.

Construction is cold-molded plywood with three layers of veneers glued over a stringered form. The stem, centerboard trunk and full-length box structures that form the seats and buoyancy chambers are prefabricated and incorporated into the building frame.

The ketch rig, with sliding gunter mainsail, is quite large but makes use of short spars and simple rigging. Spruce or aluminum can be

---

SEABOAT 225

LOA
22'6" (6.86 m.)

LWL
19'10" (6.05 m.)

Beam
6'4" (1.93 m.)

Draft
Board up: 10" (0.25 m.)
Board down: 4'11" (1.50 m.)

Displacement
1,920 lbs. (871 kg.)

Sail Area
199 sq. ft. (18.5 sq. m.)

Construction
Cold-molded plywood

Disp./Length Ratio
110

Sail Area/Disp. Ratio
20.3

JOHN WESTELL
"Treetops" Barracks Hill
Totnes, Devon TQ9 6DG
England

Stringers are attached to the male building mold but not to the stem, which becomes part of the finished hull.

The transom is held in place by cleats on the mold so that it too can be removed with the hull.

used for the spars. The long top batten in the mainsail supports a large roach and adds valuable sail area. The batten folds against the yard when furled. The jib can be of either the roller-furling or jiffy reefing variety.

A single jib sheet winch is mounted on the centerboard trunk, which also has a winch for handling the steel centerboard. The mainsheet and mizzen sheet both ride on travelers and are handy to the helmsperson. The rudder lifts up for beaching. A six to 10-hp. outboard motor can be mounted on the transom.

Buoyancy is in the form of blocks of expanded polystyrene foam fitted at the bow and stern and along both sides. It is sufficient to float the boat level and high enough to permit bailing.

The Seaboat 225 would make a challenging but manageable project for the amateur builder. The fin-

ished boat, with its great versatility, could satisfy a wide variety of boating needs, from fishing to daysailing, weekending, coastal cruising or even passage making.

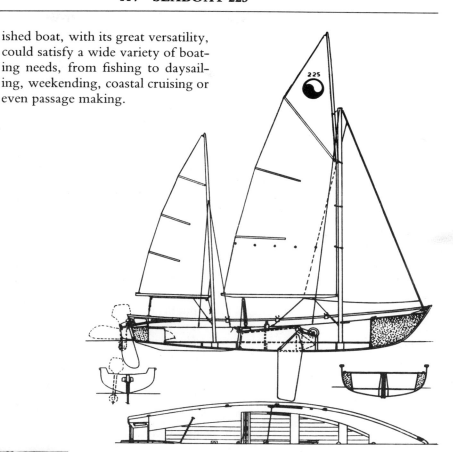

Two layers of veneers are complete and the third being applied.

PLYBOY

Plyboy, designed by Giancarlo Coppola of Italy, was chosen as the winner of the 1978 *Cruising World* Design Competition. As its name implies, it is constructed of plywood, the material chosen by nearly all of the designers who submitted entries in the competition.

Coppola's reasons for selecting plywood are that it is an easy and fast material with which to work and is much more pleasant to handle than fiberglass. Modern epoxy adhesives and coatings ensure its longevity and it does not require a great deal of finishing.

Coppola gave a lot of thought to making Plyboy both easy and inexpensive to build, while at the same time producing a boat that is both comfortable and exciting to sail. One of his first decisions was to design a light displacement boat, and with a displacement/length ratio of 134 Plyboy is extremely light. Such a boat has a faster, livelier motion than a heavier boat of the same size, but because the boat is intended for sailing in protected waters and short coastal cruises, the motion can be tolerated.

While most plywood boats have either single or multiple chines where the panels meet, Coppola's plywood panels meet at wide chine pieces, which are rounded to fair into each panel. This eliminates the hard chined look that many people find less than beautiful and enhances performance by removing sharp corners from the waterlines and buttocks. Water does not like to flow around corners.

Plyboy is, in fact, quite a handsome little boat. The cabin is a bit high but this is necessary to achieve adequate (five foot) headroom in a light boat with a shallow bilge and the necessary high cabin sole.

All plywood is ⅜-inch thick. Standard eight-foot sheets can be scarfed together for the hull but Coppola said it is worth the additional cost of buying 24-foot sheets (which are available by special order) to eliminate this difficult operation. As a further aid to the amateur builder, three basic sizes of lumber can be used to build nearly the entire boat, including the spars.

Either cast iron or lead can be used for the fin keel, and the pattern can be made by the builder and brought to a foundry. A centerboard version is being designed.

Control under sail is assured by the large, partially balanced transom-hung rudder. On the negative side, the rudder appears capable of snagging lines.

The mast is a solid, round, tapered wood spar. The 4/5 rig is enjoying a popularity revival. It reduces the number of headsails required and the amount of time spent on the foredeck changing sails. Having the halyards led aft to the cockpit also keeps the sailors in the cockpit. The mainsail shows only one reef; a second reef would probably come in handy.

By sloping the cockpit sole aft, Coppola was able to drain it through the transom, a very simple arrangement. There are no thru-hull fittings below the waterline, and thus no expensive sea cocks and fittings.

Dorade-type ventilator boxes are built into the winch bases, saving weight and cost. The bridge deck keeps water out of the companionway and provides additional space belowdecks.

On the foredeck is an anchor locker and a hatch that can open either forward or aft. Gussets and handrails prevent sheets from hanging up on the hatch.

A few interesting features highlight the otherwise conventional interior arrangement. A table that slides out of the way to starboard has a built-in chart holder and can be used either in the cabin or on deck. Another structure, which Coppola calls a settee, can serve as a seat either athwartships or fore and aft in the cabin. It can also form a leeboard for a quarter berth. Items like this save weight without sacrificing liveability.

The small portable head can be stowed under a forward berth, or set up between the berths or even in the cockpit. A hole in the cabin top (with plug) and lifting eyes on the cabin sole allow the boat to be lifted easily with a simple crane or overhead lift.

PLYBOY

LOA
22'8" (6.90 m.)

LWL
19'10" (6.00 m.)

Beam
7'9½" (2.37 m.)

Draft
3'7" (1.10 m.)

Ballast
1,000 lbs. (450 kg.)

Displacement
2,250 lbs. (1,020 kg.)

Sail Area
235 sq. ft. (22 sq. m.)

Construction
Plywood

Disp./Length Ratio
134

Sail Area/Disp. Ratio
22.0

GIANCARLO COPPOLA
Calmaggiore 25
31100 Treviso
Italy

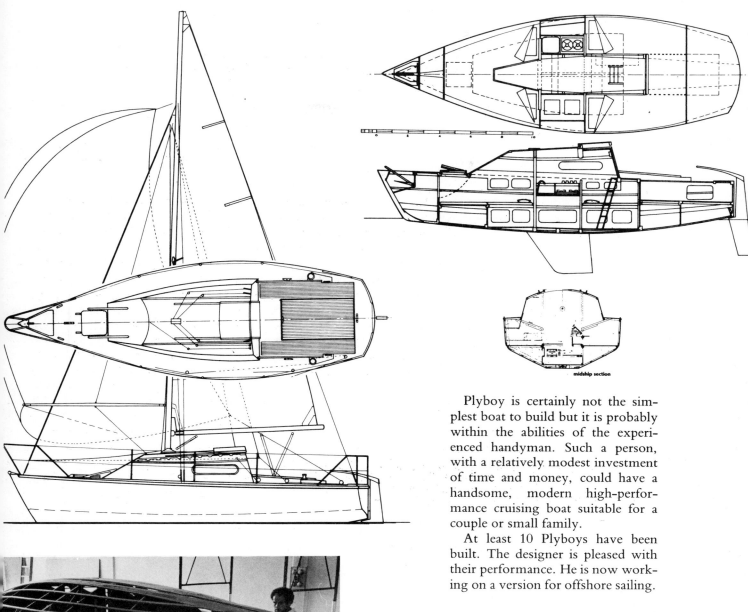

midship section

Plyboy is certainly not the simplest boat to build but it is probably within the abilities of the experienced handyman. Such a person, with a relatively modest investment of time and money, could have a handsome, modern high-performance cruising boat suitable for a couple or small family.

At least 10 Plyboys have been built. The designer is pleased with their performance. He is now working on a version for offshore sailing.

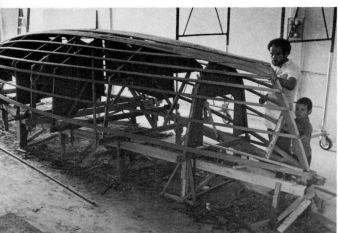

Longitudinal frames are attached to the bulkheads and frames of the inverted hull.

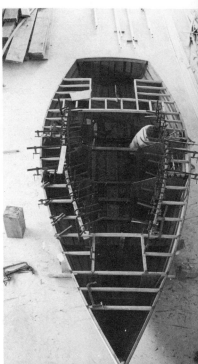

Deck beams and frames are fitted to accept the plywood deck.

The gap between the plywood hull panels will be filled with a rounded chine piece.

SOURDOUGH

Sourdough? Isn't that a strange name for a boat? Well, maybe not so strange as it seems. Although one meaning of sourdough is a delicious type of bread, the word also is used as a metonym for the old-time prospectors in Alaska who carried sourdough as a staple part of their diet.

Jay Benford designed this husky little pocket cruiser for a client in Copper Center, Alaska, for long-distance cruising, possibly as far as Hawaii. It has a single-chined, flat-bottomed hull with full keel and raised, flush deck. "Every reasonable step has been taken to make this simple and straightforward to build," the designer states, "and still maintain a vessel with good seaworthiness."

Benford has designed many craft, of varying sizes, with this dory-type hull form and says he has received good reports on their sea-keeping abilities. Pounding is not a problem with the flat bottom because when the boat is sailing and heeled over, a V-shape is presented to the water. At anchor, the chine is completely immersed in normal conditions.

The hull is constructed by cold molding plywood planking over fir longitudinal framing and bulkheads using epoxy for sealing and gluing. Ballast is concrete and scrap metal cast in shape and bolted externally. Most of the materials necessary for construction are available at a lumberyard or hardware store.

Care must be taken in comparing the displacement, and displacement ratios of Sourdough with those of many other craft. Benford points out that the figure of 4,900 pounds represents the estimated total

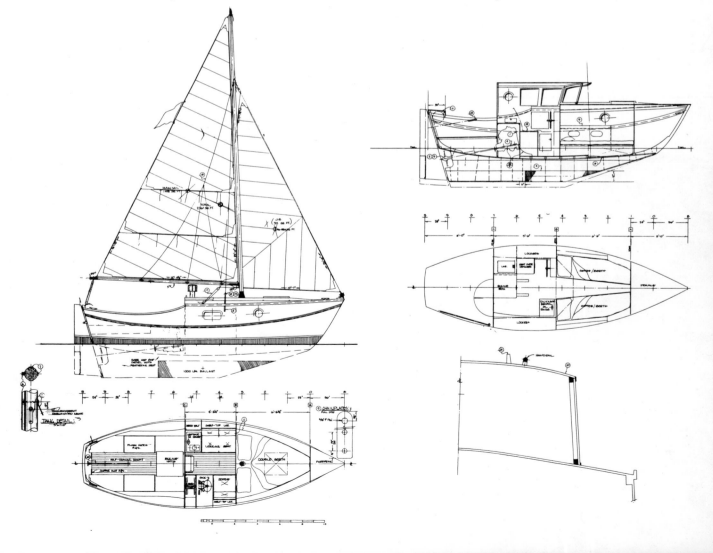

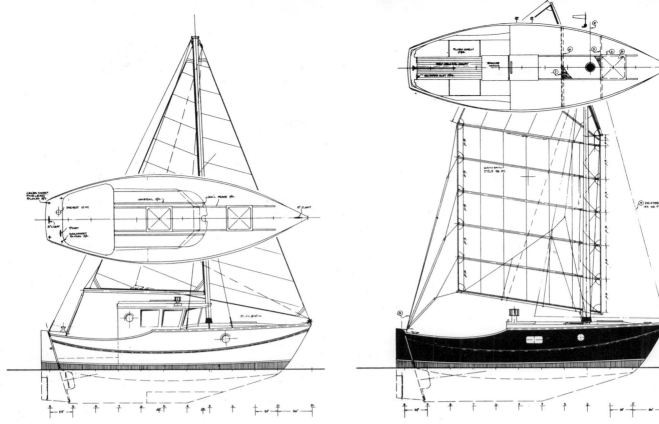

SOURDOUGH

LOA
  23'0" (7.01 m.)

LWL
  19'6" (5.94 m.)

Beam
  8'0" (2.44 m.)

Draft
  3'0" (0.91 m.)

Ballast
  1,000 lbs. (454 kg.)

Displacement
  4,900 lbs. (2,223 kg.)

Sail Area
  Fractional sloop: 236 sq. ft.
    (21.9 sq. m.)
  Masthead sloop 224 sq. ft.
    (20.8 sq. m.)
  Lug: 273 sq. ft. (25.3 sq. m.)

Construction
  Cold-molded plywood

Disp./Length Ratio
  295

Sail Area/Disp. Ratio
  Fractional sloop: 13.1
  Masthead sloop 12.4
  Lug: 15.1

JAY R. BENFORD
758 Trenton Ave.
Severna Park, MD 21146

weight of Sourdough and its contents, ready for cruising, including fuel, water, crew, gear and stores. The displacement quoted for some designs is the empty weight of the boat as it leaves the factory.

Even calculated conservatively, the weight of fuel (20 gallons) water (15 gallons), one crew, ground tackle, food etc. for Sourdough has to amount to nearly 1,000 pounds, or 20 percent of displacement. Allowing for the addition of this weight in the design of a boat is critical. A boat designed to displace 4,000 pounds and then loaded down to 5,000 pounds will have its performance and, possibly, seaworthiness seriously affected. This is especially true in a small cruiser where the added weight is such a large part of the total displacement.

Exaggerated sheer and the flush deck result in a healthy freeboard forward and aft, and a deep, well-protected cockpit. Backrests are high and angled for comfort. The shallow footwell is pitched aft and drains through ports in the transom, 12 inches above the waterline.

Headroom down below is four feet, 10 inches. To starboard are a hanging locker, sink and single seat. To port is a woodburning stove, complete with oven and wood bin and a double seat. Forward is a double V-berth. The MSD is a bucket in the cockpit locker.

With no quarter berth or settee, there would be many times at sea when the crew would have to sleep in the cockpit or on the cabin sole to avoid the motion forward. Perhaps the arrangement could be altered to include a sea berth. A pilothouse version is also shown. In addition to fractional sloop rig, Benford has drawn both masthead and lug rigs. All are very conservative in area. The small area is in keeping with the client's plans to "motorsail cruise." The eight-hp. Sabb diesel with feathering variable pitch propeller can cruise 600 miles at five knots on 20 gallons of fuel, according to the designer. Greater sail area might be preferred by those interested in higher sailing performance.

BAHAMA SANDPIPER

Once in a while a new design appears that seems to possess an extraordinary harmony among its parts. Everything fits together simply and properly. No complicated gadgets are necessary to make the boat work. Nothing stands out as incongruous with the rest of the design.

Such a design does not just happen, but is the result of a naval architect doing his homework and doing it well. The Bahama Sandpiper is truly a "concept boat" and Chuck Paine has done a marvelous job making every aspect of the design fit the concept, that of an utterly simple boat that can be trailered and beached easily.

Paine said the Bahama Sandpiper "closes the gap between full-keel yachts, which are restrained to deep waters and cannot be trailered, and more traditional shoal draft cruisers (catboats and sharpies) which lack either speed, stability, or both."

Very few beachable boats are available in this country and very few sailors know the pleasure of pulling up on a sandy shore for a little exploration, or a quiet night, or to avoid a storm. Beachability requires that the boat remain at a comfortable angle of heel when grounded, and the external ballast keel found on most boats makes this impossible.

To solve the problem, Paine chose a long, shallow hull and centerboard configuration. Maximum hull draft is only 18 inches. Ballast is in the form of 1,500 lbs. of lead (36% of displacement) encapsulated in fiberglass adjacent to and forward of the centerboard trunk. The long waterline and low displacement/length ratio assures spirited performance.

Three sail plans are available: cat ketch, sloop and cutter. The cat ketch is, I think, the most interesting and appropriate. The two short spars (tapered aluminum flagpole extrusions) can be stepped or unstepped by one person. Paine has worked out a unique system for this operation.

The mizzen mast is stayed and thus has a lighter cross section than the unstayed foremast. Being lighter, it is easily handled by one person. It is mounted in a tabernacle, which allows it to be tilted forward to a point where its head is over the foremast step. There the two-part halyard can be used to raise or lower the heavier foremast.

This rig is also self-tacking and does not require any additional sails. Booms are spruce and the mizzen boom can be used to raise an outboard motor on or off the transom. Of the 14 Sandpipers built, seven have been cat ketch rigged.

Many centerboard boats suffer from a centerboard trunk that obstructs the cabin arrangement. By choosing a long, narrow board, Paine has been able to keep the case low and almost unnoticeable. Also unnoticeable is the fact that it is located about two inches off center to starboard to accomplish a roomier layout.

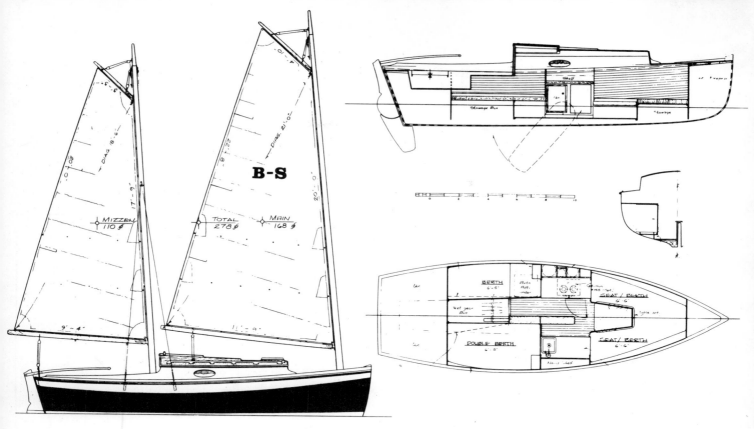

The interior is quite large for a 24-foot boat. Two quarter berths, one of normal width and one quite wide, are located aft. A V-berth with table is situated forward. A generous galley separates the two areas.

Paine Yacht Design owns molds for the Sandpiper and offers the molded fiberglass parts as a kit to the home builder or can arrange completion by a local boatyard. The boat is suitable for construction in fiberglass (C-Flex, Airex core or Str-r-etch Mesh), or cold molded plywood. A hull, deck, centerboard and a set of construction plans cost about $8,000, so the boat can be completed for about $13,000.

The Bahama Sandpiper looks like an incredibly fun boat to sail and cruise, and one that makes the possibility of owning a cruising boat more realistic for a great many sailors. With such a craft, an owner can forget about marinas and boatyards, dredged channels and crowded harbors, and return to the simple enjoyment of sailing.

BAHAMA SANDPIPER

LOA
24′0″ (7.32 m.)

LWL
22′6″ (6.86 m.)

Beam
7′11½″ (2.43 m.)

Draft
1′6″ (0.46 m.)

Ballast
1,500 lbs. (680 kg.)

Displacement
4,140 lbs. (1,878 kg.)

Sail Area
305 sq. ft. (28.3 sq.m.)

Construction
see text

Disp./Length Ratio
162

Sail Area/Disp. Ratio
18.9

C. W. PAINE YACHT DESIGN, INC.
P.O. Box 763
Camden, ME 04843

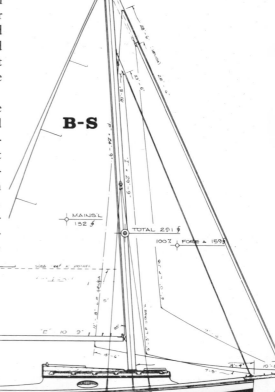

ALLEGRA

Allegra was designed by Fred P. Bingham as a development of the very popular Flicka, designed by his son, Bruce Bingham. The Flicka class, now produced by Pacific Seacraft of Santa Ana, California, is slightly smaller, being 20 feet on deck with an 18-foot, two-inch waterline and eight-foot beam. She has six-foot headroom and four full-size berths. Fred Bingham says there were many requests for a larger yet still trailerable vessel based on Flicka, and Allegra is the result.

Allegra is very similar in appearance to Flicka, but has a bit more flare and forward overhang. She is four feet longer on deck, two feet, six inches longer on the waterline, and has the same beam of eight feet (the legal maximum for trailering

without special permit). Her 6,200-pound displacement is nearly 40 percent greater than Flicka's 4,500 pounds.

The keel is full yet cutaway forward with an angled bottom profile. This should make her a stable, sea-kindly boat and responsive to the helm. Ballast consists of 2,000 pounds of lead pigs and shot encapsulated within the fiberglass keel. The rudder is large and hung outboard for ease of construction and maintenance.

The deck and cabin design of the two craft is nearly the same, but with a few small changes. Allegra's bridge deck adds security in the event the cockpit is flooded by a boarding sea. It also increases the seating area in the cockpit and storage space below. The cockpit length of six feet, six inches allows sleeping on deck. Cockpit storage space is ample with lockers on both sides.

It is in the cabin where the few additional feet of length are most noticeable. While Flicka has a toilet fitted between the two V-berths,

ALLEGRA

LOD
23'11" (7.29 m.)

LWL
20'10" (6.35 m.)

Beam
8'0" (2.44 m.)

Draft
3'5½" (1.05 m.)

Ballast
2,000 lbs. (907 kg.)

Displacement
6,200 lbs. (2,812 kg.)

Sail Area (Marconi Cutter)
337 sq. ft. (31 sq. m.)

Construction
C-Flex fiberglass

Disp./Length Ratio
307

Sail Area/Disp. Ratio
15.4

FRED P. BINGHAM
516 Arrellaga #5
Santa Barbara, CA 93103

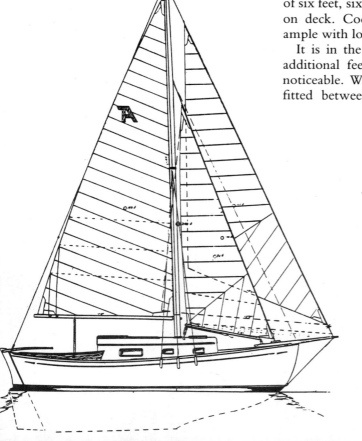

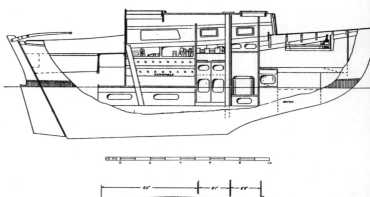

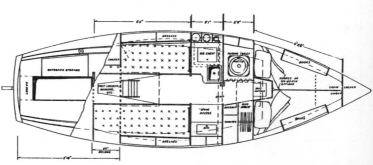

Allegra has an enclosed head. Head-room is increased from six feet to six feet, two inches, which doesn't sound like much, but makes an important difference even for those slightly under six feet tall.

The galley has room for a gimbaled stove. The forward cabin has a narrow hanging locker and dresser. Allegra's quarter berth is positioned further forward than in Flicka, making it more accessible.

Allegra can be rigged as a gaff cutter, Marconi sloop or Marconi cutter. A boomed self-tending staysail is used on the cutter and a boomed jib is possible on the sloop. Wood or aluminum spars can be used.

Auxiliary power can be either a 12-hp. Stuart-Turner diesel or an outboard motor on a bracket. There is room for two 20-gallon flexible water tanks and 15 to 20 gallons of fuel.

C-Flex has proved the most popular construction material. Molded fiberglass hulls are offered by the designer.

Allegra offers the possibility of a comfortable and seaworthy cruising boat with good performance at a reasonable price. She can be home built or purchased as a hull and deck for about $8,000. A complete boat costs about $23,500.

View of the bow reveals the hollow or concavity at the forward end of the waterline.

The Allegra prototype reaching on Puget Sound.

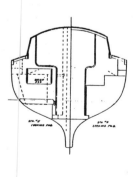

FRANCES

Appearing in *Cruising World* in October 1975, Frances was one of Chuck Paine's early designs. It attracted much attention, contributed to his growing popularity as a designer of beautiful and seaworthy boats, and is still his most popular design.

Frances was intended as a small, yet comfortable cruising boat capable of coastal or offshore cruising, with a high level of performance and a seakindly manner. Ease and economy of construction were also major considerations.

The double ended hullform combines moderately heavy displacement with superbly graceful sheer and balance. In its original flush deck, 7/8 rig configuration, it is, I think, one of the most handsome boats afloat.

In profile, the underbody appears to be that of a traditional full-keel boat. A section drawing, however, reveals slack bilges, a tight tuck at the garboards and a keel that is more like an appendage. Wetted surface is increased, but so is effective keel depth and efficiency.

The raised flush deck is both easy to construct and inherently strong.

Standing headroom aft of the mast is provided by the short trunk cabin.

This flush deck version was constructed in Japan.

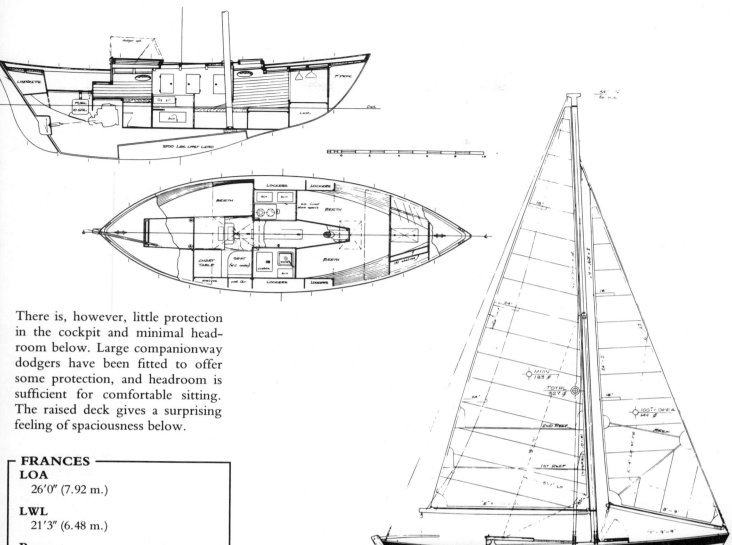

There is, however, little protection in the cockpit and minimal headroom below. Large companionway dodgers have been fitted to offer some protection, and headroom is sufficient for comfortable sitting. The raised deck gives a surprising feeling of spaciousness below.

FRANCES

LOA
26'0″ (7.92 m.)

LWL
21'3″ (6.48 m.)

Beam
8'0″ (2.44 m.)

Draft
3'10″ (1.17 m.)

Ballast
3,400 lbs. (1,542 kg.)

Displacement
6,800 lbs. (3,084 kg.)

Sail Area
337 sq. ft. (31.3 sq. m.)

Construction
see text

Disp./Length Ratio
316

Sail Area/Disp. Ratio
15.0

C. W. PAINE YACHT DESIGN, INC.
P.O. Box 763
Camden, ME 04843

A demand for more headroom and interior space led Paine to design a stout-looking short trunk cabin configuration, and later a long trunk cabin version.

Five interior arrangements are offered, with three, four or five berths. In the three-berth arrangement, a small but useful chart table is fitted to starboard with the toilet under the seat. In the four-berth plan, for the long trunk cabin, there is even an enclosed head.

Sail area is on the low side, appropriate to a small, offshore cruiser. With either the 7/8 or masthead rig, however, sailing performance should be, and has proved to be, very good. An engine is optional, with many owners choosing either an outboard motor or oars for propulsion. Much interior room is gained by not having an inboard engine on such a small boat.

Construction is either fiberglass or cold molded wood. Over 100 sets of plans have been purchased. An additional 35 boats have been built by Morris Yachts of Southwest Harbor Maine, and 17 by Victoria Yachts in England.

Frances will undoubtedly become one of the classic small cruising boats, against which others will be measured. Paine has also designed a slightly smaller, 24 foot boat called Carol. It is similar to the flush decked Frances and displaces 5,700 pounds.

SHEARWATER

With the growing popularity of the cat ketch rig, some designers and builders are simply taking conventional, existing hulls and adding two unstayed masts. Sometimes the result is satisfactory and sometimes it is less than that. To realize its full potential the cat ketch rig must be combined with a complementary hull form.

Richard Black, whose knowledge of yacht design is the result of "a self-directed program of study spanning 15 years," has been following the modern development of the cat ketch since 1974 and said he has become "something of a specialist in refining this rig to extract its full potential." This design, Shearwater, is noteworthy not only because it exhibits Black's conclusions on the properly arranged cat ketch rig and its combination with a suitable hull, but also because of the unusual but sensible design concept.

In viewing the production boats available in the popular trailerable boat market, Black felt most were inexpensively built, of questionable quality for serious sailing, and intended for the neophyte boat buyer. With an increasing number of experienced cruising and racing sailors considering trailerable boats as a way of saving dockage expenses, or as a way of sailing in distant waters even on a short vacation, Black felt that there was a need for a well-designed, well-built trailer sailer with performance to satisfy the experienced skipper. His target price was in the range of $30,000 to $40,000.

Based on the photographs and information supplied by the designer, Shearwater appears to be an elegant 27-foot, six-inch pocket cruiser with an attractive combination of high performance and ease of handling. In addition to making a fine coastal or offshore cruiser, Black said she is suitable for both single-handed and one-design racing.

Black's logic in determining the right hull for the cat ketch rig is that since this rig is less powerful than a tall, masthead sloop, the hull must be light and easily driven. An easily driven hull is long, narrow and shallow; such a hull is also tender. A tender hull should have a low and easily reefed sail plan. The cat ketch can be just that. And for trailering, the narrow, shallow and lightweight boat is ideal.

With a displacement/length ratio of 169, Shearwater is certainly in the light-displacement category. Beam was kept to eight feet for trailering but tumblehome brings the maximum beam close to the waterline for increased stability. Ballast is high at 47 percent of displacement but placed within the hull so it should not cause a violent motion at sea.

Draft with centerboard and kick-up rudder raised is only 14 inches, making launching and retrieving easy. Designing and building a skeg and rudder that can kick up, yet still be strong enough for security at sea is not easy, or inexpensive. When well executed, however, it is ideal for a seagoing trailerable. Draft with centerboard lowered is six feet.

Shearwater's low, short cabin trunk is very handsome. Headroom below is only five feet, four inches but Black did not want to sacrifice esthetics to achieve six or eight inches more headroom.

The cold-molded hull is constructed of four layers of ⅛-inch fir set in epoxy resin and sheathed in two laminations of polypropylene cloth and epoxy. Decks consist of two layers of ¼-inch plywood cored with end-grain balsa. This is covered with ¼-inch teak deck epoxy-bonded without fastenings. The transom and cabin sides are finished bright.

Now to the rig! Black has definite views on the best arrangements for the cat ketch rig, and they appear to make sense. Masts are carbon fiber and weigh only 65 pounds each; the designer said they are overbuilt and plans to test spars that weigh only 48 pounds each.

Black prefers wraparound sails to a conventional, single ply sail with track. The leading edge is cleaner and more "stall-proof" than a sail

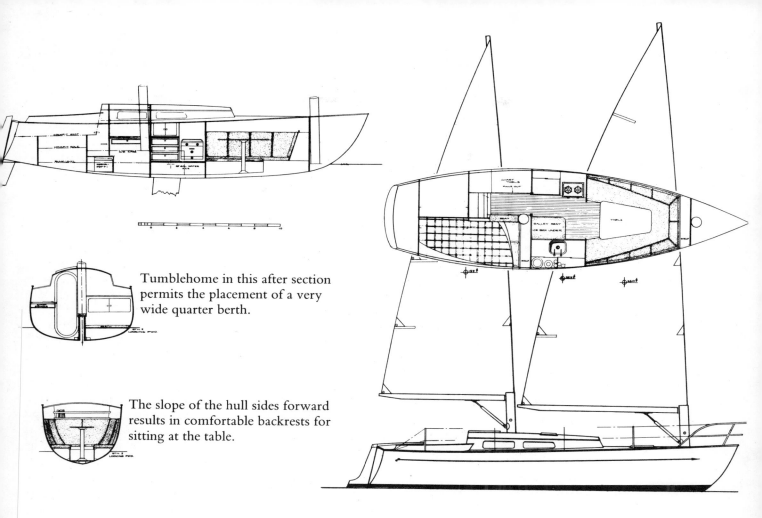

Tumblehome in this after section permits the placement of a very wide quarter berth.

The slope of the hull sides forward results in comfortable backrests for sitting at the table.

on a track. It is thus able to achieve high efficiency even with an inattentive helmsperson, sail trimmer, or self-steering device. Both sails have two sets of reef points and can be reefed from the cockpit in less than 30 seconds.

Black also reports a unique system for setting a storm trysail. The sail is kept stopped with light twine. When needed, the bundle is wrapped around the mast, outhauled and hoisted out of stops from the cockpit.

An integral part of the rig, and perhaps a controversial one, is the conventional booms with strong mechanical or hydraulic vangs. He finds this gives him much better control of the leech shape and mast bend than with wishbone booms. All reefing lines are led inside the booms and, since the booms are attached to the tabernacles rather than the masts, they and their internal lines can be left in place even when trailering. The masts stow within the length of the boat.

On the subject of performance the designer thinks Shearwater has up-

wind performance comparable to that of a "good production sloop" of similar size. Reaching, with a mizzen staysail, is her strongest point of sail. Downwind, she suffers only in light air but Black is working on a backstay that can be raised to the main masthead to carry a spinnaker in such conditions.

Let's not forget the interior. Aft are a double quarter berth to starboard and pull-out chart table to port, with a portable toilet under the companionway steps. Further forward is the galley, on both sides, all within reach of the galley seat on top of the icebox. A spacious table and settee area, presumably convertible to a double berth, is located forward. Tankage for 60 gallons of water is located amidships. Power consists of an outboard motor in an aft well.

Shearwater is a well-conceived, versatile, high-performance boat that should appeal to a variety of experienced sailors. Based on experience with Shearwater, Black has designed a 30-foot fiberglass production boat, the Anacapa 30.

SHEARWATER

LOA
27′6″ (8.38 m.)

LWL
24′0″ (7.32 m.)

Beam
8′0″ (2.44 m.)

Draft
1′2″/6′0″ (.36/1.83 m.)

Ballast
2,500 lbs. (1,134 kg.)

Displacement
5,290 lbs. (2,399 kg.)

Sail Area
390 sq. ft. (36.2 sq. m.)

Construction
Cold molded wood/epoxy

Disp./Length Ratio
169

Sail Area/Disp. Ratio
20.5

RICHARD BLACK YACHT
DESIGN
908 Vallecito Dr.
Ventura, CA 93001

SASSY

There is more than one way to skin a cat, and there is more than one way to make a boat easy to build. The usual approach is to keep the structure simple and avoid complicated fitting, which may be too difficult for the amateur builder. With Sassy, Carl Schumacher has gone further and eliminated the difficult cabin structure completely.

Schumacher's aim in designing Sassy was to create a boat that is versatile and simple with a maximum of privacy and stowage space and a minimum of fitting and joinery.

Consider what he has achieved. Here is a light displacement 28-foot boat with berths for four in two private cabins, an enclosed head, a seven-foot cockpit, and (in his own words) a "well ventilated galley." It is well ventilated because it is in the cockpit under a dodger.

These qualities have not been achieved without sacrifices. Headroom is about 4½ feet forward and four feet aft. The head is tiny (2'6" × 3') yet contains a folding sink.

Having the cockpit double as the cooking/dining area can work out well in most situations. Visibility is excellent and a tent can be added to the dodger to afford protection and privacy to the entire cockpit. Having a sink and icebox in the cockpit could be a real luxury.

The hull is constructed of ½-inch Douglas fir exterior-grade plywood; spruce can be substituted to save weight (but will increase cost). Two layers of ¼-inch ply make up the deck. Hull and deck are sheathed in fiberglass cloth.

The keel is cast lead and the spars are aluminum. Schumacher points out that the spars can be bought in kit form to save money.

Speaking of money, the designer's cost estimates for the construction of Sassy are $8,000 with an Atomic 1 inboard engine and $6,000 with an outboard motor.

With its airfoil-shaped keel and rudder, and large, modern sloop rig, Sassy should be an exciting performer. This, and her large cockpit and flush deck make her attractive as a daysailer as well as a cruiser. The deck plan shows an interesting steering arrangement, with a tiller in the cockpit connected by a linkage to the rudder.

While Sassy's type is not a new idea it is one that has not received much attention. It is an interesting alternative to the conventional small cruiser with a cabin. Its space use results in much more accommodation than is normally found on a boat of this size. You must, however, be willing to accept less protection from the elements.

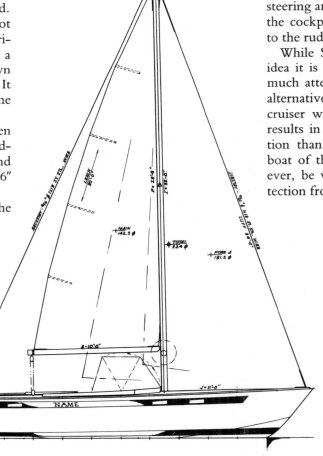

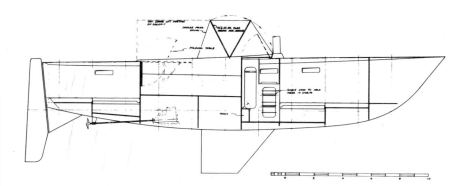

SASSY

LOA
28′0″ (8.53 m.)

LWL
23′1″ (7.03 m.)

Beam
8′0″ (2.44 m.)

Draft
4′6″ (1.37 m.)

Ballast
2,150 lbs. (975 kg.)

Displacement
4,882 lbs. (2,214 kg.)

Sail Area
324 sq. ft. (30.1 sq. m.)

Construction
Plywood

Disp./Length Ratio
177

Sail Area/Disp. Ratio
18.0

CARL SCHUMACHER
1815 Clement Ave.
Alameda, CA 94501

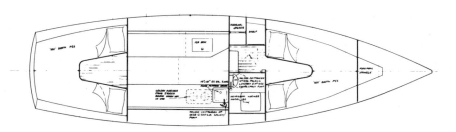

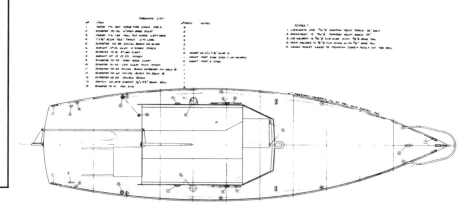

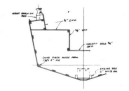

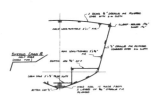

PASSAGE MAKER 28

In designing the Passage Maker 28, Tom MacNaughton attempted to create the smallest ultimately safe, true liveaboard cruising boat. While she may appear to be similar to many traditional double-ender designs, both her hull and rig are quite modern and incorporate refinements that her designer says are vast improvements over the older designs. Whereas the Colin Archer types were based upon the rescue craft of many years ago, the Passage Maker 28 is based upon the rescue craft of today—and great improvements have been made in the design of rescue craft.

It has been found that by making forward waterlines finer and aft waterlines fuller, pitching can be reduced and weatherliness improved. Combined with the cutaway forefoot, this has made today's rescue craft much more comfortable, maneuverable and easy to handle. These same qualities are much sought after in a sailing boat and MacNaughton is convinced he has achieved them.

Another feature adapted from rescue boats is the knuckle or chine in the bow area above the waterline. It allows the forward sections to be fine and V-shaped at and below the waterline, yet well flared above it to provide reserve buoyancy. The chine also acts as a spray deflector.

Ballast is all external and extends over the entire length of the keel bottom for protection in grounding. The deep, narrow rudder should be highly efficient, guaranteeing excellent control.

The displacement/length ratio of 550 certainly places the Passage Maker 28 in the very heavy displacement category. What many people don't realize, however, is that the full garboards normally found in a heavy boat often result in less wetted surface than that found on a lighter boat with hard bilges and very hollow garboards.

Two different rigs have been drawn, a double headsail Marconi rig and a Chinese lug. The Marconi rig is very high and efficient looking. The staysail is quite small, but there are reasons for this. It opens up the slot between it and the jib to make tacking of the jib easier. Also, by having the staysail stay run to the spreaders rather than to some higher point, the necessity of running or intermediate backstays is eliminated. This reduces cost and weight, makes shorthanded sailing easier, and with reef points, can convert the staysail into a storm jib.

The Chinese lug rig has a larger sail area of 530 square feet. Although the unstayed mast may be difficult to construct, the absence of standing rigging and complex fittings (gooseneck, spreader bases, tangs, etc.) makes it an economical alternative. The designer points out that since the sail takes its shape from the battens and sheetlets, it can be cut and sewn flat by the amateur sailmakers.

What appears to be a wheelhouse on the Marconi version is really a

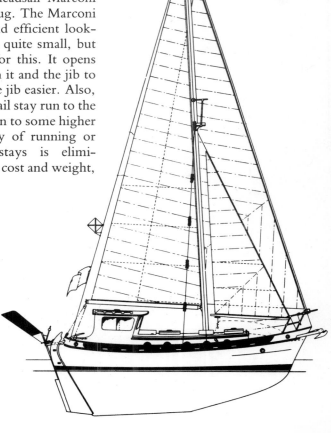

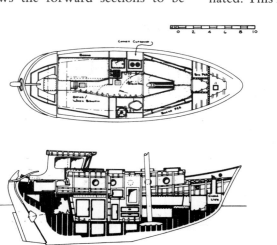

cockpit shelter with a conventional companionway below. While some disfavor a wheelhouse because of its vulnerability to waves, with this arrangement it could be swept away without sacrificing the integrity of the boat. A folding dodger as shown on the lug version also is possible.

Two interior arrangements were drawn, the first being the one for the designer's own boat. It is unusual in that it includes a large office/workbench area and also because watertight doors in the bulkheads lessen the chance of sinking in the event of hull damage.

MacNaughton points out (and illustrates himself) that there are a number of ways in which one can make a living afloat which require some sort of office or work space. This area could be designed to suit the owner's needs exactly.

Forward of the head and galley is the dining area, which can also be used for sleeping. Further forward is a very large storage area, where it

belongs, in the least comfortable area of the boat.

Arrangement #2 is somewhat more conventional, with a larger aft galley. The berths located outboard of the settees are more enclosed than normal pilot berths (see inboard profile). The designer calls them alcove berths and they each have a curtain for privacy and a Dorade for ventilation.

Both galleys have the stove placed in a "cooker cupboard," a ventilated and insulated box with a glass door. This keeps the heat of cooking from spreading through the boat, certainly something to be appreciated in warmer climates.

The boat is suited for construction in C-flex fiberglass, cold-molded wood, carvel or strip planking. She is not designed for those looking for breathtaking performance, but rather for those who desire a safe and easily handled boat that is comfortable to sail and live aboard.

PASSAGE MAKER 28

LOA
28'7" (8.72 m.)

LWL
23'0" (7.02 m.)

Beam
9'9" (2.97 m.)

Draft
5'3" (1.60 m.)

Ballast
6,600 lbs. (2,994 kg.)

Displacement
15,000 lbs. (6,804 kg.)

Sail Area
510 sq. ft. (47.4 sq. m.)

Construction
see text

Disp./Length Ratio
550

Sail Area/Disp. Ratio
13.4

MacNAUGHTON ASSOCIATES
Hampden Highlands, ME 04445

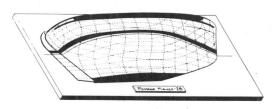

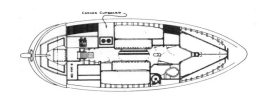

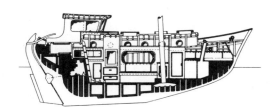

ANNIE

Chuck Paine's boats seem to possess unique charm and simplicity, are imaginative without being freakish and exhibit character without being cute. They are basically handsome, seaworthy boats, and his Annie is no exception.

Paine calls Annie "an ultimate boat for the working man . . . just large enough to become a man's home, just seaworthy enough to handle any ocean, just fast enough to offer her owner any port in the world . . . and no more." To achieve this in a boat of less than 30 feet in length is no mean feat.

His most conservative design to date, Annie is actually the result of Paine's taking what he considered the best examples of this type of boat and selecting their good points and improving their weak ones. As his examples he chose L. Francis Herreshoff's H-28, Laurent Giles' Vertue and Wanderer, Ralph Winslow's Four-Sum, and the Nicholson 31.

The H-28 lacked standing headroom and the Vertue and Wanderer were narrow and thus had small interiors. Four-Sum was his favorite but was too heavy to perform up to his standard. The latter did, however, serve as the basis for Annie.

To increase speed potential, Paine increased stability and sail area while decreasing displacement. Stability was increased by going to a slightly larger beam, using lead rather than iron for ballast, and having an aluminum mast and fiberglass hull to lower the center of gravity. While Four-Sum had a 7/8 rig, Annie has a masthead rig with 10 percent more sail area, all inboard.

Even though Paine reduced displacement, Annie is still a moderately heavy boat, a quality he considers necessary in a small cruiser. It results in a gentle motion at sea and the ability to carry heavy loads of stores and equipment. It also allows the boat to be massively built. Annie's fiberglass hull is what Paine calls "bulletproof," while the deck and cabin are plywood covered with fiberglass. Paine prefers this because it gives the pleasing look of deck beams down below.

Speaking of down below, take a look at the interior of this 29-foot boat. There are four berths, with two good sea berths, without resorting to the settees. A full-size chart table plus wet and dry hanging lockers certainly will be appreciated by the coastwise or offshore sailor. There is an enclosed head, and the forecabin has room to stand up and

ANNIE

LOA
29′2″ (8.88 m.)

LWL
24′2″ (7.35 m.)

Beam
9′4″ (2.94 m.)

Draft
4′6″ (1.37 m.)

Ballast
4,400 lbs. (1995 kg.)

Displacement
10,800 lbs. (4,898 kg.)

Sail Area
450 sq. ft. (41.8 sq. m.)

Construction
Fiberglass

Disp./Length Ratio
342

Sail Area/Disp. Ratio
14.7

C. W. PAINE YACHT DESIGN
P.O. Box 763
Camden, ME 04843

walk around. The cabin sole is wide and there is room beneath it for 50 gallons of water and 20 gallons of fuel. Side decks are at least 20 inches wide and a high toe rail surrounds the boat.

Paine said Annie's principal virtue is her healthy displacement. "Say what you will about heavy cruisers, they are the type most likely to be discovered far from their home port, and most frequently found suitable for floating homes for their owner."

Morris Yachts of Southwest Harbor, Maine, has built 11 hulls in fiberglass. Paine completed a Morris-built hull himself for his personal cruising boat.

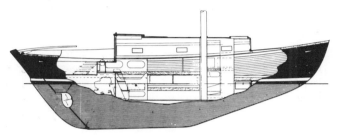

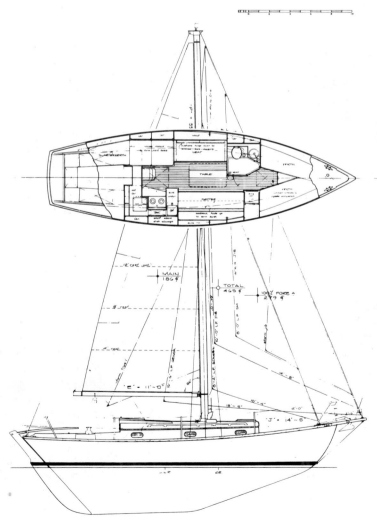

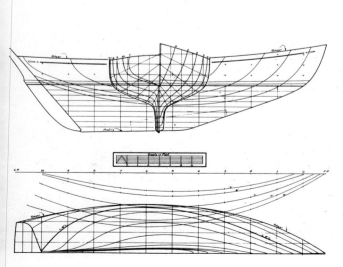

FALMOUTH CUTTER

The Pardeys' *Taleisin* is dressed and ready for launching.

While Lin and Larry Pardey were cruising the Mediterranean Sea in their 24-foot Lyle Hess-designed *Seraffyn,* they started dreaming about and planning their next boat. While they were pleased with *Seraffyn,* they wanted a cruiser with enough space for a proper, sit-down bathtub, and also enough room to carry more food, water and fuel.

Through correspondence with the Pardeys, Hess designed a boat very similar in type and appearance, but about five feet longer. The Falmouth Cutter 29 has a length on deck of 29 feet, nine inches, and is offered with a choice of gaff or Bermudan cutter rig.

The Pardeys completed their circumnavigation and sold *Seraffyn*

and have now launched their new *Taleisin* to this design. For the keelson, deadwood and frames they used locust wood that Larry cut himself in Virginia 12 years ago. Planking, decking and joiner work are teak. Floor timbers and knees between frames and deck beams are all cast bronze. Planks are fastened to the frames with copper rivets and roves. Bronze bolts are used throughout. They completed a three-and-a-half year, 5,000 manhour building period.

The hull form is one with which Hess has had a great deal of experience and success. It is based on the English Channel pilot cutters, which had to be able to put to sea and stay there comfortably in all sorts of conditions.

The bow is quite fine for weatherliness and the forefoot is slightly cut away for maneuverability. Aft sections are of the classic wineglass form. The transom-hung rudder is easy to inspect and service and can be fitted with a trim tab for self-steering.

Seamanlike bulwarks surround the spacious deck. The trunk cabin is just large enough to provide standing headroom in the main cabin. A raised scuttle forward allows headroom between the V-berths for dressing and undressing. The cutout for the cockpit footwell

is very small and would thus hold only a small volume of water.

Because the Pardeys are both short, they had Hess draw a cabin for them slightly lower than the standard one. They also chose a conventional foredeck hatch in place of the scuttle. This should allow dinghy stowage forward of the mast rather than on the cabin top, and also leave a large, open deck for lounging.

The standard Bermudan cutter rig spreads 653 square feet of sail. For esthetics and to achieve a larger

Note the trim tab for self-steering mounted on the rudder.

foretriangle the Pardeys chose to rake the mast more and to extend the bowsprit by two feet. At about eight feet long, the Pardeys' bowsprit is what many would consider a "widow-maker." They use a downhaul on the jib to reduce the need of actually venturing out onto the sprit. Larry also said the running backstays will be unnecessary and has eliminated them.

The interior shown is only one of the many possible arrangements. It features two quarter berths set well outboard with short settees and a drop-leaf table inboard. The chart table on the port side is positioned over the icebox. Opposite is the galley with an athwartships, ungimbaled stove. Many feel that a gimbaled stove takes up too much space and prefer to have a fixed stove and use a portable single-burner gimbaled stove at sea.

The Pardeys' arrangement is different with a bathtub aft and a double berth forward in place of the V-berth. As with their smaller *Seraffyn* they have chosen not to install an inboard engine, but will use an outboard motor for maneuvering in port.

In addition to the Pardeys' boat there are three more Falmouth Cutters abuilding, a gaff cutter for a Vermont owner and two Bermudan cutters in Maine.

It is difficult to imagine a more seaworthy, spacious and comfortable cruising boat under 30 feet. Judging from the time and quality materials the Pardeys have invested in *Taleisin,* it will probably cruise the oceans of the world for a few generations.

FALMOUTH CUTTER

LOA
29'9" (9.07 m.)

LWL
27'6" (8.38 m.)

Beam
10'8" (3.25 m.)

Draft
5'0" (1.52 m.)

Ballast
5,500 lbs. (2,495 kg.)

Displacement
15,800 lbs. (7,167 kg.)

Sail Area
653 sq. ft. (60.7 sq. m.)

Construction
Planked wood

Disp./Length Ratio
339

Sail Area/Disp. Ratio
15.9

LYLE C. HESS
1907 West Woodcrest Ave.
Fullerton, CA 92633

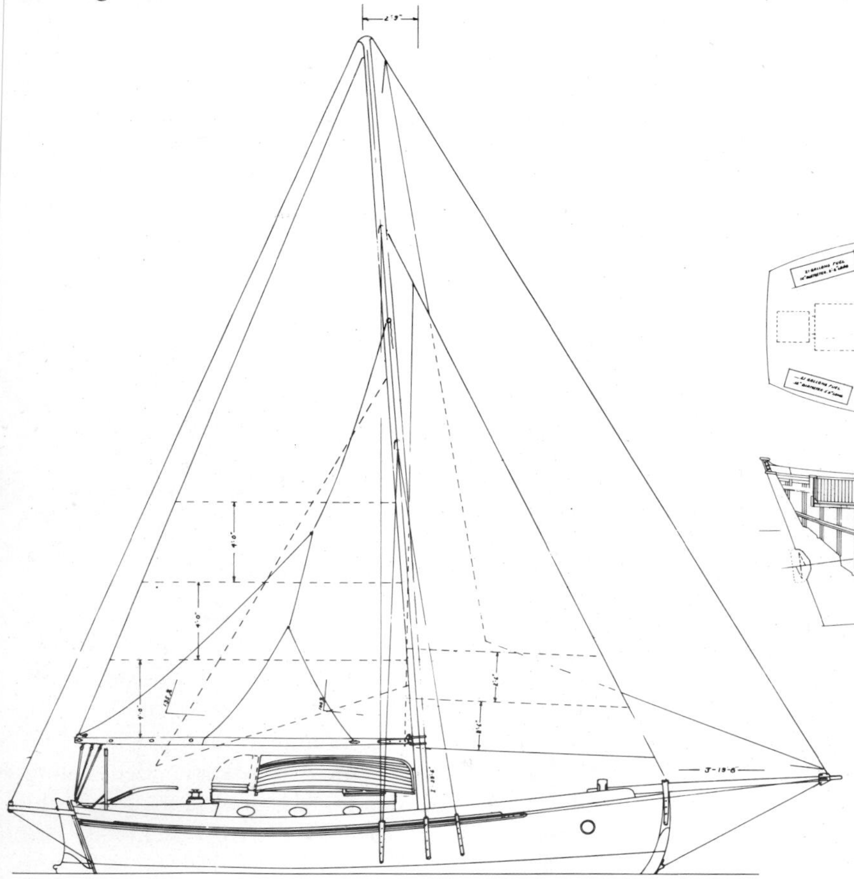

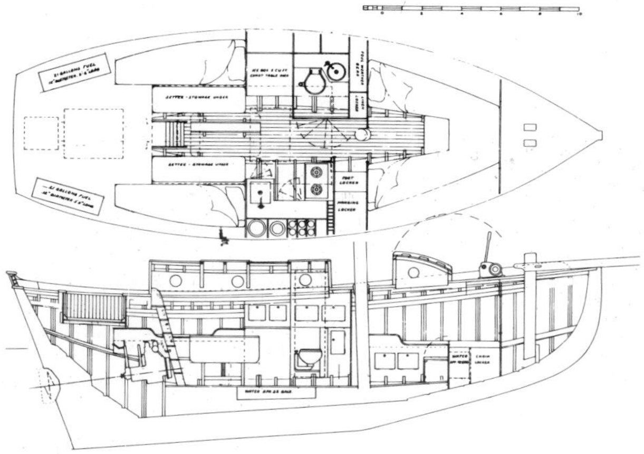

BULLDOG

Aluminum has become a very popular building material for racing yachts because of the strong, lightweight hulls that can be produced. These are nearly all curved-frame hull forms and require forming the aluminum plates into complex shapes, a difficult and expensive process.

For the cruising sailor who desires an aluminum boat but doesn't wish to (or can't) pay a high price, the alternative is chined construction. With the exception of the French, who are building chined aluminum cruising boats in great numbers, sailors have not been much attracted to this type of construction. Chined hulls are not as esthetically pleasing to those with traditional tastes and performance may be sacrificed, though only to a very small degree in a well-designed chined hull.

A compromise between the two is radiused-chine construction. In this system the hard chine where two plates meet is replaced by a radiused strip of aluminum running the length of the seam as shown in the body plan. Both appearance and performance are improved, al-though construction cost is somewhat higher than for a hard-chined hull.

Bulldog, a 30-foot sloop by Ted Brewer for a Canadian owner, was built in radiused-chine aluminum by Huromic Metal Industries of Goderich, Ontario. The owner, who plans to use the boat for long ocean voyages and as a permanent home afloat, is an experienced draftsman and presented Brewer with very detailed preliminary sketches of what he wanted.

Bulldog is quite beamy, with moderate draft and a long waterline. The underbody is typical of many Brewer-designed boats, with the forefoot and area ahead of the rudder cutaway. Freeboard is high, but well disguised by the wide sheer stripe.

In addition to the 5,000 pounds of lead, accounting for 42 percent of displacement, there is a tank for 75 gallons of fresh water in the keel. When this is full the effective ballast ratio is increased to about 47 percent. Together with the 10-foot, five-inch beam, this should make her an exceptionally stiff vessel.

Deck and cabin also are alumi-num. A sort of compromise flush deck arrangement is shown. The cabin top is flush with the foredeck while the side decks slope down to allow portlights in the cabin sides. Thus working on deck is eased and there is still light and visibility below.

The cockpit is small and secure-looking. Three-inch scuppers drain through the transom and the life raft is stored in a locker below the cockpit sole. A foredeck locker houses the anchor windlass and a pipe leads to the chain locker in the forecabin.

The interior appears to be well

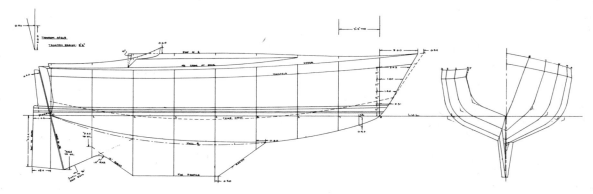

laid out for both passage-making and living aboard. Good sea berths are provided by the quarter berth to starboard and pilot berth to port. A folding double in the forecabin can be used in port. A wet locker is located behind the companionway ladder, over the engine. In the head a backpack-type sprayer is installed as a shower. To starboard in the forecabin is a workbench.

The double headsail rig is tall and well suited to shorthanded sailing. Lowering the mast is made possible by the tabernacle on deck.

Bulldog is a fitting name for this

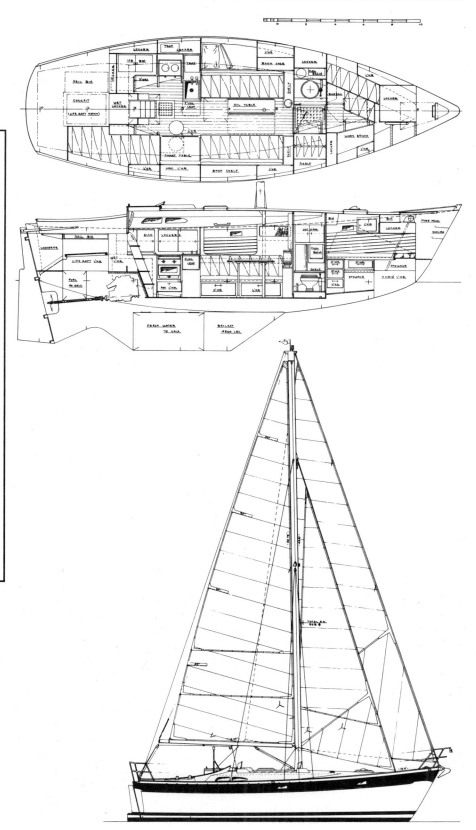

BULLDOG

LOA
30′0″ (9.15 m.)

LWL
26′0″ (7.93 m.)

Beam
10′5″ (3.18 m.)

Draft
4′11″ (1.50 m.)

Ballast
5,000 lbs. (2,117 kg.)

Displacement
12,000 lbs. (5,442 kg.)

Sail Area
528 sq. ft. (49.1 sq. m.)

Construction
Aluminum

Disp./Length Ratio
305

Sail Area/Disp. Ratio
16.1

TED BREWER YACHT DESIGNS,
LTD.
217 Edith Point Rd.
Anacortes, WA 98221

stout little cruiser. Perhaps she marks the beginning of an increased acceptance of aluminum and radiused-chine construction.

COAST 30

A customer from British Columbia asked Grahame Shannon to design a boat that would be easy and comfortable for two people to cruise. Good performance in light winds also was a design requisite. While he felt that full standing headroom was necessary in the galley and head, sitting headroom was considered adequate in the saloon.

From the waterline up, the Coast 30 has a traditional appearance with outboard rudder and rounded stem profile. Below the water, she has a shallow, easily driven hull with deep fin keel for windward ability. Displacement is light at 6,500 pounds, with 41 percent ballast.

The cockpit is small, too small to stretch out in, but well protected and with a small footwell. There is a great deal of storage space in the lazarette and lockers under the port and starboard seats.

Dodger installation is simplified by the cockpit coaming, which continues right across the cabin top. The flush foredeck offers good lounging and dinghy stowage space.

Four layers of 3.8mm (just over ⅛-inch) plywood are laminated with epoxy resin to form the hull, with additional layers in highly stressed areas. There is no interior framing other than the interior joiner work which is structurally tied to the hull. Two layers of 6mm (¼-inch) plywood on light beams form the deck. The design could be converted to fiberglass for production building.

A healthy amount of sail can be carried on the tall, fractional rig. Swept-back spreaders eliminate the need for intermediate backstays to achieve adequate headstay tension. Single lower shrouds allow mast flexibility to control mainsail shape.

The Soling-type jib sheets to a radiused track on the foredeck; it is thus self-tending without a boom.

Down the companionway, there is a galley to starboard, the head to port and an oilskin locker beneath the ladder. A hanging locker is located in the head with a cabin heater just forward.

The dining/lounging area is U-shaped and appears cozy. It could also be used for sleeping at sea. Further forward is a V-berth.

No auxiliary power is shown, as the client desired to do without. A removable outboard motor bracket which can be attached to the transom will, however, be included with the boat. Shannon has drawn plans for the installation of a small diesel inboard engine.

The first boat is being built by Tim Tuulos Custom Yachts of Surrey, British Columbia.

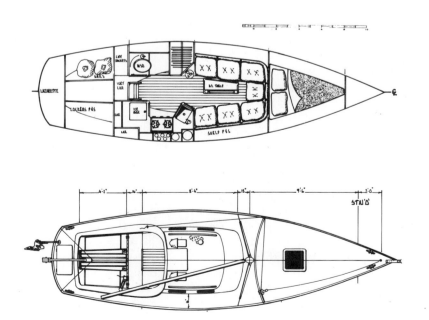

COAST 30

LOA
30′6″ (9.29 m.)

LWL
25′0″ (7.62 m.)

Beam
9′1″ (2.77 m.)

Draft
4′6″ (1.37 m.)

Ballast
2,700 lbs. (1,225 kg.)

Displacement
6,500 lbs. (2,948 kg.)

Sail Area
405 sq. ft. (37.7 sq. m.)

Construction
Laminated plywood

Disp./Length Ratio
185

Sail Area/Disp. Ratio
18.6

COAST YACHT DESIGN, INC.
215–810 W. Broadway
Vancouver, British Columbia
Canada V5Z 4C9

R9-30

What appears at first glance to be a rather conventional 30-foot "racer-cruiser" turns out to be, upon closer examination, an interesting and innovative design for a light, fast and comfortable cruising boat. She was intended to be a coastal cruiser for four, with offshore capabilities. A high priority was given to windward ability.

The hull is of solid fiberglass with a bolt-on lead keel. It is stiffened by three longitudinal stringers on each side, which double as sole and berth supports. A narrow waterline beam with much flare and tumblehome in the topsides characterizes the midship section. Forward sections are U-shaped, while the afterbody shows a deep sharp bustle and skeg for steering control. The skeg is a bronze casting bolted to the hull, containing rudderpost and gland and propeller shaft bearing. This assures strong rudder support and avoids a narrow, difficult skeg molding.

Perhaps the most interesting aspect of the R9-30 is the interior arrangement. Although the cockpit is located aft, a wide bridge deck places the companionway near midships. Rolf Eliasson, the designer, says that he based the layout on the principle that you enter the "activity area" in the middle of the boat with the lounging and sleeping areas at each end. This eliminates disturbing the off-watch when going to the galley, chart table or head.

Aft of the companionway is a large U-shaped settee arrangement that can be secluded by curtains. The backrests fold up to form pilot berths on either side. With bunk boards on the lowers and lee cloths on the uppers at sea, there are four berths in the most comfortable area of the boat. Since there will normally be only two sleeping at a time while at sea, their weight can be placed on the windward side, if desired.

Two opening ports to the cockpit allow both ventilation and communication. With the drop leaf table this also should be a comfortable dining and entertainment area in port.

Located under the forward end of the table is the diesel engine. Having it placed over the keel and near the center of pitch reduces excessive pitching motion. It is also easier on the engine to be in an area of reduced motion.

In the forward cabin is the head with toilet and pull-out wash basin, wardrobe and V-berths. Raising the seat between the berths forms a double berth for harbor use. Opening the door to the head separates this area from the forepeak.

The rig shown is for a fairly conventional, simple and efficient sloop. Mainsail area is proportionally larger than normally found on today's racing boats. A recessed locker in the foredeck, with the forestay led into it, allows a jib to be stored there temporarily. Two spinnaker poles lie in recessed troughs. A seven-foot dinghy can be stowed here.

Placing the helmsman at the forward end of the cockpit gives him good weather protection and access to the halyards and boom vang, which are led aft from the mast. Ample stowage is found under the cockpit seats and in the lazarette. A grabrail runs from the cockpit around the mast.

Light displacement and a long waterline length result in a very low displacement/length ratio of 182. Even if the rudder length is subtracted from the waterline length, the ratio is still a low 212. The sail area/displacement ratio of 16.8 is slightly less than that found on many racers but should still provide lively performance even in light wind. Indeed, lively performance, smart appearance and a unique interior arrangement characterize the R9-30.

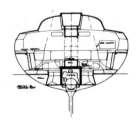

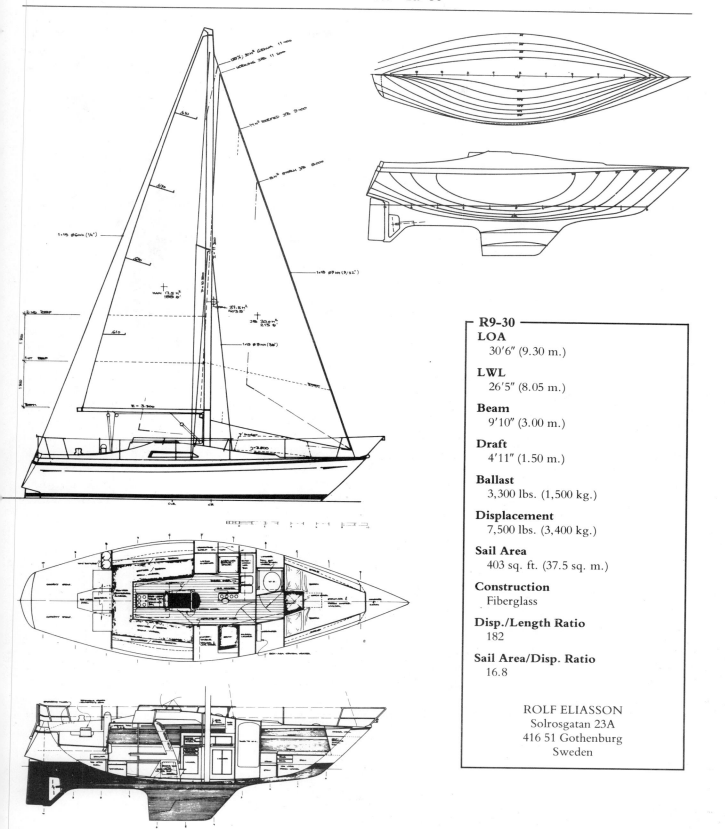

R9-30

LOA
30′6″ (9.30 m.)

LWL
26′5″ (8.05 m.)

Beam
9′10″ (3.00 m.)

Draft
4′11″ (1.50 m.)

Ballast
3,300 lbs. (1,500 kg.)

Displacement
7,500 lbs. (3,400 kg.)

Sail Area
403 sq. ft. (37.5 sq. m.)

Construction
Fiberglass

Disp./Length Ratio
182

Sail Area/Disp. Ratio
16.8

ROLF ELIASSON
Solrosgatan 23A
416 51 Gothenburg
Sweden

WYLIE 31

Stock plans offer an attractive alternative to the sailor who is not able to find a production boat that satisfies all his requirements. A stock design with some personal modifications can provide him with a custom yacht perfectly suited to his needs at a fraction of the cost of a true custom design. Additional advantages are that he can see a completed boat before finalizing the details of his own boat, and he is assured of a proven design.

This 31-foot cruising cutter was designed for one or two persons to live aboard or for four persons to comfortably cruise short distances. She could conceivably fit more people for a daysail. The hull exhibits a long waterline and low wetted surface. Strength and ease of construction are provided by the skeg-mounted, transom-hung rudder.

Thomas Wylie specifies ½-inch fir strip planking for the inside layer of the hull. This gives great longitudinal strength and results in a beautiful, natural interior finish. This is followed by three layers of ⅛-inch molded fir and mahogany on the outside.

A sort of double bottom of solid wood in the middle half of the hull distributes the loads from the mast and keel. The exterior is covered with fiberglass. This frameless construction method increases interior space and permits personal alterations to the interior arrangement.

A unique accommodation plan is made possible by placing the diesel engine under the sink and companionway steps. The space under the cockpit is occupied by a huge double berth to port and a large locker to starboard.

Working at the galley may be a little difficult with the companionway coming through the middle of it and with the stove situated to port. A wet seat and wet locker next to the stove is a useful feature at sea. Forward of the mast is a roomy head, laundry bin and hanging locker, and a double berth in the forepeak.

For someone interested in a small, high-performance cruising boat, the Wylie 31 deserves consideration. She could either be home-built by someone with good woodworking skills or contracted to a boatbuilder of his choice. In either case she should be a relatively simple boat to build and a fun boat to sail. Seven boats have been built, including one cruising the South Pacific.

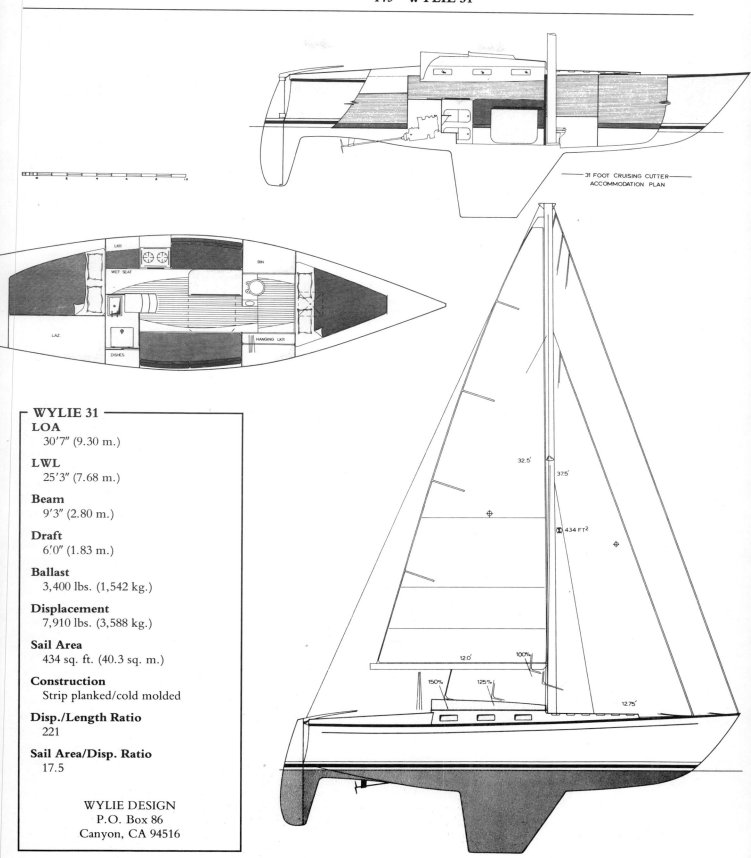

31 FOOT CRUISING CUTTER
ACCOMMODATION PLAN

LKR
WET SEAT
BIN
LAZ.
DISHES
HANGING LKR

WYLIE 31

LOA
30'7" (9.30 m.)

LWL
25'3" (7.68 m.)

Beam
9'3" (2.80 m.)

Draft
6'0" (1.83 m.)

Ballast
3,400 lbs. (1,542 kg.)

Displacement
7,910 lbs. (3,588 kg.)

Sail Area
434 sq. ft. (40.3 sq. m.)

Construction
Strip planked/cold molded

Disp./Length Ratio
221

Sail Area/Disp. Ratio
17.5

WYLIE DESIGN
P.O. Box 86
Canyon, CA 94516

32.5'

37.5'

434 FT²

12.0'

100%

150%

125%

12.75'

SARAH

Sarah was originally designed for sailing on the Great Lakes, with their prevalent light winds. So, it is markedly different from other Chuck Paine designs, intended for ocean sailing. In comparison to his Annie (page 134), Sarah is more than two feet longer overall and a foot wider, yet is 50 pounds lighter and has 10% more sail area. Her displacement/length ratio is almost 20% lower and her sail area/displacement ratio is 10% greater.

Sarah's double-ended hull form has its maximum beam well aft of amidships to keep waterlines forward quite fine and to enhance performance in the higher speed range.

Buttock lines aft are surprisingly straight below the waterline for a double-ender. The cutaway full keel and inboard rudder indicate lively but predictable performance. An aperture provides good protection for the propeller.

Above the waterline, Sarah is extremely handsome, with just the right combination of sheerline and trunk cabin. In boats of this size and smaller, achieving standing headroom and a graceful sheer line and cabin is not easy.

Side decks are quite wide, and a 5-inch bulwark all around should make deck work easy and secure. The cockpit is large enough to seat

four people without consuming all available space. The mainsheet traveller on the cabin top also serves to keep the cockpit uncluttered.

The cutter rig is quite tall, with a mainsail luff/foot ratio of just over 3. It should prove to be fast and weatherly, yet still manageable.

Simplicity and practicality characterize the interior arrangement. A large, single quarterberth is found to starboard, with its head serving as the navigator's seat. While not ideal, this is a reasonable compromise in a boat of this size.

Two settees and a pilot berth are found in the main cabin. In order to fit a head of reasonable size, Paine made the starboard settee quite short, suitable for sitting or for use as a child's berth. A drop-leaf table separates the settees.

Standing headroom is carried all the way into the forward cabin, greatly increasing its habitability. An overhead hatch also is a valuable feature.

Although Sarah was primarily aimed for light air sailing, the scantlings call for rugged construction. Her specifications could classify her as a performance cruiser. Loomis Yachts, of South Dartmouth, Massachusetts, has molds for the hull and has sold two finished boats and four kits for home completion. Plans also are available for amateur construction.

SARAH

LOA
31'4½" (9.56 m.)

LWL
25'10" (7.87 m.)

Beam
10'3½" (3.13 m.)

Draft
4'9" (1.45 m.)

Displacement
10,750 lbs. (4,876 kg.)

Ballast
4,800 lbs. (2,177 kg.)

Sail Area
500 sq. ft. (46.5 sq. m.)

Construction
Fiberglass

Disp./Length Ratio
278

Sail Area/Disp. Ratio
16.4

C. W. PAINE YACHT DESIGNS
P.O. Box 763
Camden, ME 04843

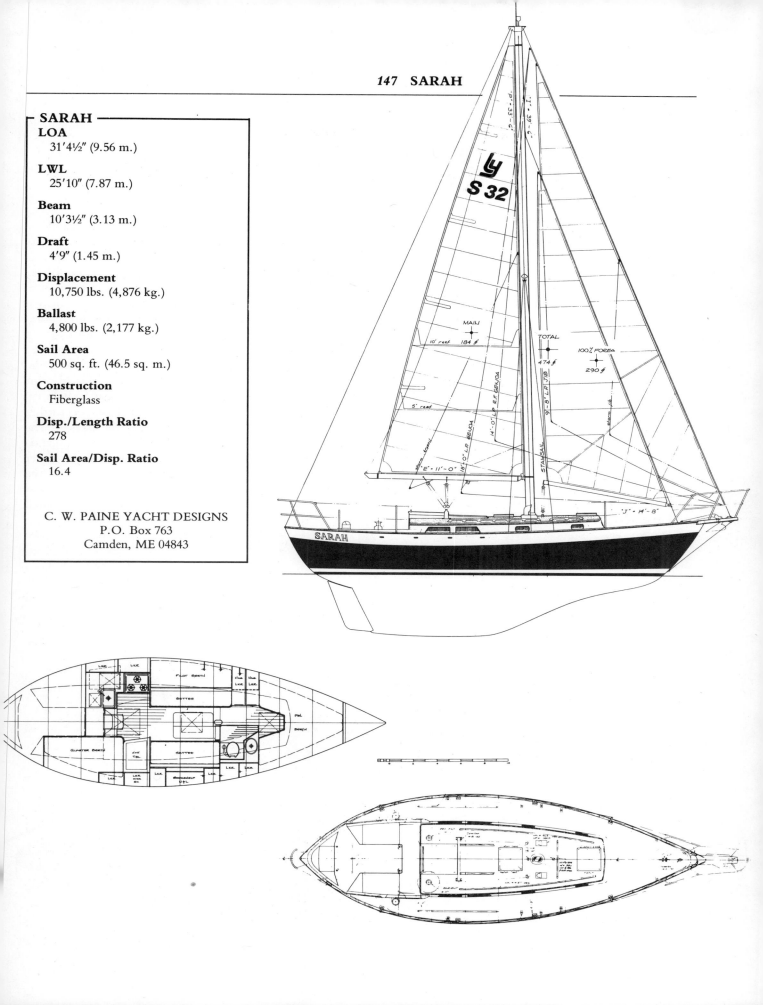

VANCOUVER 32

In response to a large number of sailors who admired the Vancouver 27 and 36, but who wanted a vessel of an intermediate size, Robert B. Harris designed the Vancouver 32. Since the designer was very pleased with the performance and appearance of the 27 and 36, the 32 departs very little from her larger and smaller sisters.

Her underbody, nearly identical to that of the 27, could either be called a full keel with cutaway forefoot and afterbody, or a long fin keel faired into the hull with a strut running to the skeg. Whatever you call it, it should give the performance of a fin-and-skeg and the strength and propeller protection of a full keel.

A Volvo diesel Sailboat Drive is shown. This fits neatly under the cockpit and is well suited to amateur installation.

The outboard rudder eases construction and service, and makes the installation of the self-steering gear more straightforward.

As with the other Vancouvers, the sail plan is moderate in area but very efficient in design. The staysail fills a quite large percentage of the foretriangle and the gap between it and the jib is a bit smaller than is often seen. This requires more careful sheeting of the headsails to achieve a proper slot, and offers a few advantages. When the wind pipes up, the jib can be furled completely without losing too much sail area forward. Area can be further reduced by reefing the staysail. The small gap makes tacking a genoa somewhat difficult, but the inner forestay can be disconnected at the tack and brought back to the mast or removed completely. A boomed staysail also is possible.

Unlike the 27 and 36, which have running backstays to take the load off the inner forestay, the 32 has a jumper strut arrangement. This makes quick maneuvering and shorthanded sailing easier.

The standard arrangement features a chart table and oilskin locker

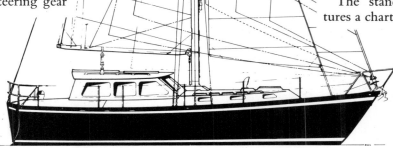

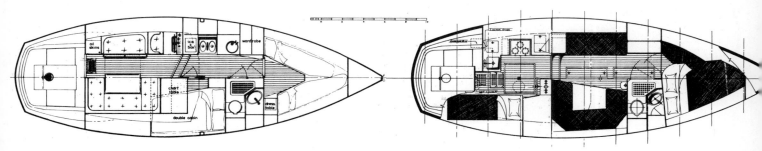

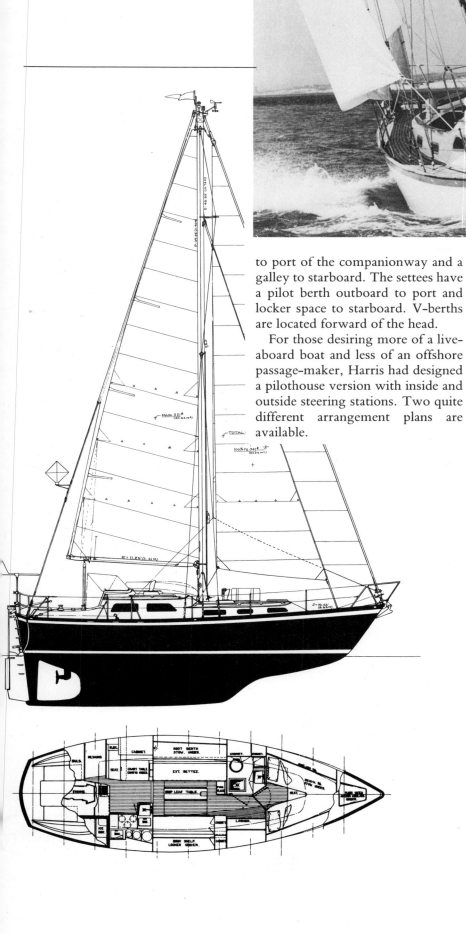

to port of the companionway and a galley to starboard. The settees have a pilot berth outboard to port and locker space to starboard. V-berths are located forward of the head.

For those desiring more of a live-aboard boat and less of an offshore passage-maker, Harris had designed a pilothouse version with inside and outside steering stations. Two quite different arrangement plans are available.

The design calls for construction in foam sandwich fiberglass, although balsa-cored fiberglass and the W.E.S.T. cold-molded systems also are possible.

Together with the 27 and 36, the Vancouver 32 completes a family of sound, seaworthy, blue-water cruising boats that can meet most sailors' needs.

VANCOUVER 32

LOA
  32′0″ (9.75 m.)

LWL
  27′6″ (8.38 m.)

Beam
  11′8″ (3.55 m.)

Draft
  4′6″ (1.37 m.)

Ballast
  6,500 lbs. (2,948 kg.)

Displacement
  14,513 lbs. (6,583 kg.)

Sail Area
  579 sq. ft. (53.8 sq. m.)

Construction
  Cored fiberglass

Disp./Length Ratio
  312

Sail Area/Disp. Ratio
  15.6

ROBERT B. HARRIS, LTD.
212-1670 Duranleau St.
Granville Island
Vancouver, B.C.
Canada V6G 2W6

CW 9.75

Cruising World's 1979 Design Competition challenged designers to come up with a sailboat capable of carrying comfortably two couples or a family of four on coastal cruises and possibly an occasional offshore passage. Stowage and tankage space, plus the ability to carry a dinghy on deck, were also important. From the many fine designs submitted, we selected the 32-foot CW 9.75.

Dudley A. Dix of Cape Town, South Africa, designed the CW 9.75 specifically for construction by an amateur using everyday tools. The result is an untraditional, very interesting-looking vessel with many innovative features.

The triple-chined hull has a fine entry and wide beam, which is carried well aft to a broad transom. Powerful after sections with a flat run indicate good performance off the wind. Wide beam and a 35 percent ballast ratio contribute to high stability.

With the rather small fin keel, directional stability could be a problem. For this reason Dix included a long, shallow skeg extending from the keel to the transom-hung rudder, which is large and partially balanced.

Displacement is moderate and is indicative of a boat that can carry a good payload. In fact, her ability to carry 195 gallons of water and 130 gallons of fuel may be a bit excessive as the tankage load alone would weigh more than 2,000 pounds. The displacement figure given is with tanks half full, which would be more than enough for most cruising situations.

Freeboard is not excessive and the six-foot, six-inch headroom was achieved with a high trunk cabin. Large portlights, plus ports in the side of the hull and two deck hatches, provide good visibility below.

Deck and cabin construction is simplified by employing straight cabin sides that merge into the cockpit coaming. This wide coaming boasts a vast amount of storage space accessible from the cockpit for winch handles, sheets, spare blocks, docklines, etc.

Cockpit seats consist of strips of teak laid over contoured frames, making them comfortable, dry and easy to make. There is a large cockpit locker to starboard and two smaller ones (one for a gas bottle) aft. A six-foot, six-inch dinghy fits on the cabin top.

The seven-eighths rig is not large, but very efficient. Since the forestay extends nearly to the masthead, neither running backstays nor a jumper strut is necessary. Swept spreaders and single lower shrouds are shown; some may prefer adding forward lowers, which would strengthen the mast but reduce mast flexibility and thus tuning options.

Wide beam and a clever arrangement result in a roomy interior. The double quarter berth, with lockers and stowage bins, has a lee cloth fitted along its centerline to make two secure sea berths, although climbing in and out of the outboard berth will be difficult.

To starboard of the companion-

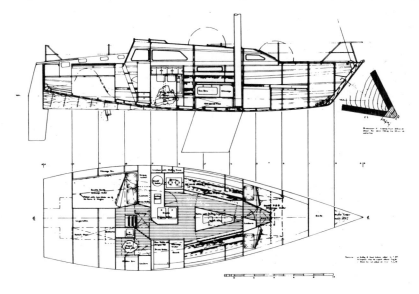

way is the navigation area and head with oilskin bin. Opposite is the galley, which is U-shaped in a fore-and-aft direction for ease of use on either tack without having to tie in the cook. The engine is located under the sinks and should be easily accessible. For noise deadening, the engine box is lined with two-inch fiberglass blanket insulation and ¼-inch perforated board. The round hole in the counter top allows access to the lockers below and holds a bowl that acts as the cover.

A table with folding leaves separates the settees. It contains the 130-gallon fuel tank in its base, with the icebox and a storage bin above, accessible from the top. With the water tanks under the settees, all tanks are amidships, where they will help reduce pitching and trim variation.

Further forward are V-berths and a sail bin. Passage forward and aft in the boat is hindered by the engine box and table, so dragging sails all the way forward would not be easy. Frequently-used sails could be kept in the large cockpit locker.

Construction is of marine plywood (12mm. or ½-inch) for the hull and deck and two layers of 6mm. (¼-inch) laminated for the cabin. Either butt or scarf joins can be used to join the length of plywood, and all plywood is coated inside and out with epoxy resin. Framing, chines, stringers and other structure are of Philippine mahogany.

The keel is fabricated of Corten steel, with 4mm. (5/32-inch) sides, 10mm. (⅜-inch) bottom and a 1½-inch-diameter steel tube as a leading edge. The lead is poured into the keel and the assembly is then bolted to the hull.

The CW 9.75 was Dix's first complete keelboat design. He has gone on to design a number of fine cruising boats, including the 34-foot steel Salty Dog II.

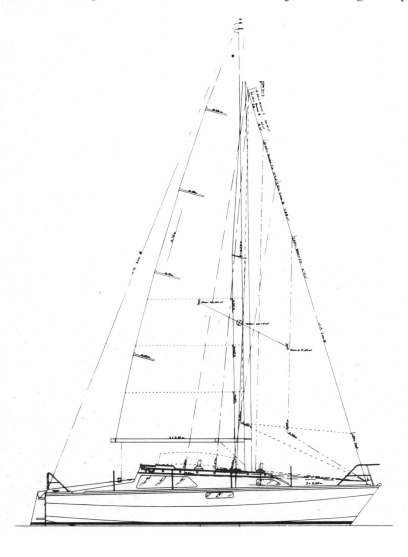

CW 9.75	
LOA	32'0" (9.75 m.)
LWL	26'3" (8.00 m.)
Beam	10'10" (3.30 m.)
Draft	5'7" (1.70 m.)
Ballast	3,241 lbs. (1,470 kg.)
Displacement	9,259 lbs. (4,200 kg.)
Sail Area	461 sq. ft. (42.8 sq. m.)
Construction	Triple-chined plywood
Disp./Length Ratio	229
Sail Area/Disp. Ratio	16.2

DUDLEY A. DIX
P.O. Box 285
Tokai 7966
South Africa

32' SAILING DORY

Jay R. Benford designed this 32-foot sailing dory for simple construction in plywood by the amateur builder or the professional boatyard wishing to set up for plywood production. It is one of a family of cruising dories, ranging from 30 to 38 feet, which Benford feels provide maximum fun, comfort and ease of construction at minimum cost.

The dory hull is characterized by its flat bottom and well flared sides. Rowing dories have reputations for being quite tender, but this design shows a much wider bottom and fuller afterbody than is found on traditional rowing dories. This, combined with a 40 percent ballast/displacement ratio, assures good stability and sail-carrying ability.

Some may look with disfavor at the flat bottom, thinking that it will have a tendency to pound. As soon as she heels, however, she presents a V-shape to the water. The chine is well immersed at the bow, reducing the possibility of pounding when at anchor or on mooring.

Simplicity of construction is emphasized. Interior bulkheads and floors in way of the keel are the only transverse frames. Although plywood is specified, Benford states that he can alter the plans slightly to make possible construction in steel, aluminum or fiberglass (foam core or C-Flex).

Both rudder and keel are airfoil sections; the keel is of lead, and bolts onto the hull. Shallow-draft and keel/centerboard arrangements are possible. Steering control should be good due to the large, wide rudder.

The rig shown is for a ketch with a gaff main. Benford likes the ketch rig for its ease of balance at the helm and the gaff main for its low center of effort. Other possible rigs are sloop, cutter or schooner (either staysail or with gaff foresail and Marconi main).

Her sail area/displacement ratio of 22.1 is very high. This should help to compensate for the relative inefficiency of the rig when hard on the wind, and make her a real speedster as soon as the sheets are cracked. The flat bottom and high prismatic coefficient promise high-speed potential. This also is indicated by the low displacement/length ratio.

Headroom below is six feet, one inch. The forecabin is occupied by a single berth and shelves. Just aft are settee berths port and starboard separated by a drop-leaf table. The galley contains an icebox, sink and wood or oil stove, well suited to cold climates. Other stoves could be used in warmer areas.

Under the cockpit is a 10-hp. Volvo diesel and 25-gallon tanks for fuel and water. The remainder of the space is used for stowage.

Some sailors may not fall in love with the dory hull form, but this 32-footer is a vessel that an amateur can build with much less time and money than would be required for other craft her size. And many can certainly appreciate her clean, purposeful appearance.

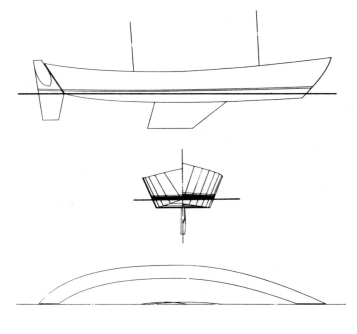

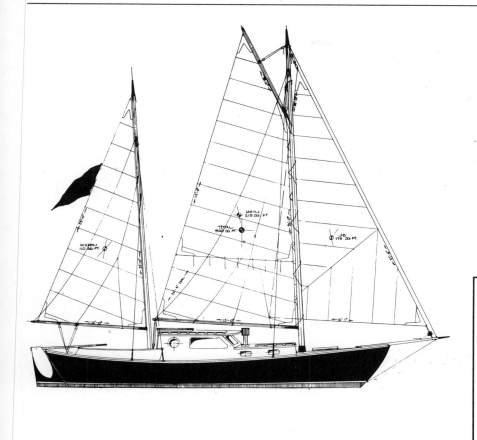

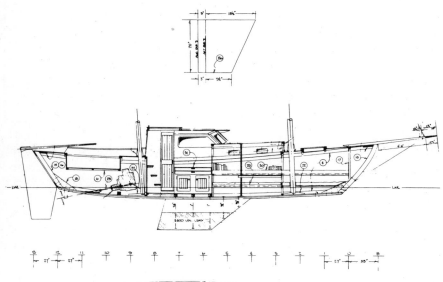

32' SAILING DORY

LOA
32'0" (9.75 m.)

LWL
27'0" (8.23 m.)

Beam
9'0" (2.74 m.)

Draft
4'0" (1.22 m.)

Ballast
2,760 lbs. (1,252 kg.)

Displacement
6,900 lbs. (3,125 kg.)

Sail Area
500 sq. ft. (46.5 sq. m.)

Construction
see text

Disp./Length Ratio
156

Sail Area/Disp. Ratio
22.1

JAY R. BENFORD
758 Trenton Ave.
Severna Park, MD 21146

SAIL-HO

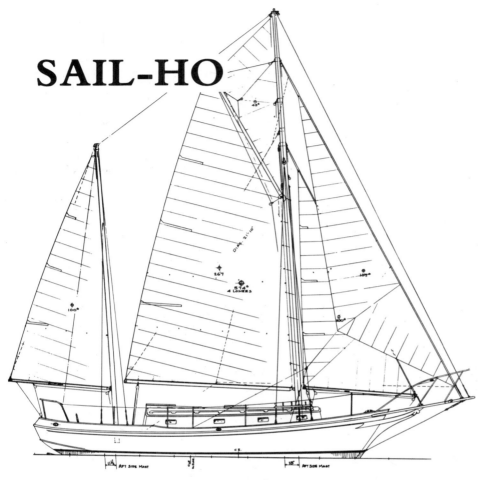

SAIL-HO

LOA
32'2" (9.80 m.)

LWL
26'8" (8.13 m.)

Beam
9'8" (2.95 m.)

Draft
4'0" (1.22 m.)

Ballast
4,500 lbs. (2,041 kg.)

Displacement
12,200 lbs. (5,534 kg.)

Sail Area
565 sq. ft. (52.49 sq. m.)

Construction
Chined aluminum

Disp./Length Ratio
286

Sail Area/Disp. Ratio
17.1

CHARLES W. WITTHOLZ
100 Williamsburg Dr.
Silver Spring, MD 20901

Unlike most welded aluminum boat construction, which requires bending and compound curvature in the plating (and thus is not suitable for amateur construction), this ketch from Charles W. Wittholz was designed with the amateur boatbuilder in mind. It is constructed from flat plate, and has a chine running from stem to stern.

With her low freeboard, springy sheer and clipper bow, Sail-Ho is reminiscent of Chesapeake Bay types, yet she is a thoroughly modern boat. A long shallow keel provides windward ability and access to shoal areas without resorting to a centerboard. The moderate beam is carried well into the ends, resulting in a rather bluff bow, but also yields large foredeck and cockpit areas. It

is also possible to increase the interior accommodations by placing the forward V-berths far up in the bow.

The hull form features a V-bottom with bow sections made rather sharp to avoid pounding, which can be a problem with a chined hull due to the flat sections. Bottom and sides are "developed" surfaces; this means that they have a curvature only in one direction at any point, and can thus be formed from flat plates. It is, therefore, possible to construct Sail-Ho from steel or plywood in addition to aluminum. These materials would, however, require some weight adjustments.

Construction procedures call for nine station frames with flat-bar longitudinals bent around them. The unusual, rounded counter stern

and clipper bow both are cut from stock plates and bars. Ballast consists of pig iron cemented inside a hollow box keel of aluminum plate.

Displacement is moderate, with a displacement/length ratio of 286. This includes the weight of equipment necessary for cruising, so will probably not be exceeded. The sleek hull without any appendages should prove to be very easily driven.

The gaff ketch rig, with a sail area/displacement ratio of 17.1, will move the boat handsomely—and it will really shine when the sheets are eased, especially when the mizzen

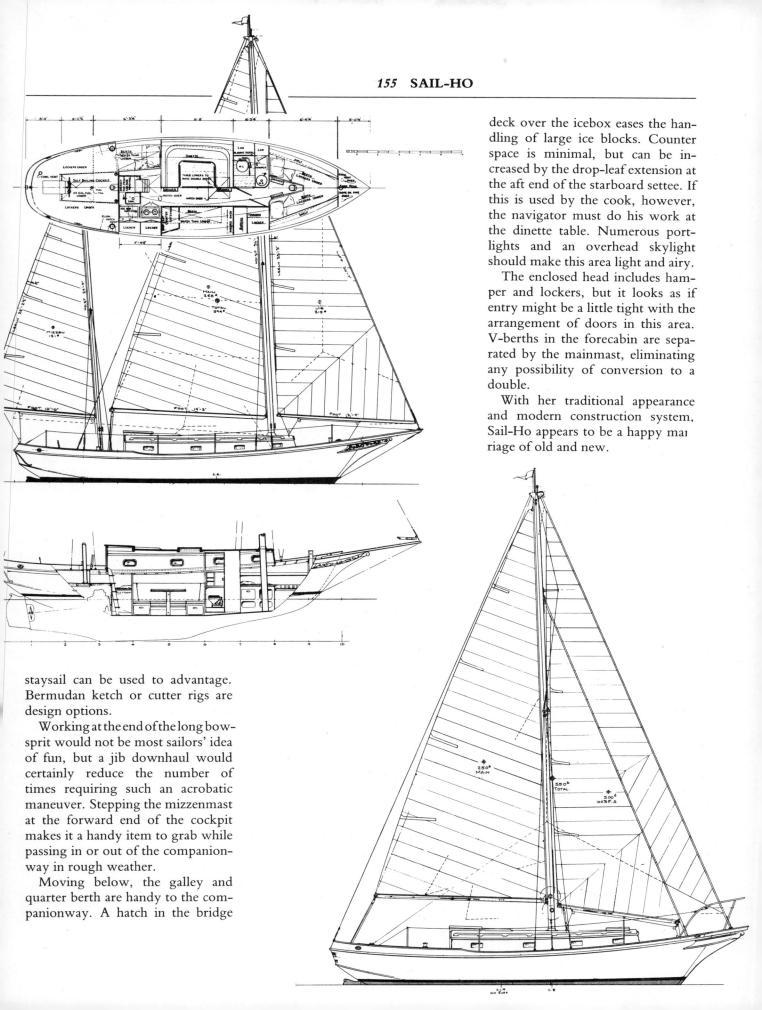

deck over the icebox eases the handling of large ice blocks. Counter space is minimal, but can be increased by the drop-leaf extension at the aft end of the starboard settee. If this is used by the cook, however, the navigator must do his work at the dinette table. Numerous portlights and an overhead skylight should make this area light and airy.

The enclosed head includes hamper and lockers, but it looks as if entry might be a little tight with the arrangement of doors in this area. V-berths in the forecabin are separated by the mainmast, eliminating any possibility of conversion to a double.

With her traditional appearance and modern construction system, Sail-Ho appears to be a happy marriage of old and new.

staysail can be used to advantage. Bermudan ketch or cutter rigs are design options.

Working at the end of the long bowsprit would not be most sailors' idea of fun, but a jib downhaul would certainly reduce the number of times requiring such an acrobatic maneuver. Stepping the mizzenmast at the forward end of the cockpit makes it a handy item to grab while passing in or out of the companionway in rough weather.

Moving below, the galley and quarter berth are handy to the companionway. A hatch in the bridge

32-FOOT ALUMINUM CUTTER

Ted Brewer, who has a great deal of experience designing steel and aluminum yachts with both chined and rounded hull forms, drew this 32-footer for a Washington builder who wanted a medium-displacement cutter of traditional appearance suited to coastal or offshore cruising.

The hull shape is based upon his successful Goderich 35 design. The rounded hull form, Brewer states, reduces resistance and eases motion in a seaway, in addition to creating a more attractive appearance.

For racing boats, aluminum is a popular building material because hulls can be constructed that are strong yet light in displacement. In a medium-displacement cruising boat like this one, the weight savings can be used to increase ballast and load-carrying ability.

Brewer designed the boat to be able to carry the large weight of stores and equipment necessary for long passages and says that if she is not used for such purposes, 750 to 1,000 pounds of additional ballast

could be added. This would increase the ballast/displacement ratio to about 45 percent.

Another advantage of aluminum construction to a client interested in a commercial production boat is that it allows a high degree of alteration. Because there are no molds used as there are with fiberglass boats, it is possible to change the fin and skeg underbody to the full-keel type with cutaway aft, which Brewer favors for off-shore sailing. A pilothouse version also could be built.

The interior shown is only one possible arrangement. With aluminum much flexibility is possible in this area. In this very practical layout, the quarter and pilot berths make two excellent sea berths. The galley looks compact and handy. A special life raft locker is found beneath the cockpit sole. Tankage of 100 gallons of water and 35 gallons of fuel is possible.

Sail area is moderate in the tall cutter rig, with single spreaders and fixed intermediate backstays. The

short bowsprit slightly increases sail area without the inconvenience or danger of a long sprit. It also makes anchor-handling easier. A 150-percent drifter of 470 square feet can be set for light airs. Either a keel-stepped or tabernacle-mounted mast is possible. In the latter case, a slightly heavier mast section must be used.

The builder, Peter J. Morrow, P.O. Box 380, Freeland, WA 98249, is prepared to offer this boat at any stage of completion, and the designer is willing to assist an owner who desires custom alterations.

This is a handsome, seaworthy vessel combining traditional appearance with modern materials. It would make a fine liveaboard and long-distance cruiser. The home builder could purchase the hull and deck and finish the interior and rigging himself at a substantial savings over buying a finished boat. The result, if done properly, would also be a very sound investment.

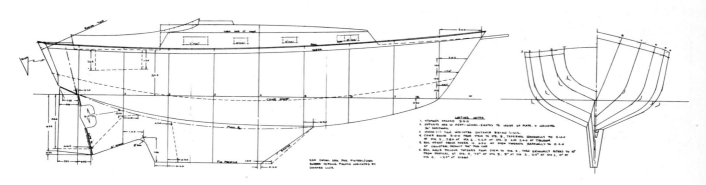

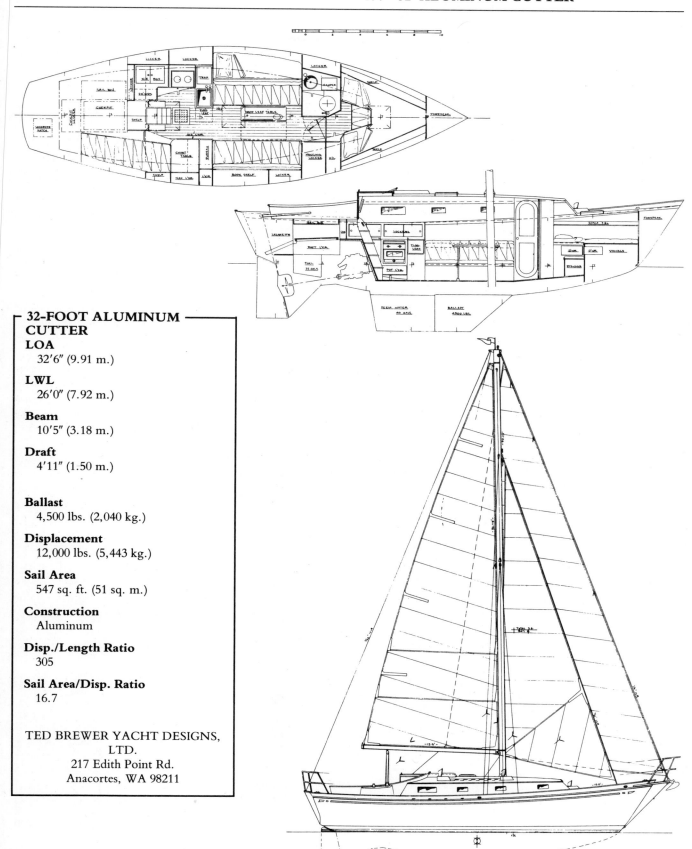

32-FOOT ALUMINUM CUTTER

LOA
32'6" (9.91 m.)

LWL
26'0" (7.92 m.)

Beam
10'5" (3.18 m.)

Draft
4'11" (1.50 m.)

Ballast
4,500 lbs. (2,040 kg.)

Displacement
12,000 lbs. (5,443 kg.)

Sail Area
547 sq. ft. (51 sq. m.)

Construction
Aluminum

Disp./Length Ratio
305

Sail Area/Disp. Ratio
16.7

TED BREWER YACHT DESIGNS,
LTD.
217 Edith Point Rd.
Anacortes, WA 98211

SUNRISE

While this boat was under construction by Tripple and Everett Marine, of Seattle, Washington, a change in the client's plans forced him to offer her for sale. Designer Jay Benford says, "It was not long after being told this (say about 15 seconds) that the lust for the boat began the wheels turning to scheme to get together enough funding to possess her. Determination must count for something for this did come to pass." That was in 1972, and *Sunrise* has served as Benford's home afloat ever since. When Benford recently moved from Washington to Maryland, *Sunrise* was trucked cross-country to follow him.

One of the most unusual features of this design is her pinky stern, in which the bulwarks are carried aft of the stern-hung rudder, resulting in additional deck space not found on a conventional double-ender. The pinky stern was originally developed on fishing craft, where the added space was useful for handling nets while also protecting the rudder. "From an esthetic point of view," Benford said, "a pinky stern also helps sweep the eye along the sheer and aids in the graceful overall effect of this line."

Sunrise was originally designed with a gaff ketch rig with square sail, and Benford sailed with this rig for about five years. He found the sail area too small for coastal cruising and the traditional square sail too difficult to set and douse at sea. He experimented with other arrangements and finally arrived at what he calls the "Great Pyramid Rig."

The gaff main and mizzen sails have been replaced by two staysails, one with its luff going from the foot of the mainmast to the head of the mizzen, and the other with its luff along the main mast and sheeted to the top of the mizzen. The greatest innovation, however, is in replacing the square sail with four triangular roller-furling sails, all set flying from the deck. Weight and windage have been reduced, and the old

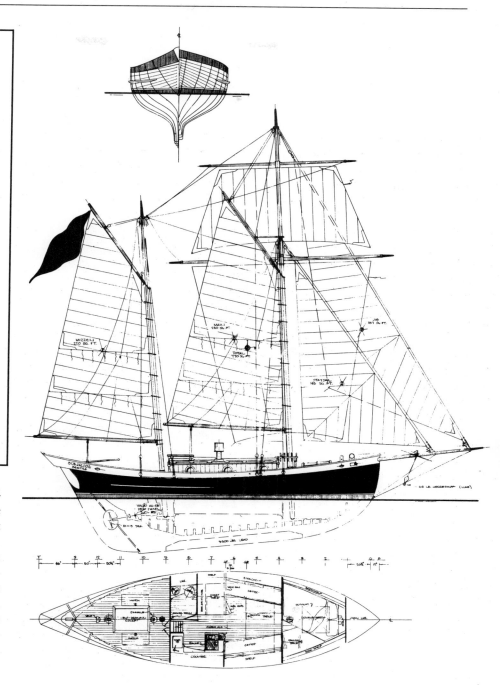

SUNRISE

LOA
34'0" (10.36m.)

LWL
30'8" (9.35m.)

Beam
11'3" (3.43m.)

Draft
6'3" (1.91m.)

Ballast
12,500 lbs. (5,670 kg.)

Displacement
31,240 lbs. (14,170 kg.)

Sail Area
770 sq.ft. (71.5 sq.m.)

Construction
planked wood

Disp./Length Ratio
484

Sail Area/Disp. Ratio
12.4

JAY R. BENFORD
758 Trenton Ave.
Severna Park, MD 21146

squaresail's 468 square feet was increased to 1,000 square feet. Yet the largest sail is still only 10 square feet larger than the original square sail.

Benford is very pleased with both the efficiency and the ease of operation of his Great Pyramid Rig. He said it can be adapted for use on other boats, if they can tolerate the weight aloft and if their spreaders can be raked aft to allow the yard to revolve at least 30° each way.

Belowdecks the boat has a large engine compartment under the cockpit. A shower/head is located to port of the companionway ladder, with the galley opposite. A wood cooking stove is fitted back-to-back with a heating stove in the saloon.

The chart table to port is designed to store and use full size, unfolded charts, and can hold more than 100 of them. This is unique on a boat only 34 feet in length.

The saloon is spacious and open for living and entertainment. The hinged table is non-intrusive. Forward, a roomy double berth under a large skylight provides comfort and a place to admire the Great Pyramid Rig overhead.

Few designers are more adept at imbuing their creations with such a charming touch as Benford. The sailor looking for salty, traditional looks and quality scantlings, plus a sumptuous live-aboard interior, will find *Sunrise* a difficult design to beat.

TIFFANY JANE

Tiffany Jayne, Paul Kotzebue's entry in *Cruising World*'s 1979 Design Competition, is an excellent example of elegant simplicity in a cruising yacht. While some sailors will find her accommodations a bit spartan for true comfort, few can deny her grace and beauty. Her performance, furthermore, should be as brilliant as her appearance.

Kotzebue is a graduate of the Yacht Design Institute and the University of California at Berkeley. He designed Tiffany Jane as his "dream yacht", a boat "light and easy to sail, with excellent performance under sail and pleasant, traditional-looking lines." He was inspired by *Istalena,* a racing boat designed by L. Francis Herreshoff, which also had a long canoe stern.

This long, narrow and nearly symmetrical hullform results in a boat that will be well balanced and directionally stable even at large angles of heel. Both the spade rudder and lead fin keel are deep and of high aspect ratio for maximum efficiency. Ease of steering should be one of the boat's strong points.

Accommodations consist of two quarter berths and two settees, all six feet, six inches long, separated by a sink to starboard and a stove and icebox to port. Fold-out tables on each side provide additional counter space for cooking and eating. The head, with privacy curtain, is forward. Headroom is just under five feet in the main cabin and less forward.

This arrangement could not be more simple but appears to offer good comfort, even at sea. Whether you want to sleep to windward for stability, or to leeward or aft for comfort, there always will be two berths from which to choose. In port, the backrest from the starboard settee can be placed between the settees to form a double berth six feet wide.

Lively performance, even in light air, is assured by the very large three-quarter fractional rig. With the small foretriangle, headsails are of convenient size and only a small sail inventory will be required. Swept-back spreaders eliminate the need for running backstays to achieve headstay tension.

Tiffany Jayne was originally designed for cold-molded wood construction and the first hull was built in that technique. C&B Marine of Santa Cruz, CA, made a mold from that hull and has constructed several fiberglass boats.

As originally designed, the boat was powered by a British Seagull outboard motor in a well just aft of the rudder. This arrangement was also altered to an inboard diesel engine at the request of C&B Marine.

Tiffany Jayne certainly provides less accommodation space than most other 34-foot cruising boats, but there are other ways to look at the design. Her light displacement, small sails and engine, and simple arrangement make it possible to build her for much less money than a more conventional 34-footer. Compared to smaller boats of similar displacement and cost, she offers greater speed and performance.

In these days of boats with enormous beams, high freeboard, umpteen berths and three heads, it is a pleasure to see a boat as beautiful and as basic as Tiffany Jane. If Henry Thoreau had been a sailor he would have appreciated this boat.

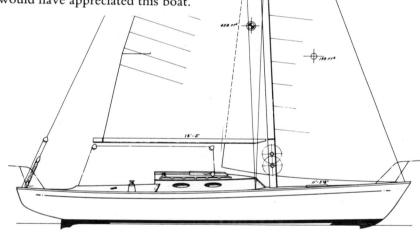

TIFFANY JANE

LOA
34'0" (10.36 m.)

LWL
25'0" (7.62 m.)

Beam
8'0" (2.44 m.)

Draft
5'6" (1.68 m.)

Ballast
3,010 lbs. (1,365 kg.)

Displacement
5,790 lbs. (2,626 kg.)

Sail Area
451 sq. ft. (41.9 sq. m.)

Construction
see text

Disp./Length Ratio
165

Sail Area/Disp. Ratio
22.4

PAUL R. KOTZEBUE
YACHT DESIGN
3364½ Upas Street
San Diego, CA 92104

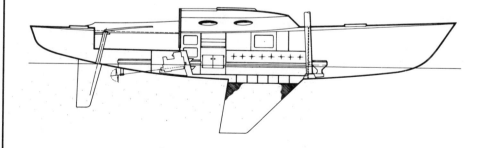

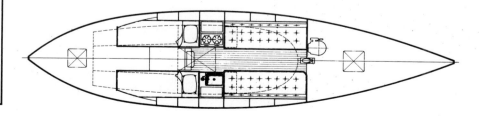

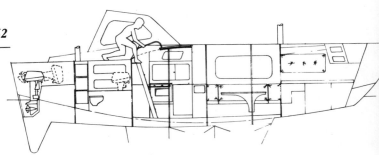

INTEGRITY

In designing a cruising boat for a client, the naval architect must first determine from him the requirements of the design. For what type of cruising is it intended? What levels of performance, comfort and security are expected? What are the client's esthetic preferences? The ultimate success of the design depends to a high degree on both the client's ability to formulate and express his needs and the designer's ability to comprehend them.

When a naval architect designs a boat for himself, however, these problems of communication and understanding are eliminated. He should know his own needs and preferences better than he does those of any client, and the design that results should be a truly unique example of his designing skills.

Integrity is the boat I have designed for myself, a "performance voyaging boat" for living aboard

and sailing shorthanded anyplace in the world. In the six years and 40,000 miles I cruised my 26-foot fiberglass cutter *Frolic,* I gradually became convinced that my next boat, for more extended voyaging to remote areas, should be steel. I saw, heard of and read about numerous instances of steel boats surviving accidents, such as groundings and collisions, that no other type of hull would have survived.

Integrity's double-chined hull form is moderate in beam, with rather fine and balanced ends. These qualities, combined with proper sail balance, will result in a boat that will steer easily even when driven hard. Thus, the helmsperson or self-steering gear will be able to steer

without great effort or frequent sail changes.

One advantage of moderately heavy displacement combined with fine proportions is that useful hull depth is great. This allows the cabin sole to be placed unusually low. Headroom can be achieved without excessive freeboard or deck height.

The keel and skeg arrangement offers an excellent combination of directional stability, steering responsiveness and useful interior volume. As in *Frolic,* the skeg is hollow and wide enough to stand in. Thus, there is standing headroom under the bridge deck and room there for a head, engine and crate stowage. This underbody also spreads displacement into the stern, increasing the prismatic coefficient while maintaining a smooth run. The long fin keel contains not only the ballast (lead set in cement) but also tankage for 90 gallons of water and a deep sump.

Integrity's deck arrangement is one of her most attractive features. I chose a raised flush deck. This is about the smallest boat on which a flush deck can be combined with standing headroom without excessive freeboard. It adds enormously to interior volume, increases stability at extreme angles of heel, provides a large and unobstructed deck

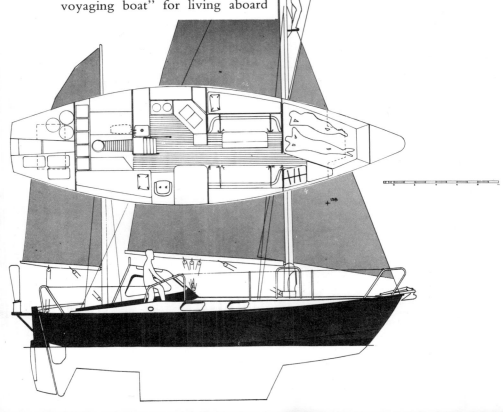

There is full standing headroom under the bridge deck, and seating under the dodger.

for sail handling and dinghy stowage, and makes construction simple and strong.

The permanent dodger is constructed of laminated plywood with large Lexan windows. It covers a bridgedeck area 4½ feet wide and 4 feet long, with 4½ feet of headroom, and rests on high, angled cockpit coamings. Visibility and protection from the weather will be excellent.

Aft of the mizzen mast is a footwell extending to the transom. At its after end is an outboard motor well. This opens through the hull above the waterline. A filler piece closing the well flush with the hull will be fitted when the motor is not in place, but will still allow the well to function as a huge cockpit drain. Cockpit lockers aft are shallow and drain into the footwell. Propane and gasoline tanks, dock lines, fenders and buckets can be carried here.

Integrity's rig is quite unusual and I think will prove to be both efficient and easily handled. More than half of the sail area is found in the very large, fully-battened mainsail. The large roach makes a running backstay necessary, but once a reef is put in the sail the backstay can be set up permanently. As the wind increases, a second and then a third reef can be put in the main. Then the mizzen can be reefed or dropped. Basic working sail will be carried up to 35 or 40 knots of wind before a storm jib or storm trysail is necessary. A mizzen staysail and large drifter or spinnaker would be the only other sails needed.

The fully battened mizzen will be useful both in strong winds—balanced with the jib—and for maneuvering in port. It can be used to keep the boat head-to-wind, under power or sail, for anchoring or for backing out of a tight spot.

Many sailors may find my choice of outboard motor power odd for a boat of this size. Simplicity, ease of repair and reduced drag under sail are my primary reasons. A motor of 15 to 25 hp. will be useful in calm weather and also motorsailing in light winds and small seas. When not in use it can be stowed in the cockpit footwell or down below.

Integrity's interior arrangement is also derived from *Frolic's,* with improvements formulated from my years on *Frolic.* The raised flush deck allows full sitting headroom in the luxurious forward berth and also in the pilot berth. The galley is designed for use at sea, with hip braces for either tack. Opposite the galley is a chart table that can also serve as a desk or eating table for two, with one sitting in the swivel chair and the other on the starboard settee. All interior furniture can be disassembled into components that will fit out through the companionway for refinishing or alterations.

Integrity's hull was constructed at the Gladding-Hearn Shipyard in Somerset, Massachusetts.

INTEGRITY

LOA
34′6″ (10.52m.)

LWL
28′3″ (8.61 m.)

Beam
10′7″ (3.22m.)

Draft
5′6″ (1.68 m.)

Ballast
5,500 lbs. (2,495 kg.)

Displacement
15,800 lbs. (7,167 kg.)

Sail Area
601 sq.ft. (55.8 sq.m.)

Disp./Length Ratio
313

Sail Area/Disp. Ratio
15.2

DANNY GREENE
Colebrook Road
Little Compton, RI 02837

VANCOUVER 36

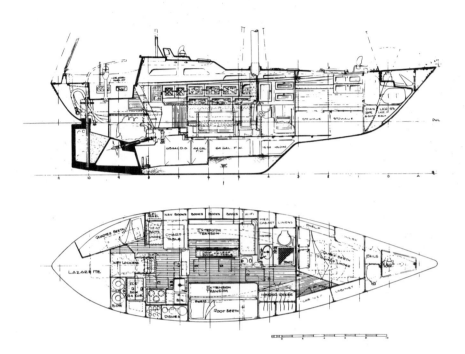

In response to his earlier Vancouver 27, which was designed to accommodate two persons on long ocean passages, Robert Harris found that many people liked the concept but wanted a boat suitable for four persons—or wanted more room for two. His solution was to add seven feet to the accommodation plan to give the needed space and another two feet at each end to eliminate the bowsprit or boomkin. Thus evolved the Vancouver 36.

Construction is of fiberglass with polyvinyl chloride (PVC) foam core. Wood construction also is possible.

Harris prefers the double-ended hull form because it is seakindly when hove-to, presents no large, flat surface when running before the wind, allows a more graceful structure with fewer hard turns and

offers no sharp corners to dock pilings. Displacement is on the heavy side, with a displacement/length ratio of 371. The sail area of 685 square feet is as large as can be accommodated without resorting to high aspect sails, a bowsprit or boomkin. The result is a moderate sail area/displacement ratio of 15.9. So she will not be at her best in very light winds, but the efficient rig should make her perform well as soon as the breeze freshens.

Two persons can live aboard or cruise in relative luxury, while there is room for four in comfort and privacy. In port, two can sleep in the forward cabin and two in the main cabin. Those forward can exit through the forward hatch and use the galley without disturbing those in the main cabin sleeping area, which can be closed off with a cur-

tain. With four persons at sea, the two off-watch crew can sleep either in the main cabin or forward, depending upon weather conditions and point of sail.

The chart table, galley and oilskin locker are all handy to the cockpit. Cooking is with bottled gas stored in a separate, gas-tight compartment vented overboard. An icebox is shown, but mechanical refrigeration can be fitted. Heat is provided by a coal-burning fireplace with louvers for heat dispersion. A low-drain fan could be used to conduct the warmed air into the head and forward cabin. Numerous cowl vents should guarantee good ventilation.

By using a V-drive, Harris was able to place the engine quite far aft under a lead-lined, sound-deadening cover. The stuffing box is still within serviceable reach.

Cutter rigged, the Vancouver 36 is set up for shorthanded sailing. The jib topsail is equipped with roller furling gear and is set on its own freestanding halyard so that it can be removed in favor of a storm sail. With its reef points, the boomed staysail should be able to serve as a storm jib under most conditions. Mainsail reefing can be accomplished completely from the cockpit.

A water catchment system is incorporated in the main boom. In a rain shower, a hose can be connected to a spigot near the gooseneck.

Locating the cockpit far aft puts the helmsman away from the spray as much as possible and handy to the self-steering gear and emergency

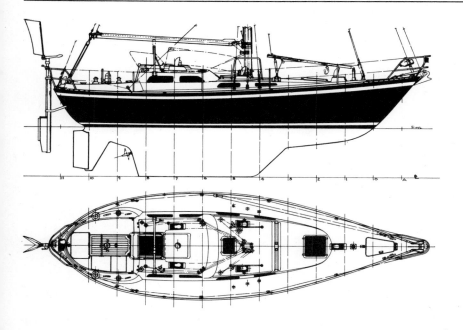

VANCOUVER 36

LOA
36′0″ (10.87 m.)

LWL
27′11″ (8.51 m.)

Beam
11′0″ (3.35 m.)

Draft
5′0″ (1.52 m.)

Ballast
8,000 lbs. (3,628 kg.)

Displacement
18,052 lbs. (8,188 kg.)

Sail Area
685 sq. ft. (63.3 sq. m.)

Construction
foam cored fiberglass

Disp./Length Ratio
371

Sail Area/Disp. Ratio
15.9

ROBERT B. HARRIS, LTD.
212-1670 Duranleau St.
Grandville Island
Vancouver, B.C.
Canada V6H 3S4

tiller. For protection in extreme climates, a hard top over the cockpit is possible.

Dinghy stowage is between the companionway and mast, while the life raft is kept in slings under the lazarette hatch, quickly accessible in an emergency. Small items can be stowed in the lazarette and starboard sea locker, while sails and larger items are kept in the port and bow lockers, accessible from belowdeck.

To maintain a clean foredeck and still allow easy anchor handling, the self-draining foredeck well houses both anchor and a hand windlass. Chain is led under the double berth.

These little items show that the Vancouver 36 is a well-thought-out boat for serious offshore cruising, and yet still is suitable to both live-aboard and coastal cruising.

MORRIS 36

Originally called the Paine 36, this design was submitted to the 1977 *Cruising World* Design Competition with a raised, flush deck arrangement similar to that of Chuck Paine's Frances designs (see page 126). Paine later drew the trunk cabin version for boatbuilder Tom Morris of Southwest Harbor, Maine.

The Morris 36 is an attempt to blend clean, traditional deck and topsides with a more modern, high-performance underbody. A long fin keel and large skeg and rudder promise not only sparkling performance but also ease of handling. What appear at first glance in the above-water view to be a transom stern without a rudder is, in actuality, a counter stern with a faired-in skeg below.

Paine said that at low speed, such as in harbor when maneuverability is desired, this part of the skeg will not be immersed. At higher speeds, when better tracking ability is desired, it will be immersed to achieve its function. It is an interesting concept.

By attaching the lead to the bottom of the hollow keel structure rather than a separate lead fin, it is possible to fit water tanks into the keel, where they contribute to stability.

Bulwarks, at least five inches high, surround the deck. With the wide, clear sidedecks and foredeck, moving on deck should be secure even in rough weather. High (13-inch) backrests in the cockpit promise comfort and protection. With tiller steering the helmsperson sits at the forward end of the cockpit, shielded from spray and wind by the cabin and dodger.

The double spreader rig features shrouds set well inboard, almost to the cabin sides. Close headsail sheeting offers a weatherliness appropriate to the highly efficient underbody.

Two interior arrangements were drawn. This, the traditional arrangement of the two, is most suitable to offshore sailing. Pilot and settee berths on each side, plus a quarter berth, provide comfortable sleeping at sea on either tack. The galley and outboard-facing chart table appear well arranged for use at sea. A sumptuous seat and bureau are included in the forward cabin.

The Morris 36 was originally designed for one-off fiberglass construction with fiberglass-covered plywood decks. Tom Morris now has molds for the solid fiberglass hull and balsa-cored deck.

Paine anticipates that the 36, with the emergence of PHRF and MHS handicapping, will be able to compete in "sensible racing such as the Marion-Bermuda race." It is, he says, his next boat.

MORRIS 36

LOA
36′3″ (11.05 m.)

LWL
29′6″ (9.00 m.)

Beam
11′7″ (3.53 m.)

Draft
5′6″ (1.68 m.)

Ballast
6,500 lbs. (2,948 kg.)

Displacement
15,602 lbs. (7,077 kg.)

Sail Area
627 sq. ft. (58.2 sq. m.)

Construction
Fiberglass

Disp./Length Ratio
271

Sail Area/Disp. Ratio
16.1

C. W. PAINE YACHT DESIGN, INC.
P.O. Box 763
Camden, ME 04843

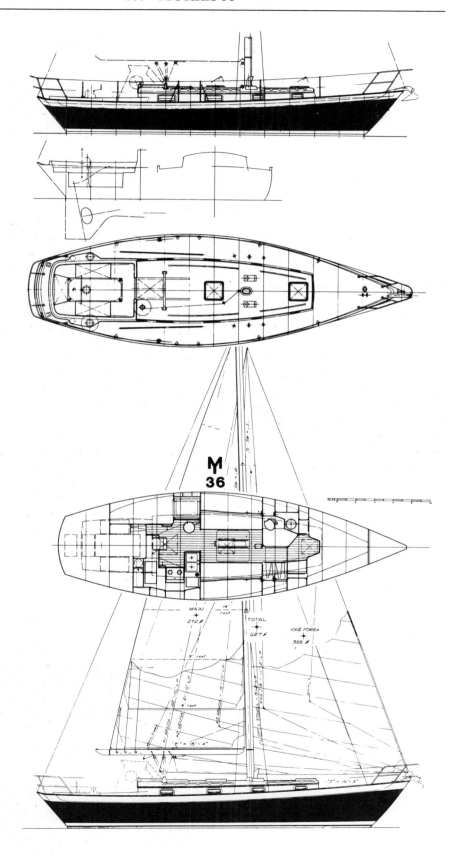

ROBERTS SPRAY 36

Boats designed by Bruce Roberts-Goodson, the Australian boatbuilder and designer who now makes his home in Maryland, have a way of turning up in just about every corner of the globe. He has sold literally thousands of sets of plans for his many designs. In just about every seaport you'll find one of his boats in the process of coming to life in someone's backyard.

Tough times have made home building more attractive these days than ever before. For the handy dreamer who is not afraid to tackle a long and complex project, building a Roberts design is the answer to work-a-day humdrum.

One of the more successful of the Roberts design is the Spray, a 40-footer. Her lines were extrapolated from those of Joshua Slocum's original *Spray,* which circumnavigated the world at the turn of the century. Following the 40-footer, Roberts came out with three sister designs in 27, 33 and 47-foot lengths. Reading Slocum's adventures convinces many sailors of the seaworthiness of the design. With modern materials for hull and rig, Roberts has tried to update and improve this classic.

Now there is a new member of the Roberts family of Sprays—the Roberts Spray 36. Like her sisters, she has matronly lines with a full keel, moderate draft and wide beam. Her clipper bow and transom stern are nearly true to Slocum's original and give her a blue-water look. She has quite low freeboard for a boat of this size and her sheer is springy and attractive. Altogether her hull is reminiscent of the coasting schooners that once plied the New England coast.

She has been drawn with three different deck and layout plans, each to suit a particular purpose. But the cutter rig remains consistent. She spreads a modest 741 square feet of working canvas, which is not excessive on a hull displacing 24,400 pounds.

Versions A and C are center cockpit plans with similar accommodations below. Both have sumptuous after cabins with transverse double berths. Forward of the cockpit is the main saloon, which is divided between the galley and the dining area forward. Note the inside steering station on version C, which replaces the navigator's station seen in A. Both designs have the head and hanging lockers forward of the main saloon.

Version B is quite different on deck and below. The large doghouse is the main saloon and will sleep a couple in the dinette to port. The cockpit and outside steering station are aft. Forward and down four steps is a second sitting area with settees and pilot berths on both sides. In the forward cabin is the master stateroom, with a large double berth tucked in between the vanity and shower.

The Spray 36 can be built in a number of different materials but the designer specifies fiberglass, with a round-chine hull, or steel or aluminum with a double-chine hull.

The designer has sold more than

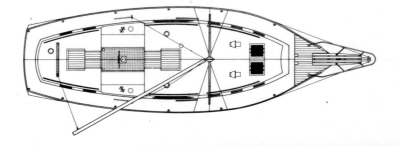

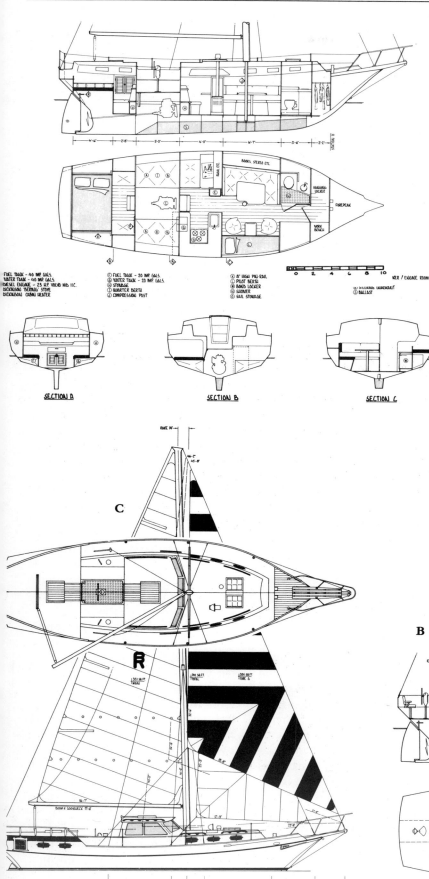

400 sets of plans for the Spray 36, and knows that at least 200 are being built, with 30 already sailing. These are quite impressive numbers. Certainly these boats will be seen in ports all over the world.

ROBERTS SPRAY 36

LOA
36′10″ (11.22 m.)

LWL
30′0″ (9.14 m.)

Beam
12′0″ (3.66 m.)

Draft
4′0″ (1.22 m.)

Ballast
8,400 lbs. (3,810 kg.)

Displacement
24,400 lbs. (11,067 kg.)

Sail Area
741 sq. ft. (68.8 sq. m.)

Construction
Fiberglass or double-chine steel or aluminum

Disp./Length Ratio
403

Sail Area/Disp. Ratio
14.1

BRUCE ROBERTS
35 Belleview Dr.
Severna Park, MD 21146

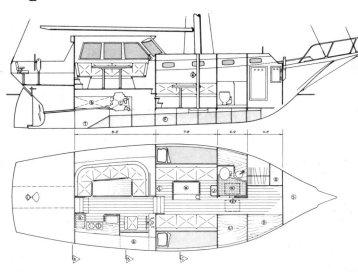

MASON 37

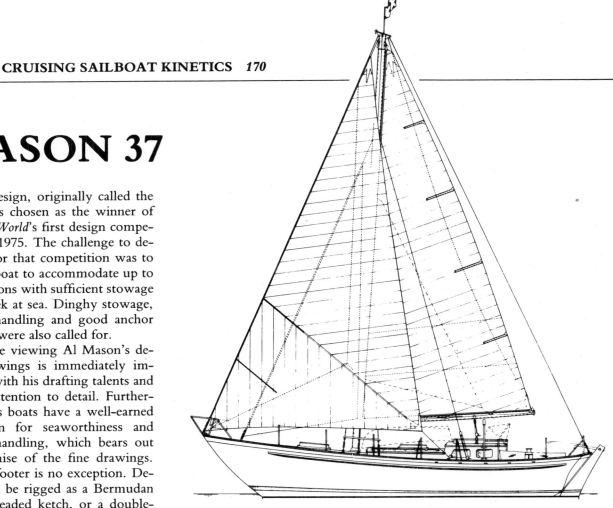

This design, originally called the S-91, was chosen as the winner of *Cruising World*'s first design competition in 1975. The challenge to designers for that competition was to create a boat to accommodate up to four persons with sufficient stowage for a week at sea. Dinghy stowage, ease of handling and good anchor stowage were also called for.

Anyone viewing Al Mason's design drawings is immediately impressed with his drafting talents and careful attention to detail. Furthermore, his boats have a well-earned reputation for seaworthiness and ease of handling, which bears out the promise of the fine drawings. This 37-footer is no exception. Designed to be rigged as a Bermudan or gaff-headed ketch, or a double-headed sloop, it is a vessel that will delight the eye of many a veteran cruising man. Displacement is heavy and the scantlings stout. Specified construction calls for Philippine mahogany carvel or strip planking over white oak frames.

The high bow allows a sweet sheer, and the designer states that the extended overhang eliminates the bowsprit and attendant problems. Moderately long overhangs, bad for an IOR racer, often serve valuable functions on a seagoing vessel, in addition to producing a very attractive hull.

This boat obviously is a no-compromise cruiser, and the moderate draft keel is flat enough to allow the boat to dry out comfortably against a wall in tidal regions for easy (and cheap) cleaning and bottom painting. It is a money-saving habit easily formed by the cruising crew away from home as the miles increase and the dollars take off on a different tack. Note that the outboard and efficiently shaped rudder are well

tucked up to avoid grounding damage. The half-entry angle at the cutwater is approximately 28 degrees, which will mean a buoyant bow. Coupled with the easy waterlines and a center of longitudinal buoyancy located just aft the midship section, these elements should produce a balanced vessel, docile on the helm when running or reaching —an endearing quality on a small cruising boat.

A high prismatic coefficient of .55 means the displacement volume is carried toward the ends, which will increase efficiency under power and in heavy winds. But the very stoutly rigged but modest sail plan means light air performance will suffer a bit. Beam is a portly 12 feet, one inch, but the displacement and relatively slack bilges and garboards should prevent this feature from creating an uncomfortable motion when becalmed. The designer has called for a 37-hp. diesel along with a 65-gallon fuel capacity, so the mechanical topsail was obviously in-

tended to be used occasionally on this boat.

Belowdecks a separate and permanent chart table can probably be partitioned off from the adjacent hatch (and weather) if desired. Oilskins hang out of the way under the ladder, and the engine housing location gives good access and creates a snug area for the cook at sea. Even a ten-ton vessel can become obstreperous when bashing into a chop.

A shorthanded crew may prefer that the starboard pilot berth be omitted, allowing a permanent settee to be located further outboard and increasing usable space in the saloon area. Even by fitting a drop-leaf table, leg room and passage space can become constricted with a two-pilot arrangement. The forward cabin incorporates enough rarely seen cabin sole area of its own to be honestly called a separate stateroom.

A curtain aft of the head door would separate this area quite handily. However, the door opening

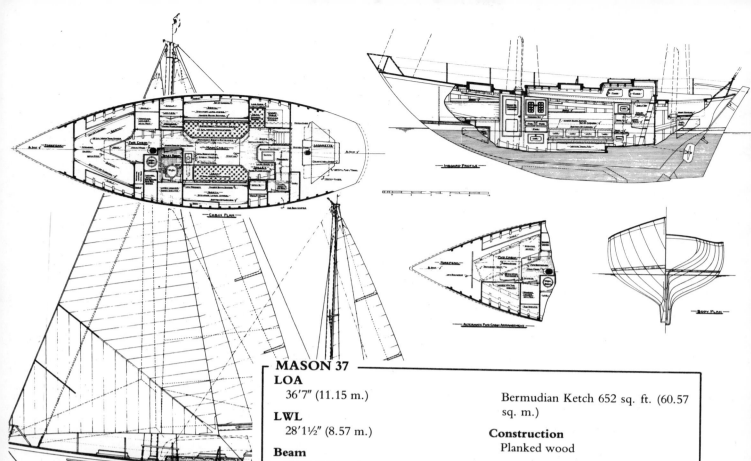

MASON 37

LOA
36′7″ (11.15 m.)

LWL
28′1½″ (8.57 m.)

Beam
12′1″ (3.91 m.)

Draft
5′4″ (1.62 m.)

Ballast
6,175 lbs. & 2,000 lbs. trimming

Displacement
21,950 lbs.

Sail Area
Sloop 586 sq. ft. (54.44 sq. m.)
Gaff Ketch 687 sq. ft. (63.82 sq. m.)

Bermudian Ketch 652 sq. ft. (60.57 sq. m.)

Construction
Planked wood

Disp./Length Ratio
441

Sail Area/Disp. Ratio
Sloop 12, Berm. Ketch 13.3, Gaff Ketch 14.

AL MASON
20281 Anza Dr.
Salinas, CA 93908

into the head area may create access problems and could easily be reversed if desired. There is enough hanging space and stowage room to keep a cruising crew happy during a voyage or while living aboard; and 119 gallons of water are carried in multiple tanks.

Concerning ventilation, there is often a great deal more asked for than delivered by the use of opening ports. Al Mason has designed fixed portlights in the raised doghouse, but the large hatch over the saloon will exchange more air than a half-dozen ports and, using an awning in harbor, it can be kept open when it rains. Additional ventilators can easily be fitted. The cockpit is small, the savings in space being more gainfully applied to increased living accommodation below.

A 37-footer is well served with a tiller, which will connect easily to a self-steering vane. Also note the permanent boom gallows on deck and provisions for stowing a rigid dinghy.

All boats are a compromise, and the Mason 37 won't be every sailor's dream ship; but few sailors will deny that the vessel is safe, comfortable, easily handled and attractive. For a cruising boat, that's compromising in the right direction. At least four boats have been built in Taiwan.

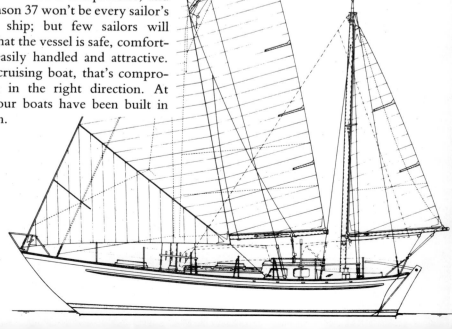

SCHEEL 37

The Scheel 37 was a development of an earlier design by Henry A. Scheel, the S30, a 30-foot daysailing cutter. Both designs have in common a long, narrow, light and easily-driven hull, combined with the unique Scheel Keel.

The patented Scheel Keel is small in lateral area and is flared at the bottom with sharp edges running down either side. Obviously, this concentrates the ballast weight low, and also restricts the flow of water under the keel from the high-pressure area on the leeward side to the low-pressure area on the windward side.

After sailing the S30 for a season, Scheel said the boat performs beyond what would otherwise be expected. He says that she sails to windward at quite a high speed/length ratio, will sail herself to windward under jib or jib and staysail alone, and under full sail has just the right amount of weather helm. She performs, he says, ". . . in an astonishing manner—partly due to the shape of the hull and partly due to some queer extraordinary contribution by the Scheel Keel's shape." Tests conducted on a boat equipped with accurate instrumentation indicate that Scheel has come up with a highly efficient hull and keel combination.

Maintaining this unique hull form, Scheel increased the length to arrive at the Scheel 37, a cruising boat with accommodations for two to four persons. Construction is of cold-molded plywood, which results in an extremely light, yet strong hull. Scheel was able to keep the displacement low; the displacement/length ratio of 178 actually is lower than that of the daysailer.

This long, narrow and light hull is certainly one of the reasons for its startling performance. It also results in a relatively inexpensive boat to build.

Sail areas are small compared to other boats of equal length and so

more easily handled. In addition to the mainsail, working jib and working staysail, Scheel recommends a lightweight 150 percent genoa, a high-cut reaching jib, a lightweight flanker and spinnaker.

Above the waterline, the Scheel 37 is quite traditional and pleasing in appearance. The cockpit is long enough to sit a group or sleep two in fair weather. Sail stowage is under the starboard seat and in the lazarette.

The bow pulpit has its intermediate tube extended to receive a snatch block from which the anchor can hang after having been broken out and hauled clear of the water. This is a great aid to the short-handed sailor on a boat without a bowsprit.

Down below, the accommodations are very simple, yet comfortable for two persons. To port of the companionway is a large icebox, which also serves as chart table. A vertical chart locker, with the charts hanging as in a file cabinet, is shown just forward of the icebox. To starboard is the galley.

A drop-leaf table is flanked by settees and Concordia berths, which were originally developed for the Concordia yawls built in the 1950s. With this arrangement, the curved slatted wood backrests can be folded down to form a berth with its own mattress supported on taut canvas. The berth can be wider than the settee, adjustable for angle of heel, and can be kept complete with bedding in the stowed position. It is a relatively expensive and heavy arrangement, but one of the best ways to combine a comfortable settee and a good berth, useful at sea.

Rogers Marine of Rockland, Maine, built the boat shown.

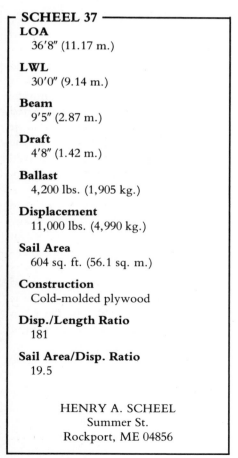

SCHEEL 37

LOA
36'8" (11.17 m.)

LWL
30'0" (9.14 m.)

Beam
9'5" (2.87 m.)

Draft
4'8" (1.42 m.)

Ballast
4,200 lbs. (1,905 kg.)

Displacement
11,000 lbs. (4,990 kg.)

Sail Area
604 sq. ft. (56.1 sq. m.)

Construction
Cold-molded plywood

Disp./Length Ratio
181

Sail Area/Disp. Ratio
19.5

HENRY A. SCHEEL
Summer St.
Rockport, ME 04856

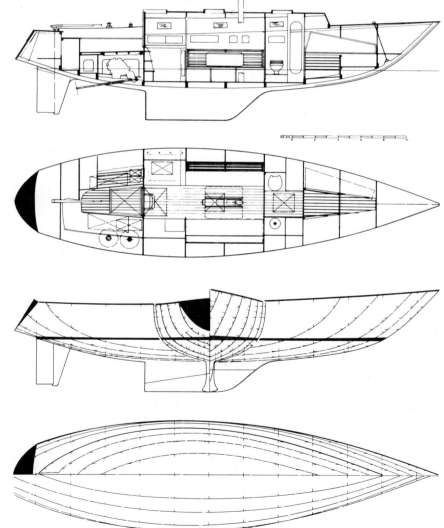

TANTON 37

More and more sailors every year are deciding that they want a sailboat on which they can live and in which they can cruise offshore. While some may be able to buy a new or used boat, many can only afford such a craft if they do some or all of the construction themselves.

In the brief modern history of sailboat cruising, a number of designs have proved to be seaworthy, comfortable and relatively inexpensive to build or buy. The Seabird Yawl and Tahiti Ketch tempted many Americans to take off for the South Pacific; many British Vertues also cruised the oceans of the world.

The French, too, produced some excellent small and inexpensive cruising boats. Many of these were chined hull forms, built in plywood or steel for economy and ease of construction. Bernard Moitessier achieved incredible feats of seamanship in his steel-hulled *Joshua,* with its telephone-pole masts.

Yves Marie Tanton has designed the Tanton 37 as his idea of the modern "getaway boat." He calls it the "Oceangoing Volkswagen" because it is a boat that the average family can afford. She can be constructed, he claims, for less than the cost of an average home.

Simplicity of construction was of great importance in the design process. Yet Tanton sacrificed little or nothing in comfort, safety and speed. This is just about the minimum-size boat that can be constructed of steel while still achieving moderate displacement. It also is about the minimum size in which a family or two couples can find privacy.

The hull is double-chined steel with a moderate length fin keel and skeg-mounted rudder. A more shallow keel-centerboard configuration is another possibility. The stern and transom are constructed of flat plate, so heavy bending is unnecessary.

Strength, light weight and ease of construction are characteristics of the flush deck. Great space on deck and below also result. The cockpit is of good size and set far aft, with propane storage in the base of the steering pedestal. No cockpit lockers are shown but there is more than adequate space under the cockpit accessible from down below. No cockpit coamings are shown but these could be added if an owner wished.

Tanton chose a cat-ketch rig for the boat because of its simplicity and performance. There are no shrouds, end fittings, turnbuckles, toggles, chain plates, etc., to buy, install or maintain. Spars could be aluminum, reinforced fiberglass or laminated wood. There is no need for a large sail inventory. As long as all the sail-handling equipment works well at sea, this appears to be an attractive rig.

With the moderate beam and flush deck, interior volume is enormous and Tanton has utilized it well. There are private double cabins forward and aft. Amidships is the galley to starboard and head with shower to port. The engine is under the chart table. In the main cabin are settees on three sides, pilot berth to port and shelves to starboard. A large drop-leaf table would fit well here.

The Tanton 37 is a well-thought-out boat. It is the right size of the right material, with the right rig, and has the right accommodations for its intended purpose. It would be surprising if it did not become quite popular.

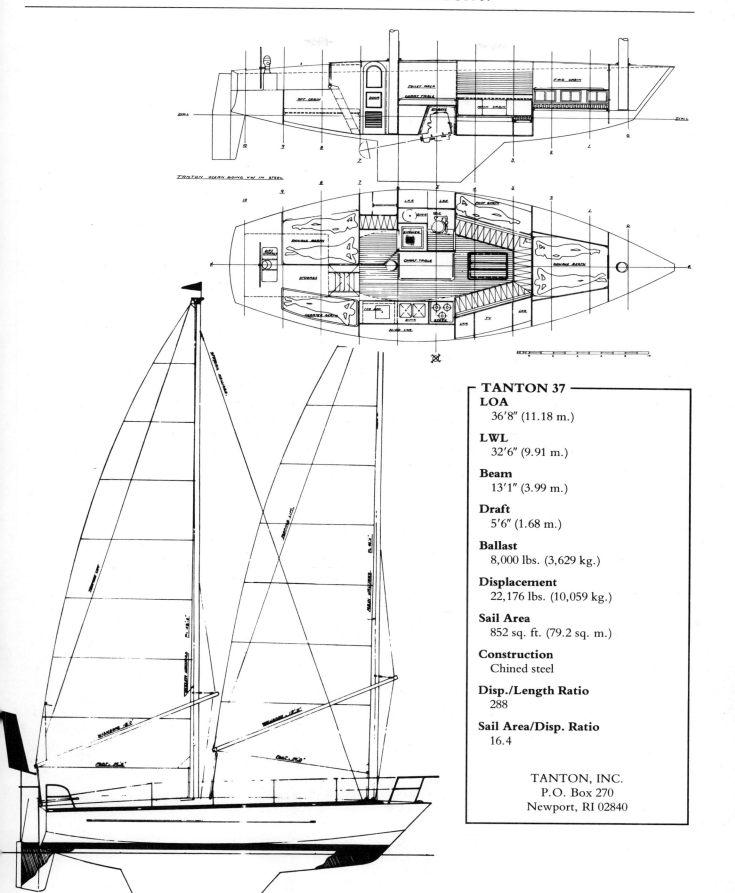

TANTON 37

LOA
  36′8″ (11.18 m.)

LWL
  32′6″ (9.91 m.)

Beam
  13′1″ (3.99 m.)

Draft
  5′6″ (1.68 m.)

Ballast
  8,000 lbs. (3,629 kg.)

Displacement
  22,176 lbs. (10,059 kg.)

Sail Area
  852 sq. ft. (79.2 sq. m.)

Construction
  Chined steel

Disp./Length Ratio
  288

Sail Area/Disp. Ratio
  16.4

TANTON, INC.
P.O. Box 270
Newport, RI 02840

MARSHALL 37

Roger Marshall originally designed this boat for a client in Connecticut and sent plans out to various builders for bids. Though a new marriage and a new mortgage forced that client to decide against building the boat, the exposure of the plans drew quite a bit of interest.

Wisner Brothers Boatbuilders of South Norwalk, Connecticut, decided to build a boat on speculation and have since sold it to a New York sailor. Launching was expected to take place late in 1984. Two other clients, one in Michigan and one in Spain, are also building boats to this design.

Wisner Brothers, whose boat appears in the photograph, are building in foam-cored construction with an inner skin of cold-molded wood and an outer skin of laminated fiberglass. This composite technique offers the warmth of a wood interior and the strength and low maintenance of cored fiberglass.

The Michigan client, who is building the boat himself, is using uncored cold-molded construction, while the boat being built in Spain is foam-cored fiberglass.

The moderate displacement hull features a fin keel and deep, skeg-mounted rudder. Three keel variations were drawn, shallow and deep fin keels of 5'6" and 6'6" draft, and a keel/centerboard arrangement drawing 4'6"/7'6". All three boats under construction are with the shallow fixed keel.

The two American boats will be fit with masthead sloop rigs, while the other will employ a very tall fractional rig. The fractional rig should be easier for a small crew to handle, because it uses smaller jibs and will require fewer sail changes. With a smaller spinnaker, however, it will probably be slower downwind, especially in light air.

The interior arrangement appears to be well thought out. There is a chain locker in the forecabin that holds 200 feet of ⅜" chain. It is positioned to keep the weight of the chain out of the bow and is fed by a pipe from the deck. To port is a single berth and to starboard are a workbench, bureau and hanging locker.

Two settees and a pilot berth are found in the main cabin. The port settee backrest can be repositioned to form a double berth. A double quarterberth, with access over the head of the berth, could be substituted for the single shown.

With its moderate displacement, high performance hull, a choice of keels and a choice of rig, the Marshall 37 could be adapted to suit the needs of many cruising sailors.

MARSHALL 37

LOA
37'7" (11.45m.)

LWL
29'11" (9.12m.)

Beam
12'1" (3.66m.)

Draft
Variations described in text

Ballast
6,600 lbs. (2,994 kg.)

Displacement
13,800 lbs. (6,260 kg.)

Sail Area
661 sq.ft. (61.4 sq.m.)

Disp./Length Ratio
231

Sail Area/Disp. Ratio
18.4

ROGER MARSHALL
Box 127A
Jamestown, RI 02835

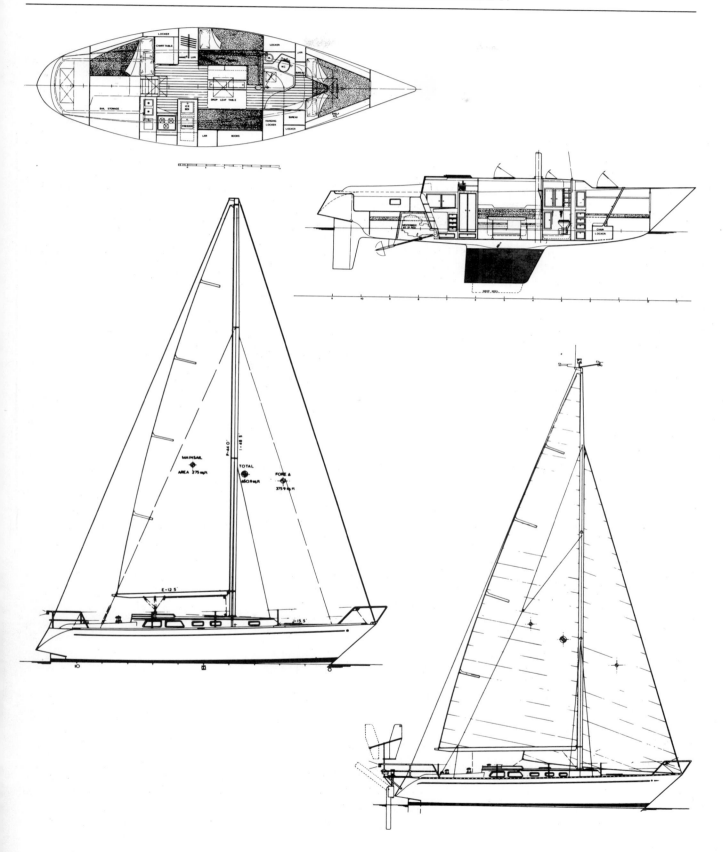

BENFORD 38

Several years ago, Paul Pfeifer started looking for a kit boat that he could finish to his own specifications. It was to serve as a liveaboard boat, and Pfeifer had definite ideas concerning what a floating, sailing home should include.

In addition to liveaboard capability, he wanted a boat with able performance so that he could enter various Southern California-to-Mexico races. He required a fin keel and skeg-mounted rudder.

When he couldn't find a kit boat that met his needs, he contacted various naval architects in search of a stock design. He considered the Benford 30, liked many of its features, but felt he needed a somewhat larger boat. At that time Jay Benford was working on a 38-foot version that seemed to be just what Pfeifer was looking for.

The most impressive feature of

the Benford 38 is its enormous innovative interior and deck/cabin arrangement. Benford has the ability to combine this with a salty and charming appearance. It is hard to imagine any designer fitting more accommodations in a 30-foot waterline boat without transforming the design into a Greyhound bus.

Her beam is healthy but not excessive, and is carried well aft. The foil-shaped fin keel and skeg with rudder are of good size. The clipper bow and what might be called "Benford stern" are short but balanced and her displacement is moderate.

Ports in the topsides and a sort of false bulwark cleverly conceal the

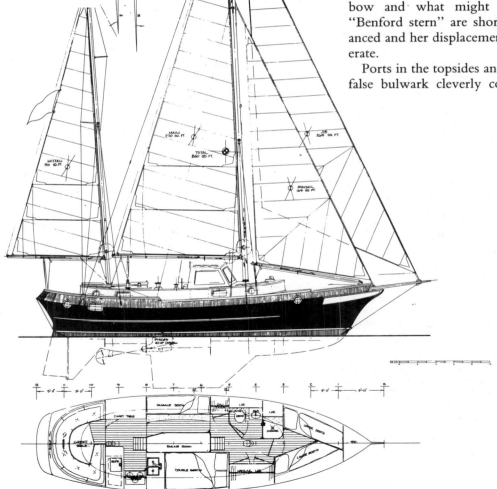

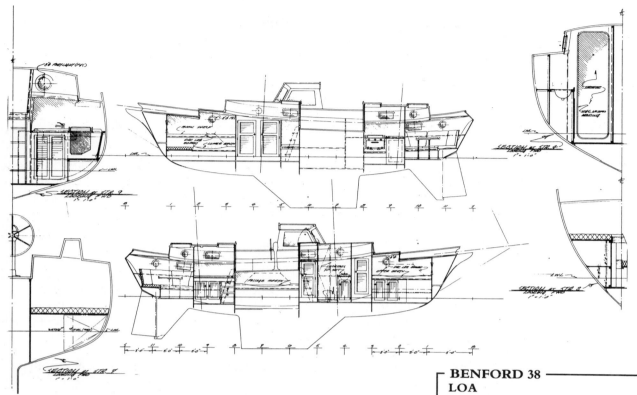

high freeboard. The complex deck and cabin structure also draw attention from the height of freeboard and cabin. Side decks are just wide enough for easy passage and the main lower shrouds lead to the cabin sides to avoid blocking the side decks. There is not much open deck space, however, for sunbathing or dinghy stowage.

Two companionways, one at either end of the cockpit, lead down below. The great after cabin is complete with what Benford calls a "great table." This looks like a pleasant, comfortable area for socializing with seating for a crowd. The spacious galley and chart table are located here, where motion in a seaway will be at a minimum.

The passage berth located outboard of the walkway and the double berth opposite are both well placed for sleeping at sea. The forward cabin contains an oilskin locker, head with separate shower stall, and a large hanging locker. Upper and lower single berths are provided in the forepeak.

With the absence of cockpit lockers and lazarette there seems to be little space for items like dock lines, fenders, jerry cans, sails, anchors and rodes. Some of these could be stowed in the forepeak but this is a poor place for objects that ought to be readily accessible.

The rig is very large and, without the mizzen, would have a normal amount of sail area for a cutter of this size. With a mizzen staysail and genoa she should be able to move well even in light air.

Miller Marine of Bainbridge Island, Washington, built the boat in airex foam-cored fiberglass and delivered it partially completed to Pfeifer for finishing. Benford says that Pfeifer has produced a fine little ship.

BENFORD 38

LOA
38′0″ (11.58 m.)

LWL
30′6″ (9.30 m.)

Beam
11′0″ (3.35 m.)

Draft
5′9″ (1.75 m.)

Ballast
6,200 lbs. (2,812 kg.)

Displacement
16,675 lbs. (7,563 kg.)

Sail Area
850 sq. ft. (79 sq. m.)

Construction
Foam-cored fiberglass

Disp./Length Ratio
263

Sail Area. Disp. Ratio
20.8

JAY R. BENFORD
758 Trenton Ave.
Severna Park, MD 21146

CONCORDIA 38

The Concordia Company, of South Dartmouth, Massachusetts, is well-known for its traditional wood yachts. Distinguished by the star and crescent moon at the ends of the cove stripe, Concordias always attract attention for their design and construction. With its elegantly fine ends and beautiful proportioned rig, the Concordia 39 yawl is the most widely known of the line and still races and cruises with rare style.

Ray Hunt, the designer of the Concordia 39, had a young crewmember on his own *Harrier* in the 1954 Newport-to-Bermuda Race. Almost 30 years later, when the former crewmember wanted a fast, offshore racer/cruiser, he commissioned this design, the Concordia 38, from C. Raymond Hunt Associates and had the boat built by Concordia. She was launched in October 1983.

John Deknatel, head of Hunt Associates, describes the design as "conceptually similar to the early Concordia yawls but in the 1980's genre." This sloop is modern yet conservative. The hull form is without any bumps or distortions to beat rating formulas, so it should be fast and well behaved. Displacement is wholesomely moderate, reflecting a seakindly motion and good carrying ability, both desirable qualities in an offshore cruiser or racer.

The fin keel, bolted onto the molded keel stub, weighs 6,000 pounds (43 percent of displacement). Steering is by tiller.

The Airex-cored fiberglass hull has skins of unidirectional glass roving and a solid, full-length backbone of S-glass. Klegecell core and epoxy resin were used for the deck. Interior furnishings coincide with hull framing for strength and light weight. Bulkheads are honeycomb core with mahogany skins.

Hall Spars of Bristol, Rhode Island, built the double-spreader rig, which features rod rigging with hydraulic backstay and boom vang. Hood Seafurl® gear on the forestay can be removed for racing.

Unusual in a racing boat but practical in a cruiser, there is an owner's stateroom forward and sail stowage aft. Sails are kept under the cockpit and are accessible through a seat locker or from around the engine. On an offshore boat, a cockpit locker that is open to the bilge must be strong, tightly sealed and well secured.

For use at sea, the settee backrests flip up to form padded leeboards for the pilot berths. With the quarter berth and settees there could be five sea berths.

Power is by a Volvo Sail Drive, which has a removable covering box for complete accessibility. Tankage for 35 gallons of fuel and 75 gallons of water is fitted.

This 38-foot sloop might be a bit too racy for many cruising sailors, and a bit Sybaritic for hard-core racers, but should serve her owner well as a high performance compromise. With her impressive lineage and example to follow, she could have a long and successful life.

In a letter to John Kiley, the designer of the boat at Hunt Associates, the owner said, "You have done a fantastic job. What other boat could be so speedy and handsome, and also be our home for three weeks with three generations of family aboard?"

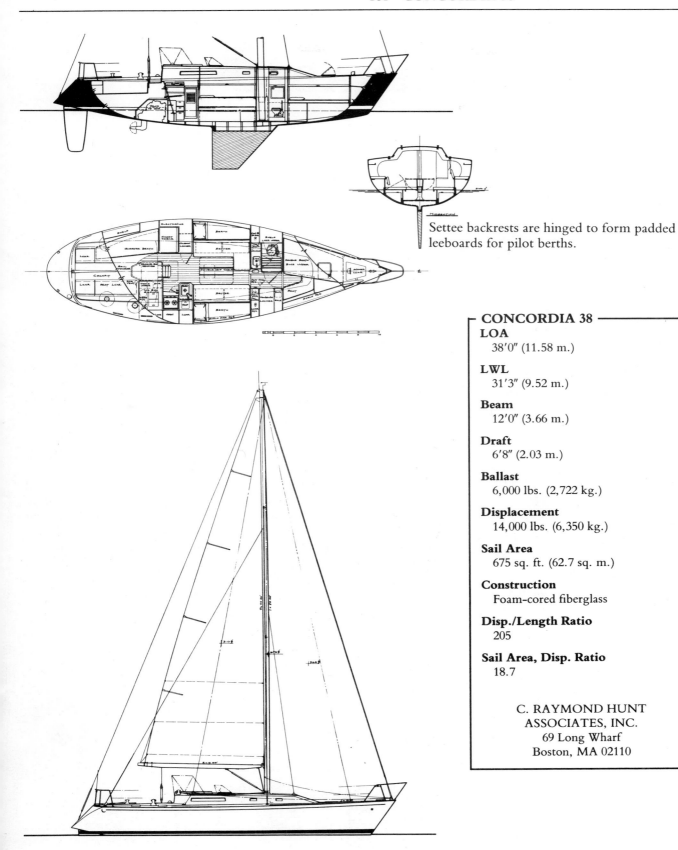

Settee backrests are hinged to form padded leeboards for pilot berths.

CONCORDIA 38

LOA
38'0" (11.58 m.)

LWL
31'3" (9.52 m.)

Beam
12'0" (3.66 m.)

Draft
6'8" (2.03 m.)

Ballast
6,000 lbs. (2,722 kg.)

Displacement
14,000 lbs. (6,350 kg.)

Sail Area
675 sq. ft. (62.7 sq. m.)

Construction
Foam-cored fiberglass

Disp./Length Ratio
205

Sail Area, Disp. Ratio
18.7

C. RAYMOND HUNT
ASSOCIATES, INC.
69 Long Wharf
Boston, MA 02110

MAXI-TRAILERABLE

Included with this design for a 38-foot Maxi-Trailerable are two preliminary versions of the boat which, designer Robert Perry says, "became obsolete as the design went through its metamorphosis from restaurant napkin to working drawings. The three progressive versions show how both the owner's and designer's perception of the boat changed as the project evolved."

A prominent Seattle sailor, Dr. Richard Philbrick, asked Perry to design him a "maximum" trailerable yacht, with a 10-foot beam, as a retirement boat. He desired a yacht that he could ship to the area he wanted to cruise or tow behind his own pickup truck with a "fifth wheel"-type trailer. He also asked for many of the features and dimensions he liked on his 52-foot sloop.

In Preliminary Version #1, Perry attempted to make the boat trailer-launchable. A draft of 18 inches was achieved by choosing a daggerboard housed in a nacelle and a removable outboard rudder. The hull is quite fine forward and full aft. The wide stern results in a large cockpit and waterplane area to aid in stability.

Indeed, adequate stability was probably the most difficult design factor to achieve. At this stage, even with 38 percent ballast (3,000 pounds out of an 8,000-pound displacement), Perry must have found that the stability was not high enough.

Two of the original features that did prove worthy are the faceted cabin and the raised dinette. The aft section of the cabin is very wide, with narrow side decks. Just aft of the mast, however, the cabin sides are stepped inboard, forming a narrow forward cabin. This permits a view forward as well as to either side from below decks.

To further increase visibility from below, the dinette is raised about a foot above the cabin sole (see sectional view).

In Preliminary Version #2 it is obvious that Perry was trying to increase stability and accommodation space, while abandoning the trailer launching capability. The stub keel/centerboard arrangement lowers the center of gravity of the ballast and removes the daggerboard trunk from the interior of the boat—but increases the draft to 30 inches.

Ballast was increased to 44 percent of displacement, and waterline length was increased to 31 feet, eight inches by reducing overhang

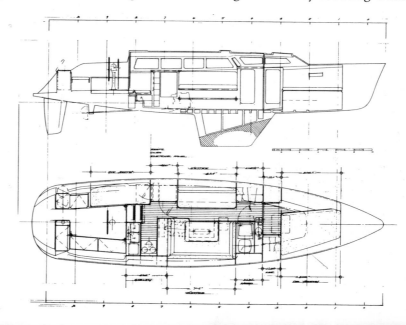

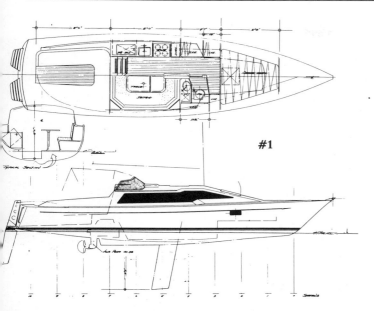

#1

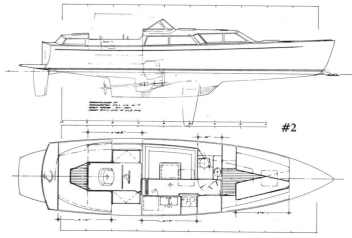

#2

forward. (A hinged stern platform for ease of boarding would increase the effective sailing length further when under way.) Bilges were made firmer and the bottom flatter. Stability certainly was increased markedly.

While the main cabin arrangement is nearly the mirror image of that in Version #1, the rest of the interior has changed. There is an after cabin with two settees, and overlapping single berths in the forecabin.

Power in Version #1 consisted of a 35-hp. Volvo diesel with S-drive. In Version #2 there is a 50-hp. Pathfinder diesel mounted off-center to port and connected by belts to a variable-pitch propeller. This configuration was ultimately rejected because Perry found that the keel foil thickness required to accommodate this type of shaft was too great.

So now on to the final version. With its small fin keel, ballast was reduced to 36 percent but the center of gravity lowered substantially. Overall and waterline lengths were increased and the aft cockpit restored.

Accommodations were increased, too, with a quarter berth aft and a settee opposite the dinette. The galley was moved aft and the forward double berth offset to starboard. The same Pathfinder diesel also is offset slightly to starboard and drives a folding propeller through a straight shaft angled in toward the centerline.

Perry added flare to the bow to keep spray down and retained the firm bilges and flat bottom. This type of hull form has a greater wetted surface than more conventional forms and is thus slower in light air. However, performance under power, and under sail when off the wind, is enhanced. With the large diesel, speed under power of nine-and-a-half knots is anticipated.

The large three-quarter sloop rig, common to all three versions, has a jumper strut for upper mast support. The mast stands on a hinged step. Spreaders are swept aft with the shrouds led to the gunwale. A roller furling, self-tacking jib with traveler is shown in addition to a large genoa.

Hull and deck were constructed of Klegecell cored fiberglass. Interior joinery is also Klegecell, cored for light weight. Tankage for 175 gallons of water and 60 gallons of fuel is provided.

MAXI-TRAILERABLE

LOA
38'6" (11.73 m.)

LWL
31'8" (3.66 m.)

Beam
10'0" (3.05 m.)

Draft
4'9" (1.45 m.)

Ballast
3,250 lbs. (1,474 kg.)

Displacement
9,000 lbs. (4,082 kg.)

Sail Area
517 sq. ft. (48 sq. m.)

Construction
Foam-cored fiberglass

Disp./Length Ratio
127

Sail Area/Disp. Ratio
19.1

ROBERT H. PERRY
6400 Seaview Ave. NW
Seattle, WA 98107

SPIRIT 39

To meet the great demand for steel cruising boat designs, especially those suited to amateur construction, Glen-L Marine Designs introduced to its catalog of designs the Spirit 39. This interesting hull features a full keel with cutaway forefoot for maneuverability and reduced wetted surface, and slight flare in the bow to keep spray down.

Beam is moderate, with maximum beam located farther forward than is common today. This allows a roomy main cabin and a relatively fine stern—and its associated sea-kindliness—without any distortion of hull lines. The large keel volume makes it possible to use inexpensive concrete and scrap steel, which is less dense than lead, as ballast.

Only the hull and deck are built of steel, with the cabin and cockpit of plywood covered with fiberglass. The relatively low freeboard keeps the center of gravity low to improve stability. Some sailors prefer an all-welded superstructure for water-tight integrity. The Spirit 39 is a compromise. The often trouble-some hull/deck joint still is welded.

Side decks and foredeck are spacious and the cockpit appears small but comfortable, with four drains. The large, flat cabin top provides excellent space for dinghy stowage.

On the high-aspect, double-head-sail ketch rig, the small mizzen is more of yawl proportion and its slight stern overhang would not interfere with fitting a self-steering gear. Tracks for the jib sheet leads are placed inboard of the rail for close headsail sheeting. A cutter rig also is shown.

The interior arrangement, with

two separate head/shower areas, is a bit unusual in a 39-foot aft cockpit boat. It does result in an entirely private stateroom forward, but some cruisers may prefer to use one of the heads for stowage, even though numerous large lockers are provided.

Large items such as oars, dinghy sailing rigs, outboard motors, awnings, etc., are difficult to stow in ordinary lockers.

The double and single quarter berths will be very comfortable at sea. A sliding chart table uses the head of the single quarter berth as a

seat. Double sinks and a three-burner stove are found in the galley.

A 35- to 40-hp. diesel is located under the bridge deck and is connected to a V-drive. Tankage for 70 gallons of fuel and 170 gallons of water is fitted.

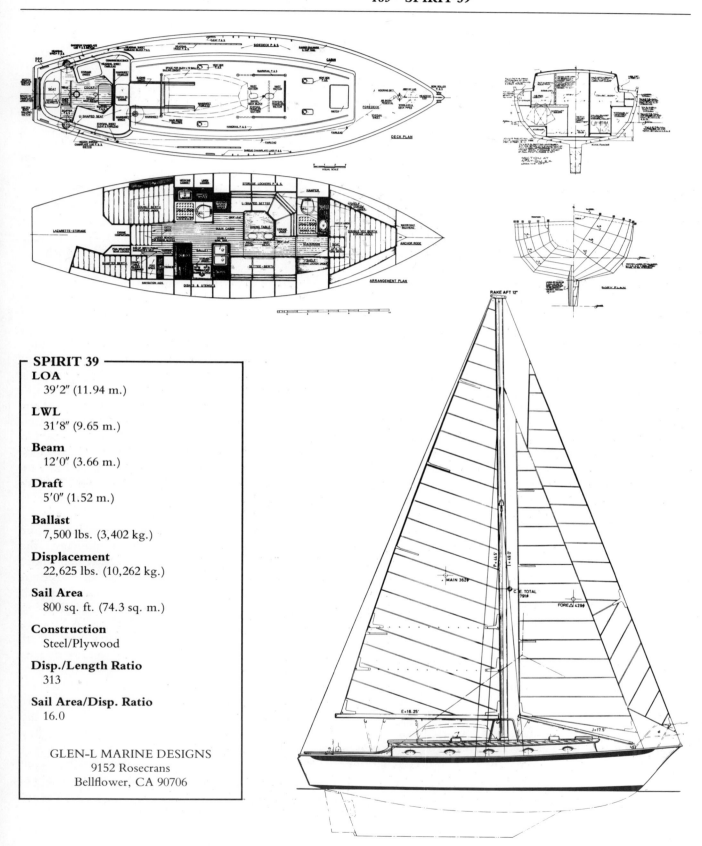

SPIRIT 39

LOA
39′2″ (11.94 m.)

LWL
31′8″ (9.65 m.)

Beam
12′0″ (3.66 m.)

Draft
5′0″ (1.52 m.)

Ballast
7,500 lbs. (3,402 kg.)

Displacement
22,625 lbs. (10,262 kg.)

Sail Area
800 sq. ft. (74.3 sq. m.)

Construction
Steel/Plywood

Disp./Length Ratio
313

Sail Area/Disp. Ratio
16.0

GLEN-L MARINE DESIGNS
9152 Rosecrans
Bellflower, CA 90706

AMBRA

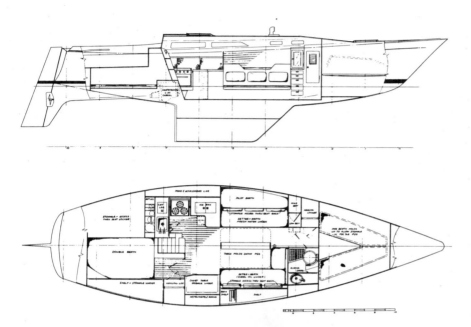

Ambra was the first design to emerge from naval architect Carl Schumacher's own design office. Previously he had worked four years with Gary Mull, participating in the design of many successful racing yachts. Schumacher states that he favors performance-oriented cruising boats that are both comfortable and practical. He likes boats with moderate displacement and a long waterline length in relation to overall length, resulting in an easily driven hull with a comfortable motion.

Ambra is an excellent example of this philosophy. Although it is obvious from this design that Schumacher has experience with racing yachts, this is not just a racing hull with cruising accommodations. The sleek, clean hull shows none of the tucks or bustles intended to exploit rating rules. The longish fin keel and large skeg-mounted rudder

should provide both windward performance and tracking ability.

Construction details call for laminated fiberglass with ¾-inch foam core in the hull and ½-inch end grain balsa in the deck. The hull/deck joint is laminated as one piece, thus eliminating bolt holes, one of the most troublesome leak areas in many boats. Floors, engine bed and longitudinal stiffeners are fiberglass laminate over nonstructural foam. This all results in an exceptionally stiff, yet light, hull.

C-Flex is used as a backbone over which the keel is laid up. Ballast is either in the form of a one-piece internal lead casting or lead pigs mixed with lead shot. Resin seals and holds the lead in place. With the lead occupying only the lower portion of the fin there is still a deep bilge in which to collect water without getting any into lockers.

The sleek deck with low cabin

profile allows unobstructed work on deck and low windage while still permitting large ports for visibility and light below. A dinghy fits neatly between the mast and companionway. To ease anchor handling and mooring operations, a powered, self-tailing winch is mounted on the foredeck.

The transom-hung rudder with tiller passing through the transom eases construction. The cockpit drains through the transom. A rather large cockpit locker is located to port.

A large, simple sloop rig is shown. The 385-square-foot foretriangle might be a bit large for the shorthanded sailor, and some may prefer an inner forestay on which to fly a staysail. Control lines, including main halyard, first and second reef lines, foreguy and jib furling line are led to winches and stoppers at the aft end of the cabin top.

With the engine in a box at the foot of the companionway, the power plant's weight is kept more central and low, and an enormous double quarter berth can be fitted. Opening ports to the cockpit bring light and air to this area. A hanging locker and large, stand-up chart table also are handy to the companionway.

The spacious main cabin has settee/berths with tankage for water and fuel under them, keeping the tanks central and low where they belong. A pilot berth to port is a valuable sea berth. Folding pipe berths in the forecastle make great sense on this boat. V-berths are often of little use and occupy valuable storage space. With this ar-

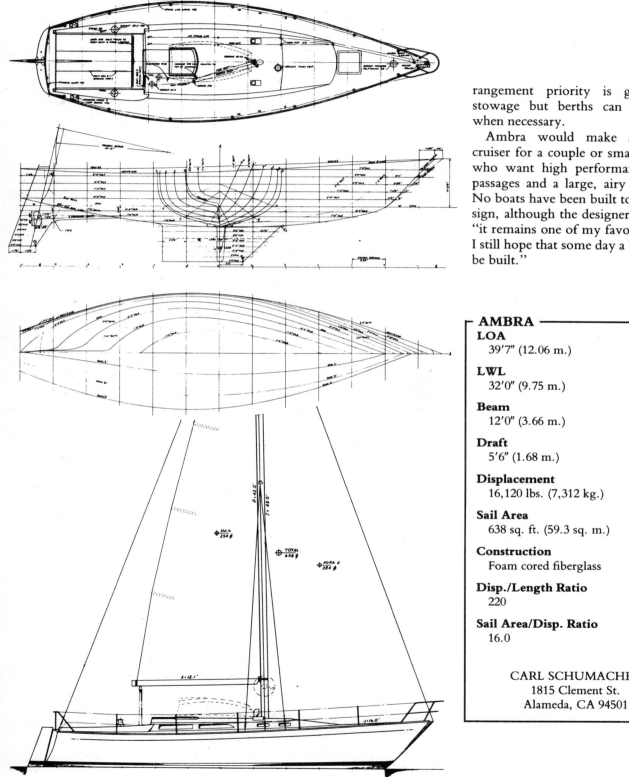

rangement priority is given to stowage but berths can be used when necessary.

Ambra would make an ideal cruiser for a couple or small family who want high performance, fast passages and a large, airy interior. No boats have been built to this design, although the designer reports, "it remains one of my favorites and I still hope that some day a boat will be built."

AMBRA

LOA
39′7″ (12.06 m.)

LWL
32′0″ (9.75 m.)

Beam
12′0″ (3.66 m.)

Draft
5′6″ (1.68 m.)

Displacement
16,120 lbs. (7,312 kg.)

Sail Area
638 sq. ft. (59.3 sq. m.)

Construction
Foam cored fiberglass

Disp./Length Ratio
220

Sail Area/Disp. Ratio
16.0

CARL SCHUMACHER
1815 Clement St.
Alameda, CA 94501

40-FOOT MOTORSAILER

In 1970 Jay R. Benford designed a 35-foot trawler yacht named *Strumpet,* which proved to be an extremely sea-kindly and fuel-efficient hull form. Interest in this boat led in 1972 to the design of a motorsailer version. The same qualities that made *Strumpet* a successful trawler made this motorsailer a fine performer.

As the next step in the evolutionary process, Benford expanded the hull in 1975 to create a 37-foot motorsailer. This also was a successful and popular design. In 1977 Benford was approached by a client who liked the 37-footer but wanted even more room. This "40-foot pilothouse sloop/motorsailer," as Benford calls it, was the result.

Although the profile drawing suggests that this is a typical long-keeled, wineglass section hull, such is not the case. The hull form is rather like a canoe body with a long,

distinctly separate, foil-shaped fin keel. This results in a greater effective lateral area and longer leading edge for windward performance. Wetted surface is slightly increased.

There is a large, protected propeller aperture ahead of the partially balanced rudder. The rather bluff bow and full canoe stern give the design a stout appearance and a large amount of accommodation space within its 40-foot overall length.

While the displacement figure is medium-to-heavy, Benford points out that it includes full tanks of water and fuel (205 and 120 gallons respectively) plus nearly a ton of stores. Some designers do not count these weights in the published displacement, so when their boats are fully loaded they can be quite a bit heavier. It always is important to know what a stated displacement includes.

As always, Benford has cleverly

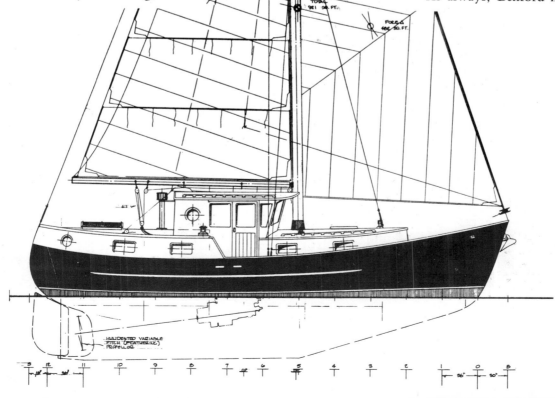

designed the deck and cabin to combine good appearance, spaciousness below and ease of work on deck. The raised deck aft allows an enormous after cabin plus some useful deck space. Bulwarks, which start at nine inches at the pilothouse and increase to 18 inches at the bow, provide security on deck.

A simple masthead sloop rig is shown. Shrouds lead inboard for close headsail sheeting and swept-back spreaders permit the shrouds to attach directly to a major transverse bulkhead. Interesting features include a roachless, battenless mainsail and a full-width mainsheet traveler. All sail handling lines lead to the pilothouse doors. A gaff sloop rig with bowsprit and topsail also is possible.

Power is provided by a Gardner diesel engine coupled to a large Hundested variable-pitch propeller.

Gauges on the engine indicate engine loading, so at any rpm propeller pitch can be adjusted for maximum efficiency. The engine is accessible from the main cabin, and a section of pilothouse sole is removable for engine service.

The roomy interior also has some noteworthy details. The navigator's station in the after cabin includes, in addition to the chart table, a typewriter counter and another counter top that hinges up to expose a workbench and tool stowage. The seat backs on the aft settees also could be hinged to form upper and lower berths.

This 40-foot motorsailer would make an extremely comfortable liveaboard boat well suited to cruising in fair or harsh climates. She will surely attract attention and compliments in any anchorage.

40-FOOT MOTORSAILER

LOA
40'0" (12.19 m.)

LWL
36'0" (10.97 m.)

Beam
14'0" (4.27 m.)

Draft
5'6" (1.67 m.)

Ballast
7,700 lbs. (3,493 kg.)

Displacement
30,795 lbs. (13,968 kg.)

Sail Area
921 sq. ft. (85.6 sq. m.)

Construction
Fiberglass or Wood

Disp./Length Ratio
295

Sail Area/Disp. Ratio
15.0

JAY R. BENFORD
758 Trenton Ave.
Severna Park, MD 21146

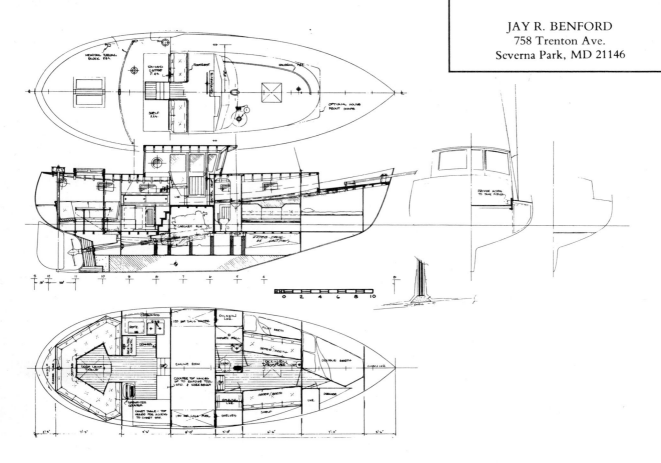

VANCOUVER 42

"Cruising sailboat" is a widely used term, yet one that can have many different meanings. Some boats are suitable for cruising in lakes, or protected coastal areas, or in warm and gentle climates. Others are suitable for cruising in almost any body of water and climate.

Robert Harris has been designing a family of similar boats that fall into the latter category. Following the success of his Vancouver 27, 32 and 36, he introduced the Vancouver 42. He calls her a "serious cruising boat," which he defines as "a small ship which should incorporate every characteristic, feature and item which will permit the owner and his party to live aboard in port or at sea, in fair weather or foul, for extended periods independent of land facilities." This is difficult or impossible to achieve in a small vessel. Yet the 42 appears large enough to fulfill this definition for up to five or six people.

The Vancouver designs are quite similar in hull form and rig, and the 42 closely resembles the 36. Thus Harris had the advantage of using the 36 as a sort of trial horse for this design.

The long fin keel should provide good windward performance and still allow the boat to support itself for hauling or drying out against a wall in areas with sufficient tide. A large skeg protects and supports the efficient, high-aspect rudder.

Beam is much less than found on many modern cruising boats and the point of maximum beam is well aft. This results in fine sections forward, and full, powerful sections aft.

The cockpit is small and well protected by the raised trunk cabin. Side decks are wide and there is a covered anchor well forward containing the anchor windlass, which can handle chain or rope from the double bow rollers. With the hatch closed there is nothing to snag sheets or stub toes.

Given a sail area/displacement ratio of 19.6, the 42 should perform very well in light airs. The inboard rig is very tall and efficient. Jumper struts at the head of the inner forestay eliminate the need for running backstays or intermediate shrouds. All mainsail reefing lines are led to the cockpit and the roller furling jib topsail means most sail handling can be performed from the cockpit.

Two interior arrangements are shown. One features a single quarter berth aft and a large double forward next to a bureau or workbench. The double is not all the way up in the bow, so motion won't be as extreme as it would be otherwise. An interesting detail is the boot drying tray over the generator set. The other arrangement has two quarter berths and a conventional V-berth forward.

The Vancouver 42 was originally designed for cold-molded construc-

VANCOUVER 42	
LOA	41′9″ (12.72 m.)
LWL	32′6″ (9.91 m.)
Beam	12′6″ (3.67 m.)
Draft	5′10″ (1.78 m.)
Ballast	10,600 lbs. (4,818 kg.)
Displacement	29,147 (13,221 kg.)
Sail Area	942 sq. ft. (87.5 sq. m.)
Construction	see text
Disp./Length Ratio	379
Sail Area/Disp. Ratio	19.6

ROBERT B. HARRIS, LTD.
212-1670 Duranleau St.
Granville Island
Vancouver, B.C.
Canada V6G 2W6

tion by Aqua Craft Ltd. of Port Co-
cuitlam, British Columbia.

A production fiberglass boat, and
a newer center cockpit version are
being built in Taiwan and imported
by Southern Offshore Yachts. A
trunk cabin configuration also has
been drawn.

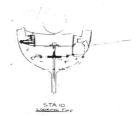

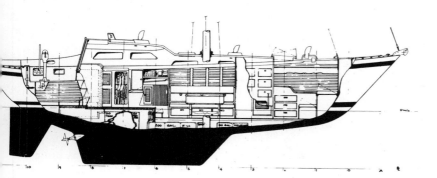

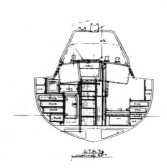

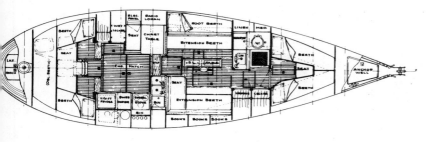

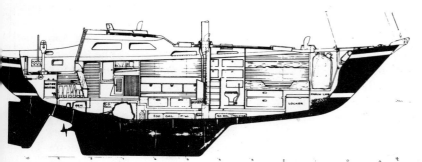

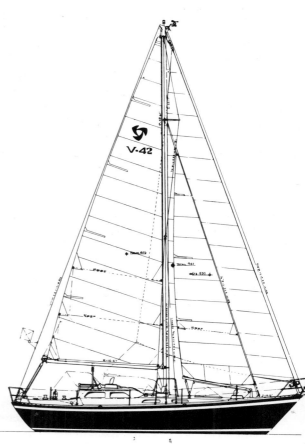

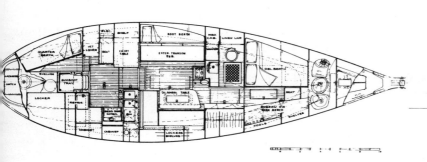

NIGHTRUNNER

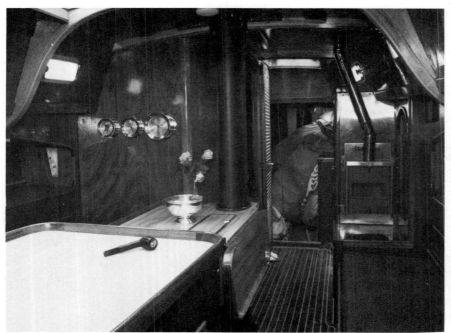

ROY MONTGOMERY

It has become increasingly common for naval architects to attempt combining a modern, high performance underbody with a traditional profile. The levels of performance and appearance vary greatly, as does their success in producing a harmonious, compatible design. Robert Perry's *Nightrunner* is an extreme example and is, in his words, "the most daring attempt by our office" and "one of the most exciting designs we have done."

The client for this design was Douglas Fryer, a Seattle attorney, who has owned an Atkin Tally-Ho Major design, *African Star,* for 15 years. He also had been involved with two Victoria-to-Maui Race syndicates, skippering Bill Lee's ultralight displacement *Merlin* to a first-place finish and new course record in the 1978 event.

With this background it was only natural that when Fryer came to Perry for a new boat, his requirements were that she be "swift, handsome and original." Fryer believes speed and weatherliness are just as important in a cruising vessel as in a racer.

Perry has given his client exactly what was called for. The hull has a very deep and efficient fin keel, with ballast totaling 46 percent of displacement and located extremely low. The upper portion of the keel is deadwood. Fryer called for a skeg-mounted rudder because, from his experience, it greatly enhances tracking ability.

Wetted surface is very low for good performance in the light air often found in the Seattle area. If you cover up the topsides and look only at the underbody, it would be difficult to distinguish it from that of a racer, except that she has no bumps or distortions for measurement purposes. The entry is fine and the run straight and clean.

Above the waterline, however, she is quite a different boat. Were it not for the fact that she was built in wood (cold-molded red cedar) some might consider it frivolous or pretentious to have such a traditional look. Fryer admits to including the bowsprit chiefly for appearance, although it does increase the sail area with very little additional weight.

While the rig does not appear too much out of character on paper, in reality it probably does. The double-spreader tapered mast is black anodized aluminum. All halyards are internal. Chain plates and genoa track are set well inboard. The design specifies rod rigging and numerous winches. The sail area is very large, with a sail area/displacement ratio of 19.5.

Having the companionway offset to starboard with the cabin trunk extending aft of it on the port side permits a large after stateroom. The boat was designed to be comfortable for Fryer and his wife and occasional guests and racing crews. Two settees plus a pilot berth in the main cabin and a pipe berth in the forepeak should satisfy this requirement.

A 40-hp. Westerbeke diesel is positioned under the galley counter. This may make it a bit noisy down below, but a boat that can sail as

NIGHTRUNNER

LOA
41'11" (12.78 m.)

LWL
36'1" (10.97 m.)

Beam
12'5" (3.79 m.)

Draft
7'2" (2.18 m.)

Ballast
11,121 lbs. (5,044 kg.)

Displacement
24,000 lbs. (10,886 kg.)

Sail Area
1,015 sq. ft. (94.3 sq. m.)

Construction
Cold-molded wood

Disp./Length Ratio
229

Sail Area/Disp. Ratio
19.5

ROBERT H. PERRY
6400 Seaview Ave. NW
Seattle, WA 98107

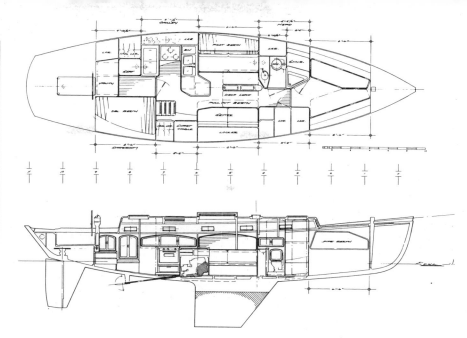

well as this one should seldom need to power. Also, engine access is excellent. Perry's design is both interesting and extreme. She was built by Cecil Lange of Port Townsend, Washington. There is little doubt she will satisfy Fryer's requirements of speed and appearance, even if she is in some ways a bit incongruous.

ROY MONTGOMERY

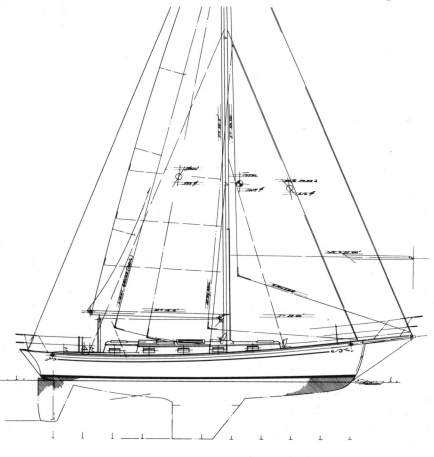

FIDELITY

The parameters established for *Cruising World*'s 1980 Design Competition called for an ideal retirement sailboat. It was to be a comfortable liveaboard boat for an older couple, yet it still had to be a capable sailer, perhaps with the ability to make an occasional offshore passage. While initial cost was not a major consideration, ease and cost of maintenance were deemed important. In conclusion, the boat had to be a sound financial investment, an alternative to a retirement home or condominium for people who prefer to live afloat.

Designs were submitted that offered greater comfort than the one eventually chosen. Some boats could sail faster. Others would cost less to build. Some were more beautiful. The chosen winner, Fidelity, best combined good looks, fine performance, liveability and ease of maintenance. It is this combination that also assures that she will retain her value and thus be a wise investment.

Fidelity has a pleasing appearance in a modern/classic sort of way. She would not look unusual or out of place in an anchorage today and probably will not in 10 or 20 years.

It is the modified rig, deck and interior layout that make Fidelity a good boat for a retired couple. C. John Simpson, the designer, said he created Fidelity specifically for "a couple in their 50s or 60s, who are still quite active and without any handicaps which might not only restrict them in the use of this vessel but boating in general."

Simpson describes the hull design as "based on proven parameters and offering excellent seakeeping quali-

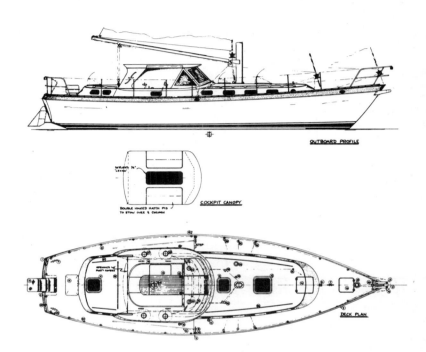

ties, good directional stability and quick response to the helm." He chose fiberglass construction for its strength and ease of repair. A hull cored with Airex foam and a deck cored with balsa are shown in the plans, but the hull and/or deck could be built in solid fiberglass if desired.

One unusual feature of Fidelity is her cockpit hardtop. It is of the "T-type" found on many sports cars today, with double-hinged panels port and starboard that fold inboard and stow on the centerline. A Lexan skylight positioned on the centerline admits light and permits visibility aloft. Sliding or removable Lexan

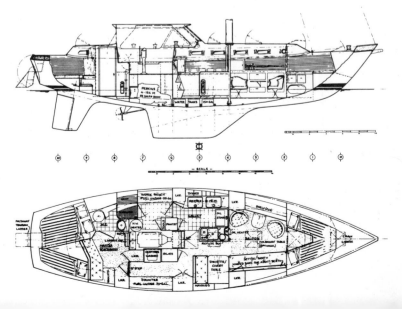

panels close off the after end of the hardtop. Snap-on side curtains, for use in port, would make the cockpit a pleasant living area even in the foulest weather.

The cabin top is as wide as possible, allowing accommodations to be spread far outboard while still permitting adequate side decks. Wide cockpit coamings further increased usable space below. A life raft can be stowed on the afterdeck and a 7-foot dinghy will fit on the after cabin top. A folding boarding ladder is included in the transom.

An easily-handled, well-stayed and efficient cutter rig is shown. All sails are roller furling and controlled from the cockpit, which has six winches.

While the upper and intermediate shrouds are led to the outboard edge of the deck for a wide and strong staying base, the lower shrouds terminate well inboard. This permits a much easier passage fore and aft.

Dual companionways lead forward and aft from the cockpit. Aft is the spacious master stateroom, with double and single berths, settee, vanity, lockers and a head with shower. A second access to the head is through the shower, from the engine room area.

A workbench with standing headroom and tool cabinets is to port of the engine. The engine and V-drive installation appears to be quite cramped but adequate removable inspection panels could ease

servicing. To starboard of the engine is the passageway with room for a washing machine and counter. Tankage for 120 gallons of fuel is located under the counter and the workbench.

Further forward is the large, U-shaped galley and dinette/chart table. An athwartships-mounted stove is shown. This could be gimbaled or a small auxiliary gimbaled stove could be used at sea.

The dinette will seat only three persons, so having guests for meals would be a problem. An alternative is to substitute a larger dining area for the easy chair arrangement in the

main saloon. The settee opposite has a backrest which folds up to form upper and lower berths. Tankage for 150 gallons of water is placed under the cabin sole.

Simpson has also drawn a double-chined steel version of Fidelity. Six boats, three in fiberglass and three in steel, are completed or under construction.

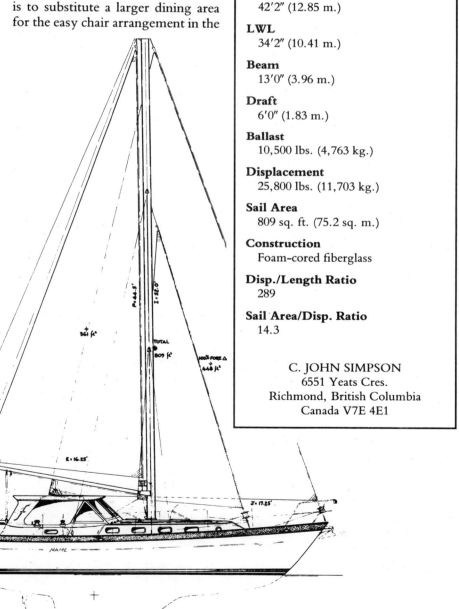

FIDELITY

LOA
42'2" (12.85 m.)

LWL
34'2" (10.41 m.)

Beam
13'0" (3.96 m.)

Draft
6'0" (1.83 m.)

Ballast
10,500 lbs. (4,763 kg.)

Displacement
25,800 lbs. (11,703 kg.)

Sail Area
809 sq. ft. (75.2 sq. m.)

Construction
Foam-cored fiberglass

Disp./Length Ratio
289

Sail Area/Disp. Ratio
14.3

C. JOHN SIMPSON
6551 Yeats Cres.
Richmond, British Columbia
Canada V7E 4E1

HARRY TABARD

Harry Tabard (he was the innkeeper in Chaucer's Canterbury Tales) was designed for an experienced Boston yachtsman who wanted a bluewater cruiser with comfortable accommodations and good performance. Paine described the hull form as combining "an utterly traditional style above the waterline with a powerful hull of moderate displacement and judiciously reduced lateral plane area."

This is where the judgment and experience of a designer comes into play. If he makes the keel and rudder/skeg too small in lateral area, directional stability is reduced to the point where steering is difficult and the helm must be constantly tended. If he makes them too large, the boat can be unresponsive and slow in light air. It appears that Paine has, indeed, been judicious.

Wide side decks and bulwarks all around, measuring 14 inches at the bow, should make deck work secure. The accompanying photographs show chocks for a dinghy to be stowed on deck between the mast and the companionway. No dodger is shown but one could be fitted.

The cutter rig is moderate in area and nicely proportioned. A short bowsprit enables the center of sail area to be kept low without making headsail handling too inconvenient. The photo shows two anchors stowed on the sprit.

A boomed staysail is shown on the sail plan but the owner chose a boomless arrangement. On a small foredeck, a swinging boom can be a dangerous item.

Paine said this is about the smallest boat that can have a true owner's

HARRY TABARD ★ BOSTON

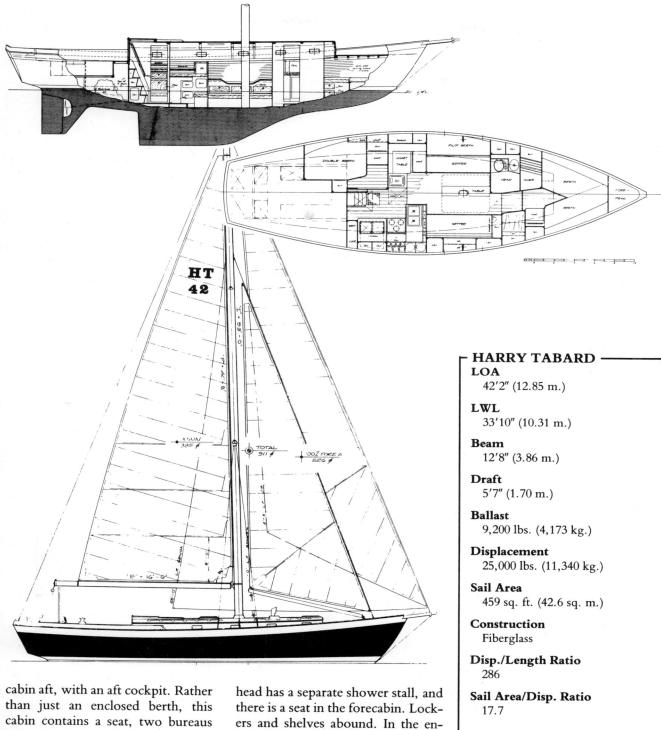

HT 42

HARRY TABARD

LOA
42'2" (12.85 m.)

LWL
33'10" (10.31 m.)

Beam
12'8" (3.86 m.)

Draft
5'7" (1.70 m.)

Ballast
9,200 lbs. (4,173 kg.)

Displacement
25,000 lbs. (11,340 kg.)

Sail Area
459 sq. ft. (42.6 sq. m.)

Construction
Fiberglass

Disp./Length Ratio
286

Sail Area/Disp. Ratio
17.7

C. W. PAINE YACHT DESIGN,
INC.
P.O. Box 763
Camden, ME 04843

cabin aft, with an aft cockpit. Rather than just an enclosed berth, this cabin contains a seat, two bureaus and some shelves. Opposite is a wet locker and a spacious galley. A large navigator's station with lockers and shelves is located beside the fireplace at the aft end of the main cabin. The head has a separate shower stall, and there is a seat in the forecabin. Lockers and shelves abound. In the engine room are tool racks and even a seat for the chief engineer.

Sea trials have convinced the designer and owner that the *Harry Tabard* makes an ideal passage-maker.

ALASKA 43

The chined custom hull is probably the quickest and least expensive to build. The choice of material—plywood, steel or aluminum—depends upon boat size, use, price and individual taste. A flush deck arrangement also is easier to construct than other cabin configurations.

Thus, when an Alaskan couple came to Ted Brewer looking for a rugged, economical boat for living

aboard and for extensive cruising, this double-chine steel hull with flush deck and iron ballast was a logical design. The high-sided hull, which can look awkward in chined construction, has been well disguised by the wide sheer stripe, opening ports and rub rail.

Short overhangs and a long waterline length serve to reduce the displacement/length ratio, which

can get high in a steel vessel, to a moderate 285.

By cutting away keel area forward and aft, Brewer reduced wetted surface and increased windward efficiency. Moderate draft permits extensive gunkholing and canal cruising.

A small open cockpit and enclosed wheelhouse were chosen for comfort in a harsh climate. In fine

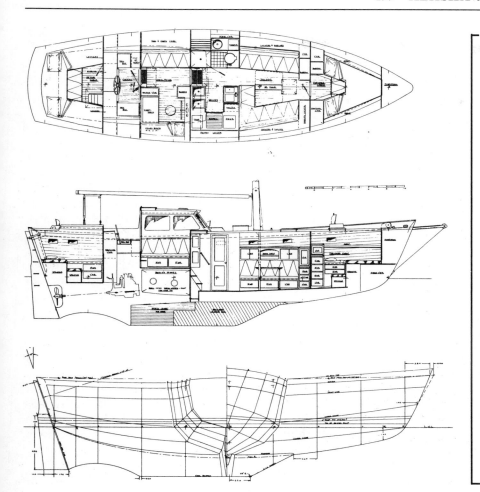

ALASKA 43

LOA
42'10" (13.06 m.)

LWL
38'0" (11.58 m.)

Beam
12'11" (3.94 m.)

Draft
5'6" (1.68 m.)

Ballast
11,000 lbs. (4,989 kg.)

Displacement
35,000 lbs. (15,876 kg.)

Sail Area
1,048 sq. ft. (97.4 sq. m.)

Construction
Double-chined steel

Disp./Length Ratio
285

Sail Area/Disp. Ratio
15.7

TED BREWER YACHT DESIGNS,
LTD.
217 Edith Point Rd.
Anacortes, WA 98221

weather the acres of open deck space make up for the small cockpit. Inside the wheelhouse, the helmsman can swing around on his stool and face the chart table. There is a small four-foot, 10-inch berth to starboard, settee and lockers to port, and an oilskin locker beside the entrance.

Aft, and accessible only from the cockpit, is the after cabin. It contains two single berths and some lockers, and appears roomy and comfortable.

Forward of the wheelhouse are the galley and head. Double sinks, refrigerator and freezer are shown in the galley, with a separate stall shower in the head. The double forward cabin is also large and spacious with numerous lockers. More than adequate ventilation is provided by 10 Dorade vents, 12 opening ports and three opening skylights.

The sail plan is modest in size but efficient and easily handled. All sails except the largest jib are under 500 square feet in area. The mainsail and boomed staysail have slab reefing. Double spreaders and fixed intermediate backstays support the aluminum mast, which is mounted in a tabernacle.

The 30-hp. Sabb diesel is small for a vessel of 15 tons, but it drives a large-diameter, controllable-pitch propeller. This type of propeller allows efficient powering in varying conditions and good maneuverability. Fuel consumption will be extremely low so the 180 gallons of fuel will go a long way. Tankage for 275 gallons of water also is fitted.

It is easy to picture this boat anchored snugly in an Alaskan fjord, ice-capped peaks all around, and a wisp of smoke drifting up from the Charley Noble.

CARTWRIGHT 43

While the Cartwright 43 may resemble other Jerry Cartwright designs from the waterline up, with its mostly flush deck and small deckhouse, below the waterline it is quite different from what many people associate with a Cartwright boat. Most of Cartwright's designs have had traditional full keels and moderate-to-heavy displacements, and all create the impression of strength and massiveness.

Jerry Cartwright has spent enough time at sea to know the necessity of having an enormously strong vessel if one wants to venture offshore, especially singlehanded. That is just what Jack Sweeney had in mind when he commissioned this design. But he also specified light weight for high performance.

Making a sailboat strong takes careful design and quite a bit of construction material. In a boat of moderate or heavy displacement, the designer does not have to be quite so careful when adding strengthening members, because weight is not so critical. The 43, with a displacement/length ratio of 212.9, is a light boat and weight must be controlled carefully.

The hull is constructed of C-Flex fiberglass planking over a male mold with three layers of 24-ounce woven roving added on the outside and one layer inside. An adhesive paste of resin and milled fibers is used between layers for lamination strength. On the inside, foam frames are set on 18-inch centers throughout. They are very strong for their weight and result in a stiff, lightweight hull.

The keel is deep and short for windward ability but could be made shallower and longer if an owner preferred. It is secured to the hull by 11 bolts.

C-Flex was also used for the deck, with a ¾-inch balsa core. Plywood replaces the balsa in areas where hardware is mounted. The deck is set on a three inch flange, held by ⅜-inch bolts on five-inch centers, and heavily glassed-in. Several grab poles and a tie rod add strength without adding much weight.

Spaciousness characterizes the interior arrangement. The galley and navigation areas are enormous and the quarter berth provides two excellent sea berths. Tools, sextant and batteries are stored in the companionway steps with an oilskin locker behind.

While not shown in the plans, the 43 had pipe cots under sail bins in the forecabin. The chain locker in the bow and combustibles locker in the stern are air/watertight to the interior and they drain overboard.

The sail plan is simple and efficient, with a detachable inner forestay. All sail changes take place in

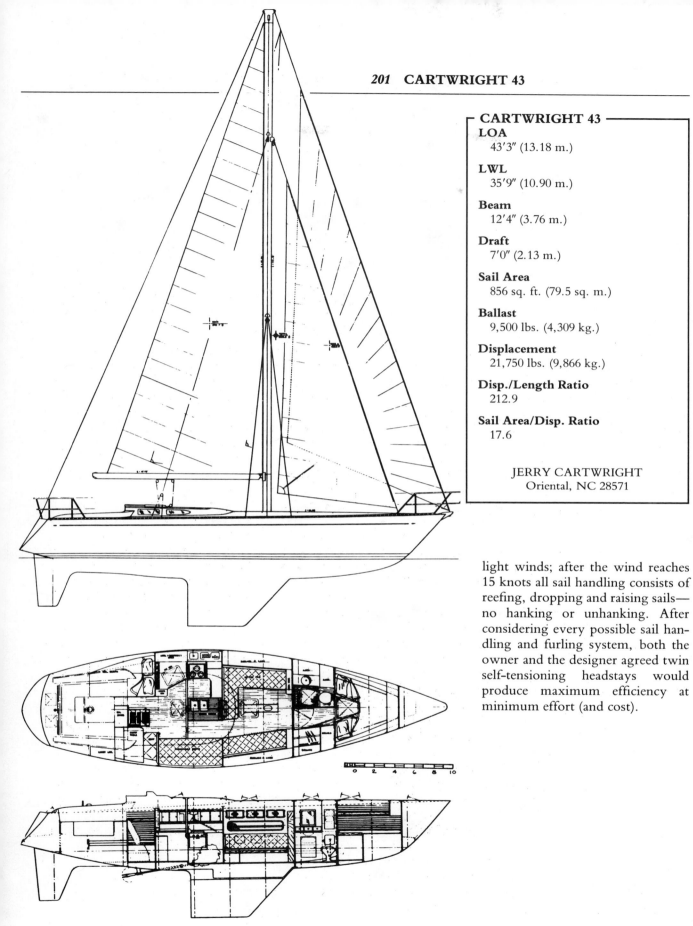

CARTWRIGHT 43

LOA
43'3" (13.18 m.)

LWL
35'9" (10.90 m.)

Beam
12'4" (3.76 m.)

Draft
7'0" (2.13 m.)

Sail Area
856 sq. ft. (79.5 sq. m.)

Ballast
9,500 lbs. (4,309 kg.)

Displacement
21,750 lbs. (9,866 kg.)

Disp./Length Ratio
212.9

Sail Area/Disp. Ratio
17.6

JERRY CARTWRIGHT
Oriental, NC 28571

light winds; after the wind reaches 15 knots all sail handling consists of reefing, dropping and raising sails—no hanking or unhanking. After considering every possible sail handling and furling system, both the owner and the designer agreed twin self-tensioning headstays would produce maximum efficiency at minimum effort (and cost).

SANDPIPER 44

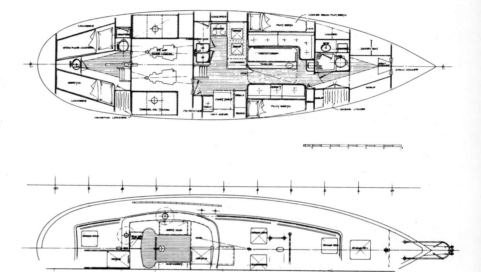

The Sandpiper 44 was designed by the design firm of Seaton-Neville for a Florida physician who wanted a shoal-draft cruising ketch for island-hopping along Florida's west coast and in the Bahamas. Her draft with the board up is only three feet, eight inches and will permit her to explore areas inaccessible to many boats half her size.

It is quite a challenge for a naval architect to design a centerboard yacht that offers an adequate level of stability and safety, efficiency under sail and ease of maintenance. Seaton seems to have met the challenge quite well.

Stability is provided by a healthy amount of ballast (41 percent of displacement) positioned at the very bottom of the shallow keel. In addition, the waterlines are very full aft and there is a moderate amount of tumblehome from amidships aft, revealed in the reverse curves at the aft end of the outer buttock lines.

To assure sailing efficiency, Seaton chose a tandem centerboard arrangement, which affords a greater amount of control over the yacht's lateral plane. Both boards are high aspect-ratio foils with hydrodynamically designed sections for maximum lift.

Many sailors do not care for centerboarders because of the increased complexity and maintenance. In this design the centerboard trunks extend well above the waterline so that the boards can be serviced at sea by removing access covers. In defense of the tandem centerboard arrangement, Seaton points out that the increased ability to balance the yacht under most sailing conditions can eliminate the need for self-steering gear or autopilot.

The high-aspect ketch rig combined with the easily driven hull form should assure some fast passages. The well-raked masts are independently stayed and the mainsail is a manageable 301 square feet. A large mizzen staysail increases the working sail area considerably.

Five opening hatches are located on deck for ventilation in warm climates. A permanent Bimini top frame, with cloth laced to it, also is shown. The cockpit is small and well protected, and has a seat locker to port and ice chest to starboard.

Down below, the after cabin contains two berths and an unenclosed head. An enclosed head arrangement would have necessitated a much larger cabin. Forward of the engine room are spacious cooking and navigation areas. Pilot berths are located outboard in the main cabin, with a head and hanging locker forward. The forepeak is devoted to storage and the chain locker is divided for rope and chain rodes.

Power is provided by twin 22-hp. Sabb diesels coupled to variable-pitch propellers. This guarantees good handling in tight spots and greater reliability. Feathering the props reduces drag under sail. An alternate arrangement is a single, larger diesel plus an auxiliary generator.

The boat was built in fiberglass at Liberty Yachts of Riviera Beach, Florida.

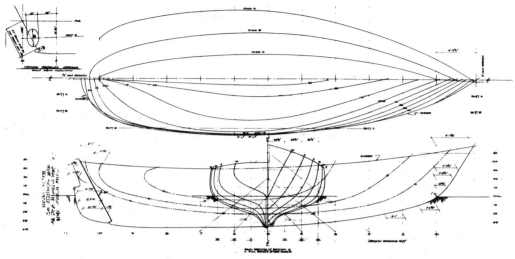

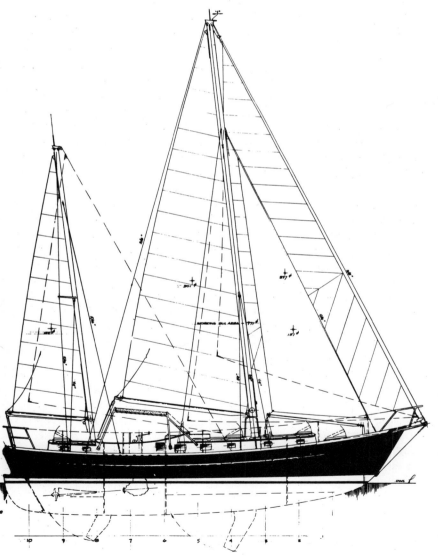

SANDPIPER 44

LOA
43'9" (13.34 m.)

LWL
37'6" (11.34 m.)

Beam
12'8" (3.86 m.)

Draft
3'8" (1.18 m/3.13 m.)

Ballast
11,750 lbs. (5,330 kg.)

Displacement
28,680 lbs. (13,009 kg.)

Sail Area
971 sq. ft. (90.2 sq. m.)

Construction
Fiberglass

Disp./Length Ratio
243

Sail Area/Disp. Ratio
16.6

SEATON-NEVILLE
NAVAL ARCHITECTS, INC.
316 N. Bayshore Blvd. #207
Clearwater, FL 33519

'APENNY DIP

Robert Harris was commissioned to design this boat to win its monohull class in the 1984 Observer Singlehanded Transatlantic Race. She also was to have accommodations for fast cruising when not racing.

Harris chose a fairly narrow hull for its inherent weatherliness and ease of steering, with a broad stern for power off the wind. The fin keel is quite deep and narrow, while the rudder is large and well supported. Originally named *Soleil Capricorne* but renamed *'apenny Dip,* the vessel was constructed by Hi Tech Boats of Noank, Connecticut, a company with a great deal of experience building lightweight IOR racers. Construction is of fiberglass cored with Airex foam and aluminum core material. High-stress glass weaves are used in place of normal woven roving mat and cloth to achieve high strength and light weight.

At first it was planned to build the boat with an absolutely minimal interior, to be completed after the 1984 OSTAR. The saloon was to consist of a simple bench to port, with stove, icebox, sink and workbench to starboard. John Heineman of Hi Tech convinced the designer, however, that by using modern materials the weight of joinery could be kept low, and that it would be both difficult and expensive to complete the interior at a later time. Doors and a few other items will be removable for racing.

The most unusual feature of the interior arrangement is the inside steering position. Just forward of the companionway ladder is a wheel and pedestal, and an elevated helmsman's seat. Portlights on three sides and a clear bubble overhead provide good visibility. Immediately to starboard is a huge chart table with stool and a wet locker. To port is the pilot berth with batteries under. Aft is the 45-hp. Pathfinder diesel with V-drive.

A wide bridge deck in the cockpit permits placing a quarter cabin to port and a voluminous head/stowage area to starboard. It also greatly reduces cockpit volume. Gas bottles are kept in a vented compartment in the lazarette, with the life raft under the helmsman's seat.

Pipe berths and a workbench are located in the forepeak. A double berth was to have been fitted here after the OSTAR. Other changes to be made at that time included enlarging the quarter berth to a double and possibly reducing the draft.

Without any rating rule constraints, Harris drew a very large sail plan, with Hood Sea Furl II on the jib and staysail and a Sto-way mainsail. A second headstay, just forward of the jibstay, is used for setting lightweight headsails.

It was intended that *'apenny Dip* race in the 1982 Round Britain Race, but the owner was not able to make that competition. Harris reports that the OSTAR plans also are off and the boat is up for sale.

'APENNY DIP

LOA
45'0" (13.72 m.)

LWL
37'6" (11.43 m.)

Beam
12'2" (3.71 m.)

Draft
8'0" (2.44 m.)

Displacement
19,000 lbs. (8,618 kg.)

Sail Area
1,003 sq. ft. (93.6 sq. m.)

Construction
Cored fiberglass

Disp./Length Ratio
161

Sail Area/Disp. Ratio
22.2

ROBERT B. HARRIS, LTD.
212-1670 Duranleau St.
Granville Island
Vancouver, B.C.
Canada V6H 3S4

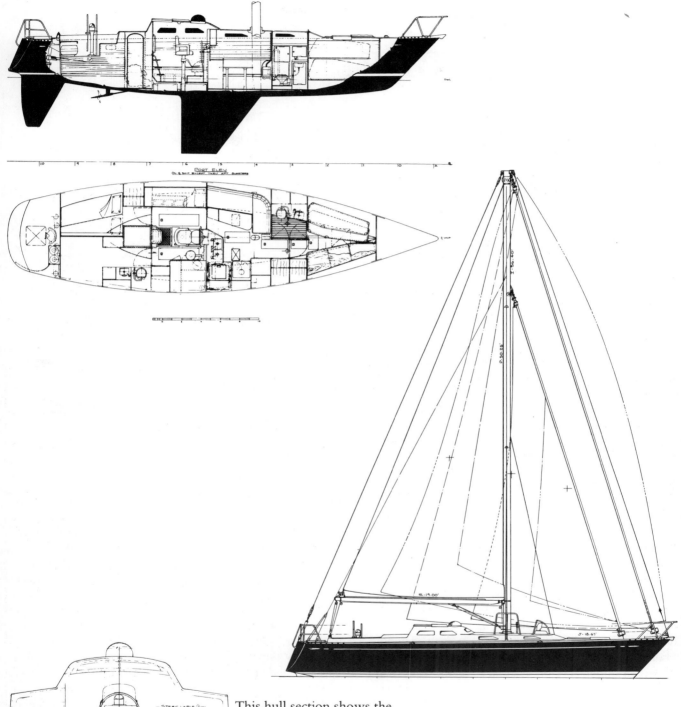

This hull section shows the elevated inside helmsman's seat, adjacent to the chart table, with overhead bubble.

INSCRUTABLE

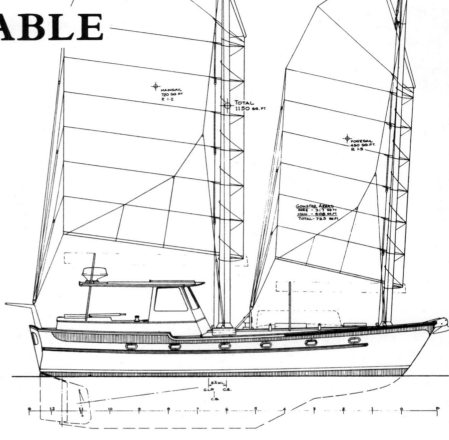

Inscrutable, another impeccably drawn vessel from the board of Jay R. Benford, was designed for a cruising couple who had spent six years sailing the South Pacific on their Spencer 35. Marg and Dale McNeil came to Benford with definite ideas concerning their next boat. Dale, who had been a draftsman at Boeing Aircraft, had prepared detailed sketches to illustrate their ideas.

While the hull and rig are certainly of interest and worthy of discussion, let's start with a tour of the interior. The general arrangement and numerous unique details are obviously a product of the owners' experience and reflect their views on the ideal cruiser.

Inscrutable was intended to be a home afloat, suitable for coastal cruising and ocean crossings. During passage-making, the middle third of the boat is devoted to sea use. This is the area of least motion, and thus greatest comfort.

There are two single sea berths, one over the engine box and one outboard of the port passageway. The port passageway contains the head, sink and bathtub, plus a special area for equipment and spare parts stowage. This passage can be closed at either end for privacy.

Forward of the companionway ladder, on either side of the mainmast, are the navigation area to port and galley to starboard, each with a clear overhead hatch. A washer/dryer is fitted between the galley and the head. Nearly all sea functions will be performed in these areas. The cabin sole is designed to drain to a low point at the companionway ladder.

Aft is the owners' cabin with huge double berth, overhead hatch, ports in transom, and numerous large lockers, bins, shelves and other stowage areas. Forward is the saloon area with settee, folding table, lounge chairs and Franklin fireplace. The forecabin contains workbenches on either side, a wood stowage bin, chain locker, clear overhead hatch and many small lockers. In the forepeak is a deep, self-draining anchor locker.

The pilothouse is actually more of a rigid dodger and, since the cockpit is self-draining, it could be removed with no sacrifice to the boat's integrity or seaworthiness. A Lexan-covered chart table and radar screen are located under the pilothouse shelter.

Steering is by telescoping tiller,

connected by a linkage to the partially balanced rudder. An autopilot also can be connected to the tiller under a hatch below the tiller.

Athwartship rails on deck forward of the pilothouse allow deck water to drain overboard or into water tanks. Stowage for a large dinghy is possible under the forward boom gallows.

In profile the hull looks like a long-keeled boat with cutaway forefoot. In section, however, it appears more as a separate fin faired into the hull with a small fillet. This raises the center of buoyancy and increases initial stability.

The hull is constructed of Airex-cored fiberglass with the core omitted in the keel and hull/deck joint. In high-stress areas the skins are joined for added strength. Decks are balsa cored with solid wood and plywood inserts in heavily loaded areas, and C-Flex is used diagonally to resist twisting.

The McNeils had experience on a lug-rigged boat and chose the Hasler/McLeod type for this boat. Hoisting, reefing and lowering of sails can be done from the cockpit. In light airs drifters can be set from the mastheads to add 725 square feet of sail. A cutter rig also is shown.

A 60-hp. Ford diesel will provide a speed of a little more than eight knots. A more economical 30-hp. Sabb diesel will deliver about seven knots. Tankage for 300 gallons of water and 205 gallons of fuel is located under the cabin sole.

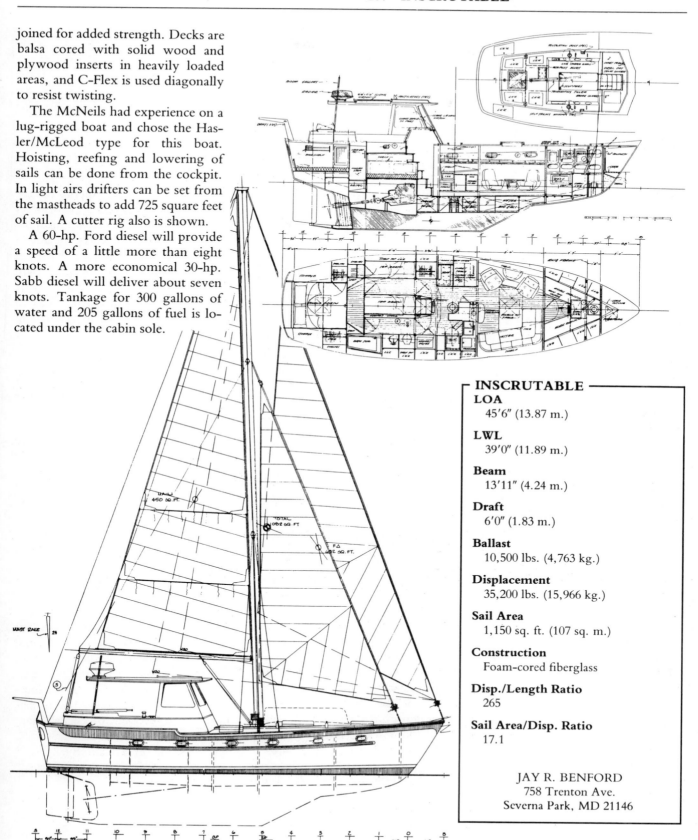

INSCRUTABLE

LOA
  45'6" (13.87 m.)

LWL
  39'0" (11.89 m.)

Beam
  13'11" (4.24 m.)

Draft
  6'0" (1.83 m.)

Ballast
  10,500 lbs. (4,763 kg.)

Displacement
  35,200 lbs. (15,966 kg.)

Sail Area
  1,150 sq. ft. (107 sq. m.)

Construction
  Foam-cored fiberglass

Disp./Length Ratio
  265

Sail Area/Disp. Ratio
  17.1

JAY R. BENFORD
758 Trenton Ave.
Severna Park, MD 21146

GALAXIE

Galaxie was designed by Mc-Curdy & Rhodes, Inc., for a New England owner who wanted a strong and comfortable cruising boat for East Coast and Caribbean sailing. He also wanted to be able to take part and do well in occasional day races. It is obvious that Mc-Curdy & Rhodes is an experienced firm and the owner an experienced sailor, for *Galaxie* is extremely well thought out and a sensible answer to the design requisites.

Long, balanced overhangs plus a graceful sheer give *Galaxie* a handsome, traditional look. Underwater she has a rather long and shallow fin keel and large skeg-hung rudder. Beam is moderate, as is her displacement.

Construction is in welded aluminum by Paul E. Luke, Inc., of East Boothbay, Maine. A longitudinal framing system with heavy transverse members was used.

The designers combined a traditional-looking trunk cabin with a mid-cockpit/after cabin arrangement. While it may look a bit boxy in the profile view, it will most likely not appear so in reality; the curvature of the plan view (looking down from overhead) and the presence of stanchions and lifelines will change the impression markedly.

Galaxie's side decks are wide and the fore and after decks very large. The after deck not only provides a spacious lounging area separate from the cockpit, but also room for stowing a good-size rigid dinghy while under way. Decks are covered with Treadmaster, a high-traction, low-maintenance mat that is bonded to the deck. A full-width folding dodger protects the companionway and cockpit.

The interior arrangement is highlighted by an owner's private stateroom aft, which truly is private. Accessible from both an aft-facing companionway and an interior passage, it has single and double berths (the double can be divided by a leeboard), head, shower, bureau, hanging locker and chart stowage.

In the passageway forward is a workbench, oilskin locker and engine access. Forward of the galley and navigation area is the drop-leaf table with settees port and starboard and jumpseats at each end. There is also a pilot berth to starboard. Joiner work is butternut, a blond wood, with teak trim; together with numerous opening deck hatches and cowl vents, she should have a light, airy interior.

Forward is another spacious cabin with head, shower, hanging locker, bureau and V-berths. The chain pipe coming down between the feet of the V-berths mars an otherwise ideal arrangement. Surely the windlass, pipe and chain locker could have been rearranged slightly to avoid this.

Galaxie is rigged as a ketch, but just barely so. The support for the mizzenmast just clears the rudder quadrant and she is closer in proportion to a yawl. Her spars are aluminum with rod rigging and a twin headstay. A large sail inventory will be used for racing and a removable roller furling drum can be attached for cruising. Numerous self-tailing winches are fitted.

A 48-hp. Westerbeke diesel drives a three-bladed feathering propeller through a 2:1 reduction gear. Her refrigerator and deep freeze are mechanical but also can run on shore power. Hot water can be drawn from an engine intercooler or shore power. A diesel-fired heater serves the entire boat. The autopilot is hydraulic and has wind vane steering capability. Tank capacities are 100 gallons of fuel and 200 of water.

Galaxie is certainly an expensive vessel to build and outfit, but when money is spent on such a well-designed and well-built boat it is a sound investment in sailing pleasure and resale value.

The designer reports, "Since her launching, *Galaxie* has been doing what she was intended to do: south in winter, New England in summer." A near-sister ship in fiberglass sandwich construction has crossed the Atlantic twice and spent four years cruising the British Isles, Scandinavia, France and Spain.

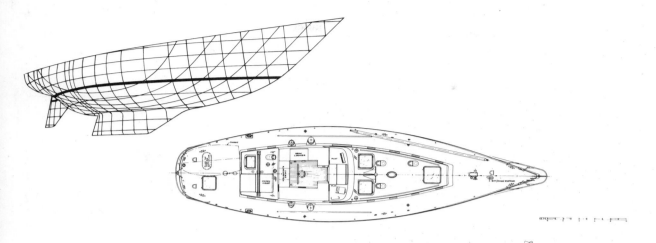

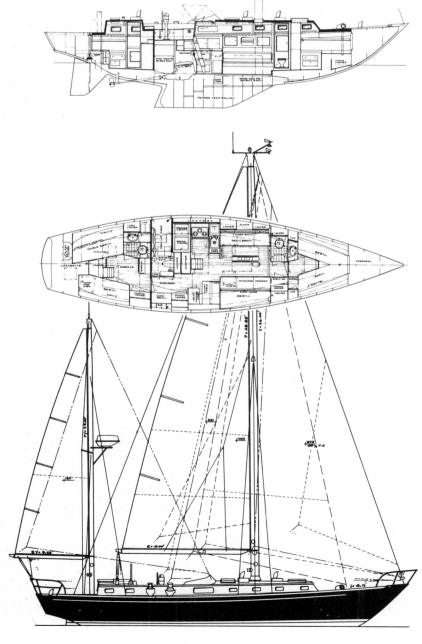

GALAXIE

LOA
46′4″ (14.12 m.)

LWL
34′3″ (10.44 m.)

Beam
12′10″ (3.91 m.)

Draft
5′9″ (1.75 m.)

Ballast
11,800 lbs. (5,352 kg.)

Displacement
29,500 lbs. (13,381 kg.)

Sail Area
1,035 sq. ft. (96 sq. m.)

Construction
Aluminum

Disp./Length Ratio
328

Sail Area/Disp. Ratio
17.4

McCURDY & RHODES, INC.
P.O. Box 206
Cold Spring Harbor, NY 11724

NORTHEAST 47

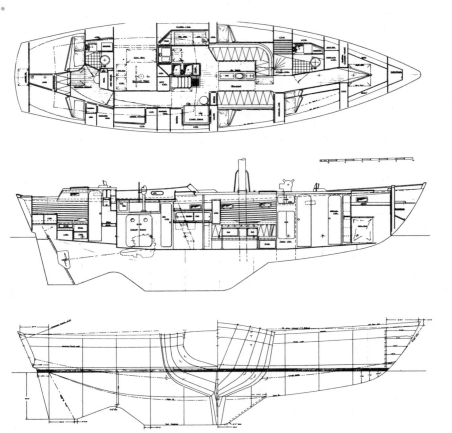

NORTHEAST 47
LOA
47'3" (14.40 m.)

LWL
40'0" (12.19 m.)

Beam
13'7" (4.14 m.)

Draft
6'6" (1.98 m.)

Ballast
13,500 lbs. (6,123 kg.)

Displacement
40,000 lbs. (18,144 kg.)

Sail Area
1,178 sq. ft. (109 sq. m.)

Construction
Steel

Disp./Length Ratio
279

Sail Area/Disp. Ratio
16.1

TED BREWER YACHT DESIGN
217 Edith Pt.
Anacortes, WA 98221

One of the most interesting aspects of studying cruising boat design is observing the great variety of craft that, though vastly different in appearance, are all well suited to a particular type of cruising. To illustrate, I've chosen two designs that are nearly identical in dimensions, both designed by experienced naval architects, and both representing good examples of boats that are popular today.

Ted Brewer designed the Northeast 47 for a Canadian owner who wanted a go-anywhere, long-range liveaboard boat. The hull is constructed of steel using the radiused chine method, with which Brewer has much experience. Sharp chines are replaced with steel plates bent to a large radius, giving the appearance and slightly reduced resistance of a rounded hull form.

Bruce Farr designed the 48-foot sloop for a California sailor who wanted a boat for fast, comfortable cruising and racing with his family, as well as daysailing with large groups of friends. It was to be built to a strict budget, competitive under both IOR and PHRF rating rules, and suited to West Coast downwind racing. Farr chose a light-displacement, fractionally rigged, foam-cored fiberglass boat to meet these needs.

Neither boat is extreme, but both are rather conservative examples of widely differing types. The Northeast 47 is only moderately heavy, and the 48-foot sloop, with just half of the former boat's displacement, is light but not ultra-light.

Even though the dimensions of the boats and the sail areas are nearly the same, one weighs twice as much as the other. What does this mean to the cruising sailor? Many things.

The heavier Northeast 47 can be built with much less concern for weight and thus can be made much stronger, equipped more lavishly, and will carry much more stores. These are all qualities necessary in a go-anywhere boat. On the negative side, more materials and equipment cost more money and must be carried around. Larger anchors and more chain must be used, and a windlass is necessary. All this adds greatly to the price and reduces the performance of the boat.

While the 48-foot sloop may not be able to withstand a grounding or collision as well as the Northeast 47, it is strong enough to survive more normal forces and at less weight. It will sail faster and more responsively in nearly all conditions. Anchors are lighter, less expensive and do not demand a windlass. She could be built to a more strict budget and still be properly equipped and fitted out for her intended type of cruising.

Sail area is almost evenly divided between mainsail and fore triangle on the Northeast 47's cutter rig. Only two rather shallow reefs are shown on the 513-square-foot main, but a storm trysail is shown. In addition to the two working headsails, a genoa or drifter, a small Yankee and a storm jib would make an adequate inventory. The sail area/displacement ratio of 16.1 reflects a boat that will take a bit of wind to move but which also will take a great deal of wind to overpower. An interesting, abbreviated staysail boom allows a self-tacking arrangement without a pedestal.

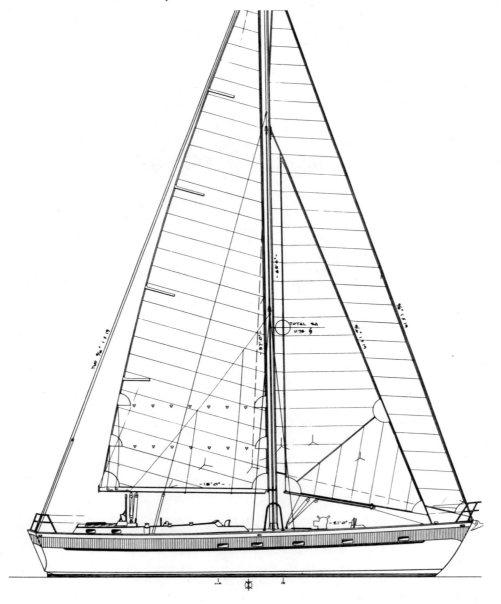

48-FOOT SLOOP

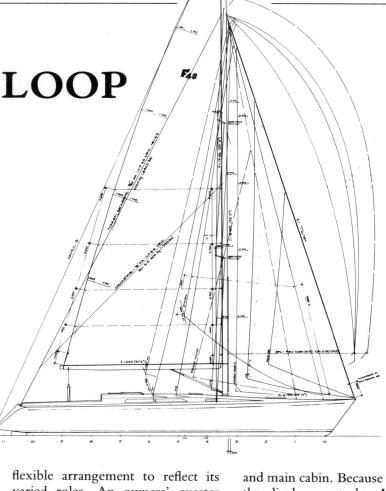

With slightly less sail area but much less displacement, the 48-foot sloop has a very high sail area/displacement ratio of 24.5 and 60 percent of the area is in the 680-square-foot mainsail. The sail plan shows a great variety of headsails (five genoas and four spinnakers) but most are only for racing. For cruising or daysailing, Farr says that the self-tacking #4 jib could be used from five to 35 knots. Four sets of reef points allow a quick reduction of sail area, without leaving the cockpit.

Swept-back spreaders on the sloop support the mast fore and aft so that she can be jibed with both running backstays off. But the runners are necessary for proper headsail tension. Running backstays on the cutter would probably only be necessary in heavy weather.

Speed and sail area are not the only performance factors to be considered. There is also sea-kindliness, responsiveness, ease of handling and ease of work on deck. The 48-foot sloop, with its deep and narrow fin keel and spade rudder, will be the more lively, spirited sailer, fun for daysailing and well suited to coastal cruising with the family or for offshore racing when fully crewed. With its slightly cutaway full keel, the Northeast 47 will be steadier on the helm, more forgiving in heavy weather but probably not the boat for tacking through a crowded anchorage or racing to Hawaii.

Both boats have large open decks for sail handling, sunbathing and dinghy stowage. High bulwarks are found all around the steel cutter.

In plan view, the two arrangements appear similar in size, and indeed both look spacious and comfortable. Brewer's sloop has a flexible arrangement to reflect its varied roles. An owners' quarter cabin has a double berth and pipe berth over. The opposite quarter berth pulls out to form a double and also has a pipe berth over. Galley and navigation areas are huge. There are two pilot berths in the main cabin and two more pipe berths forward.

The Northeast 47 has a large, private after cabin, fixed berths for seven, two heads and a large galley and main cabin. Because it has twice the displacement, by Archimedes' law the underwater portion of the hull has twice the volume. It doesn't appear to make much difference in the arrangement plan but it means that where the sloop has shallow bilges and little under-berth stowage, the cutter has deep bilges and all sorts of lockers and drawers and bins under the berths.

Deep bilges and lockers allow more tankage and tend to keep the

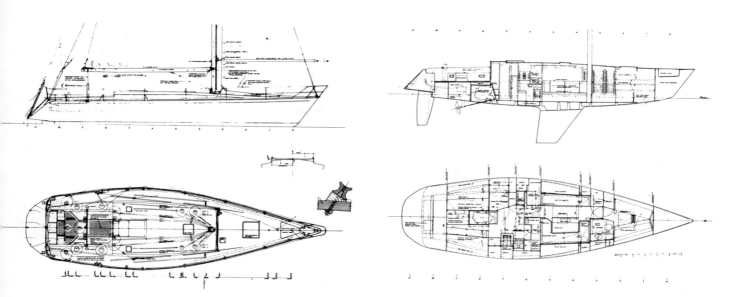

bilge water in the bilge, where it belongs. The cutter carries 180 gallons of fuel to the sloop's 45, and 250 gallons of water compared to 164. Cases of food could be stowed away on the cutter while space is severely limited on the sloop.

This is not to say that the sloop is not capable of ocean passages, only that it is self-sufficient for a shorter time. The Northeast 47 could spend

many months in remote areas while the 48-footer would have to visit supply ports more often.

The California sailor would have little use for the heavy steel cutter, and the Canadian would have little

use for the light fiberglass sloop. Only by carefully considering his particular needs and situation can the cruising sailor choose the boat best suited to him or her.

Variety is the spice of boat design!

48-FOOT SLOOP

LOA
48′4″ (14.73 m.)

LWL
38′10″ (11.83 m.)

Beam
13′11″ (4.24 m.)

Draft
8′0″ (2.44 m.)

Ballast
8,314 lbs. (3,771 kg.)

Displacement
20,111 lbs. (9,122 kg.)

Sail Area
1,130 sq. ft. (105 sq. m.)

Construction
Foam-cored fiberglass

Disp./Length Ratio
152

Sail Area/Disp. Ratio
24.5

BRUCE FARR & ASSOCIATES, INC.
121 Eastern Ave.
P.O. Box 3457
Annapolis, MD 21403

PATRICE

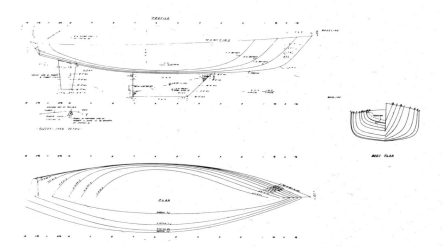

When sailors today think of a high performance boat they often think of the IOR-type racer. While such a boat can, indeed, achieve high speeds, it often requires a large crew, a large sail inventory, expensive hardware and an attentive (and strong) helmsman to maintain this performance. High performance in a traditional sense implies a boat that will sail quickly with a minimum of work, with few sail changes and little wrestling with the helm.

Patrice, designed by Paul R. Kotzebue, promises the latter type of high performance. The hull is long and narrow, with a long fin keel and a deep skeg-mounted rudder. Displacement is low but not excessively so. Long, graceful bow and stern overhangs will add appreciably to the effective sailing length when under way. Stability is achieved with a ballast/displacement ratio of nearly 50 percent.

Low freeboard contributes to reduced weight and windage. Wide side decks are left outboard of the low trunk cabin. The cockpit is over 10 feet long and could hold quite a few people comfortably.

The rig, too, promises high performance in a traditional sense. It is large and has a comparatively low-aspect ratio; the mainsail will be a powerful and versatile sail. While reaching and running, the full main is more effective than a tall, narrow mainsail, and thus less reliant on headsail changes and spinnakers to maintain speed. In strong winds, the rig is sensible because it takes fewer crew to reef the main than to change jibs.

A tapered aluminum mast with double spreaders is specified. Running backstays are shown in addition to a small jumper strut. The runners would probably only be needed in rough weather.

The interior arrangement is conventional, but quite practical for a variety of possible uses. Double and single quarter berths, settees, pilot berths and a V-berth forward offer both good sea berths and good privacy in port. Strategically placed curtains could create three separate cabins.

Patrice is designed to be built in cold-molded wood. The hull is strip-planked with ¾-inch cedar and then covered with three layers of ⅛-inch spruce diagonal planking followed by a linear polyurethane finish. Balsa-cored plywood with a teak overlay will be used for the deck.

Power is provided by a lightweight Pathfinder 42-hp. diesel. Tanks for 120 gallons of water and 50 gallons of fuel are fitted.

Patrice is a graceful, well-behaved boat for those sailors who want high performance but don't want to have to round up a large crew just to go sailing.

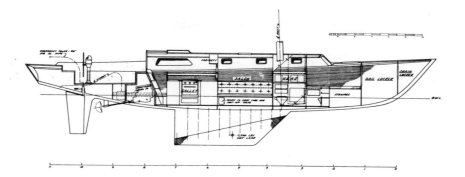

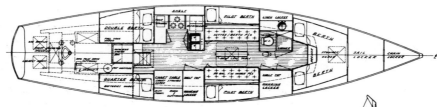

PATRICE

LOA
49'0" (14.94 m.)

LWL
37'6" (11.43 m.)

Beam
12'0" (3.66 m.)

Draft
6'0" (1.83 m.)

Ballast
11,300 lbs. (5,126 kg.)

Displacement
23,000 lbs. (10,433 kg.)

Sail Area
1,073 sq. ft. (99.7 sq. m.)

Construction
Cold-molded wood

Disp./Length Ratio
195

Sail Area/Disp. Ratio
21.0

PAUL R. KOTZEBUE
YACHT DESIGN
3650 Hancock
San Diego, CA 92110

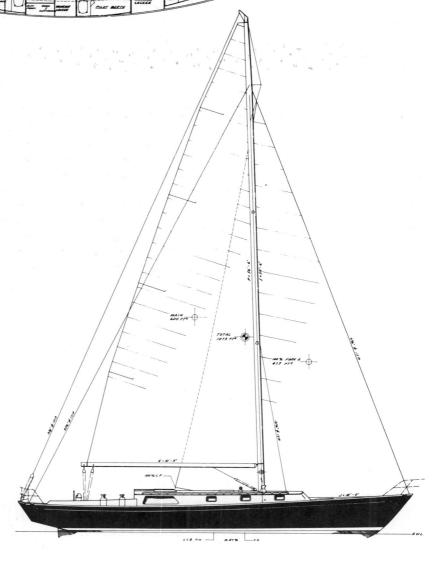

49-FOOT STEEL KETCH

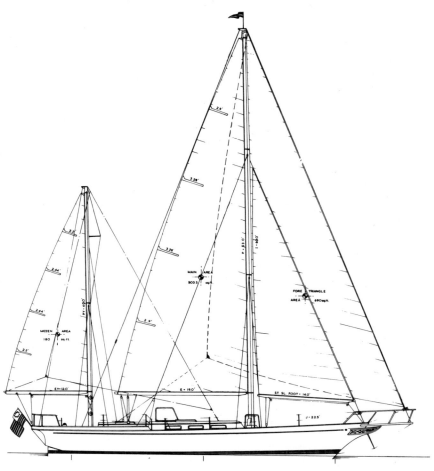

Roger Marshall designed this handsome vessel for a client who wished to build the boat himself. Steel was chosen because the client had welding experience and already had constructed a steel boat.

Original plans called for a chined hull form. But this was modified to a plating form, which replaces the chine with a 42-inch-radius steel plate at the turn of the bilge. This, combined with a slight curvature in the topsides and a small amount of fairing, will result in a hull that will not be recognizable as steel.

Marshall has drawn a boat with the popular combination of traditional topsides and modern underbody. The small but subtle sheer, clipper bow, raised sheer aft and well-raked transom give the boat a sleek and purposeful appearance. This is enhanced by the large, flush foredeck and low cabin trunk, which also is constructed of steel for watertight integrity.

With a long waterline length, moderate displacement, efficient keel/centerboard arrangement and large sail plan, its performance

should be a credit to any cruising boat. The deep rudder, located far aft on a deep skeg, assures excellent steering control.

By making the cockpit very small and placing it as far aft as possible, Marshall has been able to create an enormous amount of deck and accommodation space. There are two companionways, one from the bridge deck to the after stateroom and one from the cabin top to the main cabin, offering privacy and flexibility.

Companionways of this type,

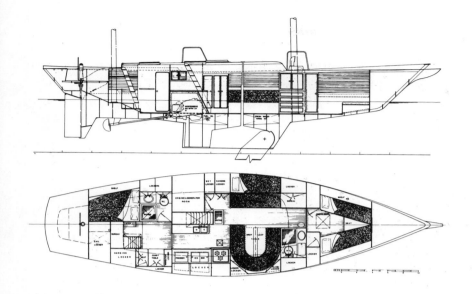

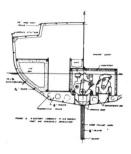

49-FOOT STEEL KETCH

LOA
49′2″ (14.99 m.)

LWL
40′0″ (12.19 m.)

Beam
13′9″ (4.19 m.)

Draft
6′3″/9′9″ (1.90/2.97 m.)

Displacement
40,907 lbs. (18,555 kg.)

Sail Area
1,374 sq. ft. (127.6 sq. m.)

Construction
Steel

Disp./Length Ratio
286

Sail Area/Disp. Ratio
18.7

ROGER MARSHALL
Box 127A
Jamestown, RI 02835

through flush or nearly flush deck hatches, result in long ladders. It is 10 steps down the main hatch. Another disadvantage is that if companionway dodgers are to be fitted they must rise over three feet off the deck to permit easy passage. Without such dodgers, quite a bit of rain and spray can find its way down below.

Side decks are unusually wide and there is room on the cabin top for a nine-foot rigid dinghy, leaving the foredeck clear for sail handling and sunbathing. The bowsprit is an anchoring platform constructed of welded steel tubing and mesh.

With a large sail area and the proportions of a yawl, sailing efficiency will be high. Both the mizzen and double-spreader mainmast are keel-stepped. The 500-square-foot main-sail and divided foretriangle promise easy shorthanded manageability. The jib shown seems to have quite a bit of roach in the leech for a battenless, roller-furling sail.

The interior arrangement looks spacious and comfortable. Cabin soles are wide and the walk-in engine room is unusually large. Numerous large storage areas are provided. While headroom in the main and after cabins is well over six feet, in the forecabin and forward head it is only about five feet, 10 inches, a sacrifice to the flush foredeck.

An 80-hp. Westerbeke diesel with a 2:1 reduction is fitted, along with a 5.5-kw. Westerbeke generator. Fuel and water tanks are integral and located in the keel to enhance stability and a sea-kindly motion.

VANCOUVER 50

Robert B. Harris, well known as the designer of the Vancouver series of blue-water cruising boats, is less well known as the co-designer of the 61-foot steel tandem center-board cutter *Angantyr*. This vessel, pictured and described in Arthur Beiser's *The Proper Yacht,* proved to be an exceptionally seaworthy, comfortable and versatile boat in her many thousands of miles of cruising.

As a logical step up in the Vancouver series and as a little sister of the well-proven *Angantyr,* Harris designed the Vancouver 50. The long, shallow full keel combined with tandem centerboards allows access to small harbors and canals normally off limits to such a large cruiser, sufficient draft for good windward performance and excellent helm balance.

By raising and lowering the forward and after centerboards, the balance between the sails and the hull can be adjusted for ease of steering and self-steering. In extreme conditions, the boards can be used to make the boat assume the desired attitude to the wind and waves under reduced sail or bare poles.

With no sail set, the forward board raised and the after board lowered, the Vancouver 50 probably would run very easily before high winds and large waves. Her canoe stern is well-suited to this maneuver. With the forward board down and after board raised, she probably would lie ahull with her bow close to the wind.

Some sailors dislike the centerboard's vulnerability to damage. Harris has attempted to allay these fears by making the boards and their trunks incredibly strong. Both board and trunks are constructed of two-inch-thick steel plate. The great weight of all the steel is concentrated low in the keel, where it acts as ballast.

Aft of the large propeller aperture is a semi-balanced rudder. The large aperture increases maneuverability and assures a good flow of water to the propeller, while the semi-balanced rudder contributes to a light helm. A trim tab built into the trailing edge of the rudder could be connected to a wind vane or autopilot to achieve self-steering with only a small amount of wind or electrical power required.

The deck is flush from stem to stern except for the small doghouse. The cockpit consists of U-shaped seating around the binnacle and does not interfere with the accommodations below. There is room under the staysail boom for a skiff of about 11 feet, with deck boxes, hatches and Dorade vents on each side.

The well-proportioned cutter rig features a tabernacle-stepped mast placed well aft. By locating the mast nearly amidships, Harris has kept the mainsail area down to just over 500 square feet. With the mast in the widest part of the boat, the shrouds can be set inboard of the rail for easy passage forward and aft.

The jumper strut at the upper spreaders eliminates the need for running backstays on the double-spreader rig. The self-tending, boomed staysail sheets to a radiused track on deck and can be reefed in heavy weather.

Main halyard, outhaul, reefing tack and outhaul lines all are led to two winches and an assortment of stoppers on the top of the doghouse.

Six more winches are arranged around the cockpit sheets.

Gallows frames for the main and staysail booms are shown. The triangular form supporting the staysail boom gooseneck also protects the forward hatch.

Twin poles for spinnakers or winged jibs can be stowed vertically against the mast. Each has its own topping lift, fore guy and after guy so that the poles need not be handled during a jibe or while dousing sail. For upwind passages, the poles can be stowed on deck.

There are three independent rain catchment systems. For use under sail, a trough in the upper side of the main boom catches water off the mainsail and channels it forward to the gooseneck, where a threaded fitting can be connected by hose to a water tank. A second system uses the doghouse top. A low railing all around leads the water to the forward corners, which drain to a tank. Finally, the scuppers from the main deck can be diverted to fill tanks.

Various accommodations are possible in a hull of this size. The one shown was arranged for an owner from Vancouver, British Columbia. It features a large galley, chart table and pilot berth in the doghouse. Two single berths, a head and voluminous storage are found in the after cabin. In the main cabin there is a dropleaf table, settee and shelves to port, and transom and pilot berth to starboard.

Further forward are the head and two hanging lockers. A workbench and upper and lower berths are found in the forepeak.

In another arrangement, created for chartering, the dining area is in the doghouse with three double cabins forward.

The Vancouver 50 is an expensive boat to build but would certainly be a practical craft well suited to passage-making, gunkholing and canal cruising.

VANCOUVER 50

LOA
  50'0" (15.24 m.)

LWL
  37'1" (11.30 m.)

Beam
  15'6" (4.72 m.)

Draft
  4'7"/8'3" (1.40/2.51 m.)

Ballast
  14,000 lbs. (6,350 kg.)

Displacement
  40,630 lbs. (18,429 kg.)

Sail Area
  1,246 sq. ft. (116 sq. m.)

Construction
  Foam-cored fiberglass

Disp./Length Ratio
  356

Sail Area/Disp. Ratio
  16.2

ROBERT B. HARRIS, LTD.
212-1656 Duranleau St.
Granville Island
Vancouver, B.C.
Canada V6H 3S4

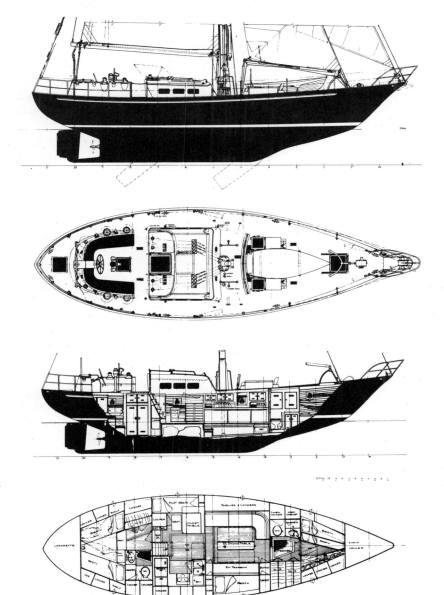

50' D.E. KETCH

The designs of Jay R. Benford are usually easy to recognize but difficult to describe precisely. They definitely have a traditional look about them yet don't resemble any particular type of traditional craft. Often they look like caricatures of boats—the kind of boats you see in children's books.

No insult is intended. On the contrary, Benford's boats all seem to have some sort of magical quality, a unique character all their own that defies definition.

Take this 50-foot double-ended ketch as an example. One is immediately struck by its salty charm. There is no single feature that causes this, but rather a harmonious combination of many small details that fit together nicely to create an overall effect.

Yacht design is more than esthetics, however. The boat must also perform its desired task. Here again Benford seems to score high marks. This ketch appears to be a comfortable and seaworthy craft.

As a development of an earlier 45-foot Colin Archer-type that Benford had designed, the 50-footer has a more cutaway forefoot and a relatively lighter displacement. Sailing reports on the 45-footer were quite complimentary and Benford has high expectations for the 50.

She was designed for a merchant ship engineer who wanted lots of accommodation and stowage space, large tanks for fuel and water, and a ship-size engine room. He certainly got what he wanted.

The hull and deck of this boat are constructed of ferro-cement, but

Airex-cored fiberglass, the W.E.S.T. system and conventional planked construction can also be used. Spars are hollow spruce put together in a box section.

For potential charter work, there are three double cabins, each with double bed. With boards to divide the doubles at sea, there are four quarter berths right at the most comfortable part of the boat. In addition, there are settees and pilot berths in the main cabin.

The engine room has a full-length workbench, lighting plant and large bank of batteries surrounding the 85-hp. Caterpillar diesel. Although the engine room is located underneath the cockpit, a long bridge deck at the forward end of the cockpit results in standing headroom throughout much of the engine

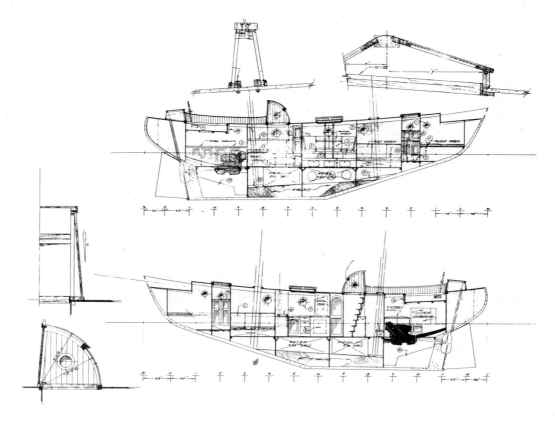

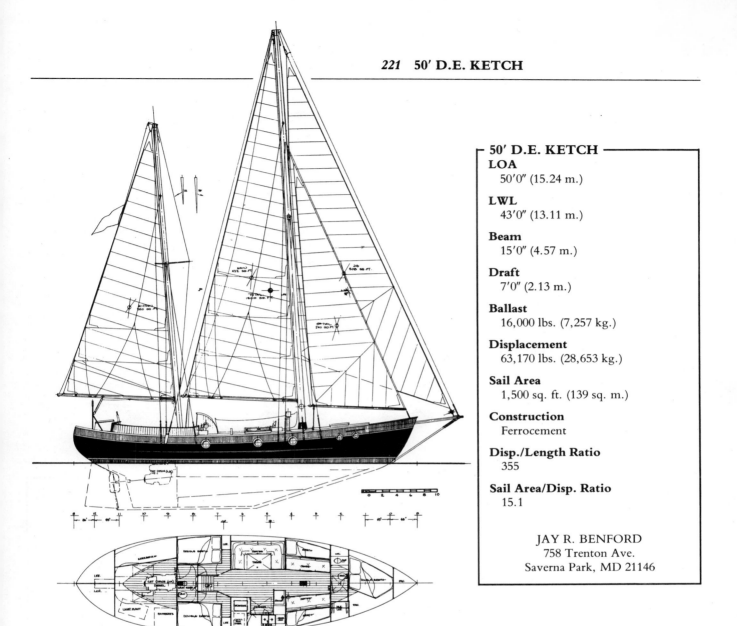

50′ D.E. KETCH

LOA
50′0″ (15.24 m.)

LWL
43′0″ (13.11 m.)

Beam
15′0″ (4.57 m.)

Draft
7′0″ (2.13 m.)

Ballast
16,000 lbs. (7,257 kg.)

Displacement
63,170 lbs. (28,653 kg.)

Sail Area
1,500 sq. ft. (139 sq. m.)

Construction
Ferrocement

Disp./Length Ratio
355

Sail Area/Disp. Ratio
15.1

JAY R. BENFORD
758 Trenton Ave.
Saverna Park, MD 21146

room. It also creates a small cockpit footwell, which will not hold a great amount of water in the event of a boarding wave, and a bridge deck that is very comfortable for lounging.

Fuel tankage for 590 gallons results in ranges under power of 900 miles at eight knots, 1,500 miles at seven knots and 2,200 miles at six knots. At reduced speed, the boat can be quite economical to power. Water capacity is 450 gallons.

The tall ketch rig has 1,500 square feet of sail for a moderate sail area/displacement ratio of 15.1. By hav-ing a large mizzen, the sails are broken down into manageable sizes. The club staysail and roller-furling jib make handling this large craft somewhat easier. Main and mizzen sails have straight leeches with no roach and no battens. The mizzen has an unusual diagonal reef to raise the after end of the boom high enough to clear a self-steering vane.

On the negative side, there does not seem to be a chart table anywhere. The navigator of a 50-foot boat should not have to work on the dinette table. Also, the galley sink is located far outboard and will prob-ably not drain well when heeled to starboard. With 10 ports in the topsides and a skylight over the main cabin, there should be adequate light down below, but all-around visibility is not achieved. One would have to go on deck to see what is happening ahead or astern.

Other configurations of this boat are also possible, including a cargo-carrying version. Benford says the possibilities for different interiors, hull materials and rig "are practically endless."

PALAWAN

Thomas J. Watson is an experienced sailor whose previous *Palawan* was a 67-foot ocean cruiser also designed by Sparkman & Stephens. This is, in fact, the sixth design by S&S for Watson. It probably is safe to assume there is a fine understanding between client and designer, and that the product of their sixth collaboration reflects the enormous amount of sailing and designing experience represented. *Palawan* is not a disappointment.

After his larger boat, Watson wanted a comfortable, seaworthy cruiser that two couples could handle. Excellent directional stability and a wind vane self-steerer also were called for.

You might be tempted to call this full-keeled ketch conservative, but on closer study you will notice there are many thoughtful and innovative details. The hull is constructed of welded aluminum alloy by the renowned Paul Luke yard in East Boothbay, Maine. While aluminum is popular for racing boats, because it reduces weight while retaining a given level of strength, in this boat aluminum is used to increase strength while keeping its weight within reasonable limits for a 50-foot cruising boat.

Decks and cabin also are welded aluminum with a teak overlay on deck. The short cabin leaves large fore and after decks. A fixed shelter at the forward end of the cockpit

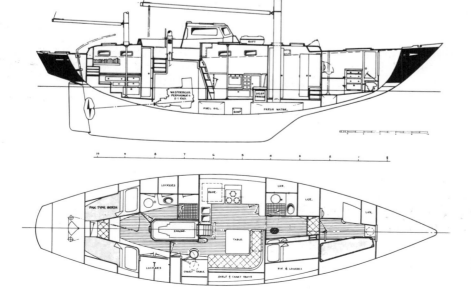

PALAWAN	
LOA	50'0" (15.24 m.)
LWL	36'0" (10.97 m.)
Beam	14'2" (4.32 m.)
Draft	6'9" (2.06 m.)
Ballast	15,000 lbs. (6,804 kg.)
Displacement	40,264 lbs. (18,263 kg.)
Sail Area	1,105 sq. ft. (103 sq. m.)
Construction	Aluminum
Disp./Length Ratio	385
Sail Area/Disp. Ratio	14.4

SPARKMAN & STEPHENS, INC.
Design Dept.
79 Madison Ave.
New York, NY 10016

provides protection from foul weather but still permits a true outside cockpit. Triple lifelines are shown.

Under the cockpit is a 90-hp. Westerbeke diesel driving a three-bladed Luke feathering propeller. A diesel-fired, forced air heater also is fitted.

Accommodations are provided for two couples with complete privacy. Aft is the owner's cabin with two berths, head, separate shower and voluminous storage space. The port berth is of the "fan type"; it is pivoted at the inboard corner of the foot and the head can be swung inboard to form a double berth for use in port.

Forward of the main saloon is the guest cabin with upper and lower berths, head with shower and more big lockers. The forepeak contains sail stowage and a workbench, plus a pipe berth, head and folding sink for possible crew use.

All the major weights are concentrated amidships, between the engine and the mainmast, for reduced pitching motion. Fuel (150 gallons) and water (300 gallons) are each kept in two separate tanks welded integral to the hull under the main cabin sole. A four-cubic-foot freezer and the ship's batteries are located under the L-shaped settee. The galley contains a seven-cubic-foot refrigerator and gimbaled gas stove. A portable seat can be used at the chart table or at the dining table.

The moderate sail plan shows a relatively small mizzen and large mainsail. The largest headsail shown is a high-clewed, 420-square-foot Yankee just overlapping the main. The mizzen boom was kept inboard to allow for the self-steerer. The single spreader mainmast is stepped on the keel while the mizzen stands on deck. Both have steps to the top. Large hull ports, to add visibility in the main cabin, were also fitted.

A large, high-quality yacht such as *Palawan* is not inexpensive to build or equip, but can repay her owner in dependability, safety, comfort and performance. Fast, trouble-free passages are indicated.

KAY

PHOTO-BOAT

KAY

LOA
51'4" (15.65 m.)

LWL
37'6" (11.43 m.)

Beam
13'6" (4.12 m.)

Draft
7'9" (2.36 m.)

Ballast
19,400 lbs. (8,800 kg.)

Displacement
43,700 lbs. (19,822 kg.)

Sail Area
1,135 sq. ft. (105.4 sq. m.)

Construction
Double-planked teak

Disp./Length Ratio
370

Sail Area/Disp. Ratio
14.6

SPARKMAN & STEPHENS, INC.
Madison Ave.
New York, NY 10016

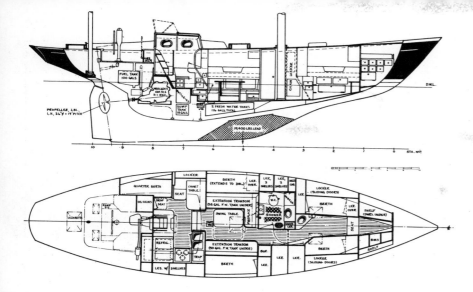

Kay was built in Thuro, Denmark, in the yard of Aage Walsted. Although she is traditional in appearance, with a long graceful sheer and overhangs seldom seen these days, her construction employs some modern materials.

The hull is double-planked in teak with the keel, backbone and frames of laminated oak. Three stainless steel web frames and a stainless steel mast step weldment add strength and integrity. Bulkheads and deck are constructed of plywood, with a teak deck overlay and a teak deckhouse.

In designing the hull, a long, deep keel was combined with several features to enhance performance and handling. The relatively shallow, cutaway forefoot should enhance tacking qualities and the nearly vertical rudderpost greatly improves steering over the raked-aft rudder often found on full-keel boats. Concentrating all the lead ballast within

a short longitudinal length will also improve the motion of the boat in head seas.

The displacement length ratio of 370 indicates a rather heavy boat. However, her long overhangs will increase the waterline length markedly under sail and reduce the boat's effective displacement length ratio. An increase in waterline length of 18 inches reduces the ratio to 305.

Spars are hollow spruce with 1 × 19 stainless wire rigging. Norseman end fittings are specified for ease of replacement at sea. Sailing efficiency was obviously a major consideration with the tall double-spreader rig.

The minimal mizzen sail is well separated from the mainsail to keep it in clean air. A sail area displacement ratio of 14.6 is on the low side, but the efficient rig and narrow, easily-driven hull must be considered.

Generous interior space and a large, uncluttered deck are provided

by the mostly flush deck arrangement. Yet the small deckhouse protects the cockpit and gives excellent visibility from the navigation area and galley.

Locating the anchor windlass and chain locker just forward of the mast serves a variety of purposes. It keeps the foredeck clear of obstructions and allows the windlass operator to work in a well protected position with less motion.

Removing the weight of windlass and chain (considerable in a boat of this size) from the bow also reduces excessive pitching in head seas. A large winch on the afterdeck (not shown) handles stern anchors and dock lines.

In the raised deckhouse the galley is equipped with an alcohol stove with oven, foot-activated water pumps, and chill and freezer boxes powered by an engine-driven compressor. An oilskin locker and dropseat are located adjacent to the companionway. Batteries and tanks for fresh and sump water are located amidships and low, beneath the cabin sole.

Two extension transom berths and two wide pilot berths (one extendable to form a double) are located in the main cabin. A fireplace in the bulkhead between main cabin and head keeps both areas warm and dry.

By having the forecabin slightly aft of its normal position, two single berths with a walkway and seat between are possible in place of V-berths. A sink also is found here, certainly a good idea on a 50-footer with one head.

Shortly after *Kay's* launching in 1975, her owner received a most attractive offer for her. He couldn't refuse, so he sold her. He immediately went back to S&S and Walsted and ordered a duplicate. When asked what changes he would like, he replied, "I am so pleased with the boat I would not change one single item."

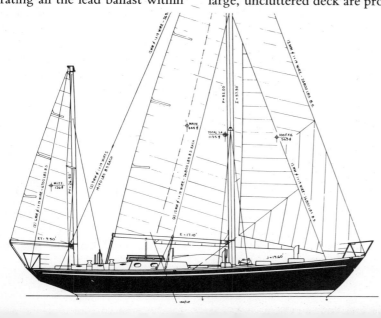

FALCON II

FALCON II

LOA
62'0" (18.90 m.)

LWL
50'5" (16.62 m.)

Beam
16'3" (4.95 m.)

Draft
8'0" (2.43 m.)

Displacement
92,000 lbs. (41,733 kg.)

Sail Area
1,823 sq. ft. (170.4 sq. m.)

Construction
Aluminum

Disp./Length Ratio
321

Sail Area/Disp. Ratio
14.5

MacLEAR & HARRIS, INC.
28 West 44th St.
New York, NY 10036

Falcon II was designed by Frank MacLear and built by Palmer Johnson for Ben Heineman of Chicago, who specified a large, superbly-equipped cruising boat able to be handled easily single or double-handed.

That Frank MacLear has experience designing such large easily-singlehanded yachts is obvious from the numerous unique and imaginative details of this design. Much could be said about such areas as the accommodations, cockpit design, galley, navigation equipment, deck layout and ground tackle (the design and equipment description for *Falcon II* runs to 58 pages). But it is the rig and the sail-handling equipment that truly distinguish this boat from other luxury yachts.

The boomless cutter rig, developed by MacLear and refined through a number of previous designs, represents a logical solution to handling large mainsails. All sails are roller furling. How else could a person work with a mainsail of 700 square feet and a headsail of 2,000 square feet? All sail control is performed with electric winches. This includes halyards, sheeting and sheet lead positioning. There are manual backups for all functions.

Since all the sails are roller reefing except the drifter, and because high-aspect (tall and narrow) sails roller reef better than low-aspect sails, a rather tall sail plan with small headsails was chosen. The largest genoa is only 145 percent.

The mainsail, set on a jackstay parallel to and seven inches abaft the mast, is boomless. It is trimmed with sheets running to the triple backstays. Vertical travelers on the backstays allow adjustment of the sheet leads. These sheets easily absorb the shock of jibes, especially without the weight of the boom flying across.

Furling the sail outside the mast reduces friction between the sail and the mast (and thus the torque required to reef) and allows examination of and access to the whole rig. Tack and head reinforcing also can be made thicker and larger. MacLear admits there is a four- to six-percent loss in mainsail drive caused by the gap, but claims that since the mainsail often contributes only about 20 percent of the total drive, the overall loss is on the order of one percent.

There are three roller-furling headstays, two to the masthead and one to the upper spreaders. The foremost carries the enormous drifter, which has a foot as long as the boat. Because it never is partially furled or reefed, the large size does not cause the bagging problem experienced with low-aspect, roller-reefed headsails. With the small gap between the two headstays the drifter probably would have to be jibed rather than tacked.

The inner headstay is for the genoa. A 145-percent genoa is used for coastwise cruising and in light winds; a 125-percent genoa is used for singlehanded offshore sailing. A spare mainsail can be set as an 85-percent jib and the storm mainsail as a 65-percent genoa.

Luff padding stitched into the sail just aft of the luff takes up sail bagginess as it is reefed. It builds up a larger spindle diameter to absorb more sail where necessary. Additional bunt padding was added in the middle of the sail after two weeks of sailing trials.

A winching platform is located aft of the helmsman's seat, with bins to catch the tails of all lines.

Either a heavy-weather staysail or storm staysail could be set on the inner forestay. Although all sails can be raised and lowered by their halyards, they seldom are. Rather, the appropriate genoa and staysail are chosen before the cruise starts and are furled and reefed as needed.

Five self-tailing winches (electric and manual) are used for sheets. All are within reach of the helmsman in his sumptuous seat. Electrified winches move the headsail sheetlead blocks on their tracks and the mainsail blocks up and down the backstay travelers.

In a halyard cockpit to port of the mast, electric/manual winches feed the halyard tails to large stowage reels. All winches are of the drum type.

In the event of a power failure

(unlikely with the two 15-kilowatt generators), all sail handling can be performed with manual winches. MacLear claims that one person with an electric winch is worth five to seven persons working manually. He also said that rather than feeling shame, the skipper should feel much the master of the situation, less at the mercy of the elements and huge sails. The sheer size of *Falcon II*'s sail plan calls for the use of electric winches, although some super athletes may disagree.

Just as the larger offshore racers develop equipment and techniques that eventually find their way onto smaller racing and cruising boats, sail plans and gear designed to make large yachts like this easily manageable often can be applied to other, smaller vessels.

Sailing in only five knots of wind, Falcon II's enormous drifter is unrolled.

DEERFOOT 62

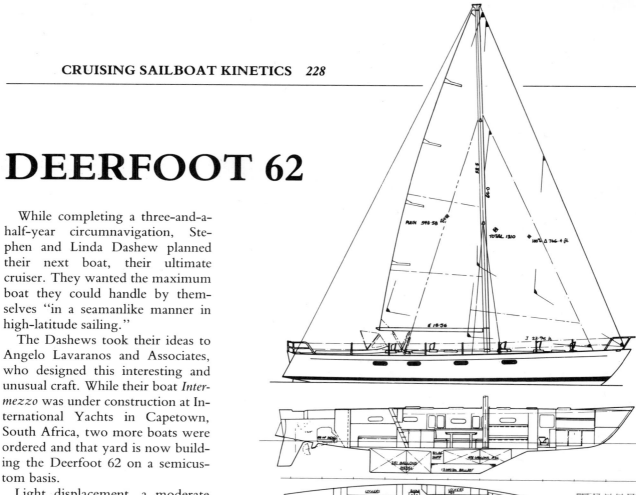

While completing a three-and-a-half-year circumnavigation, Stephen and Linda Dashew planned their next boat, their ultimate cruiser. They wanted the maximum boat they could handle by themselves "in a seamanlike manner in high-latitude sailing."

The Dashews took their ideas to Angelo Lavaranos and Associates, who designed this interesting and unusual craft. While their boat *Intermezzo* was under construction at International Yachts in Capetown, South Africa, two more boats were ordered and that yard is now building the Deerfoot 62 on a semicustom basis.

Light displacement, a moderate beam and a long waterline result in a very easily driven hull, so that a relatively small and easily handled sail plan will power the boat nicely. The long, shallow fin keel provides good directional stability and the five-foot six-inch draft allows cruising in thin waters. A partially balanced spade rudder was chosen.

The stern is quite wide, permitting placement of the engine room under the cockpit, which is spacious

This view of the hull under construction shows the longitudinal framing system, with widely-spaced heavy transverse frames and closely-spaced longitudinals.

but short. A skirt added to the bottom of the transom serves to increase waterline length underway with little additional weight. Using a static waterline length of 52 feet, the displacement/length ratio is a low 159. With an effective sailing waterline of about 55 feet this ratio is reduced further to 134. This certainly is a light-displacement boat.

Ballast consists of 12,000 pounds of lead in the lower, forward part of the keel cavity. This figure, 24 percent of displacement, is increased by fuel and water tanks also located in the keel.

Hull and deck are constructed of welded aluminum with plate thicknesses of one inch in the keel, $5/16$-inch in the bilge area, and $7/32$-inch topside. The topsides are insulated with $1\frac{1}{2}$-inch polyurethane foam. Tanks are welded integral with the hull.

In an effort to eliminate all leaks, there are no fastener holes in the hull or deck except for the companionway hatch runners. All other fittings are either welded in place or bolted to plates that are welded to the hull or deck.

There are two watertight bulkheads in the boat, one at the forward end of the engine room, and one at the after end of the forepeak. This means that these two areas only are accessible through deck hatches but they also isolate flooding if either area is holed.

It is obvious that a great deal of thought and experience went into the planning of the machinery installations. An 85-hp. Perkins diesel turns a 24-inch feathering, variable-pitch propeller through a Borg Warner V-drive. Belt-driven off the engine are a refrigeration compressor, an AC generator and two DC alter-

The broad stern with "skirt" attached makes an excellent spot for boarding.

DEERFOOT 62

LOA
62'3" (18.97 m.)

LWL
52'0" (15.85 m.)

Beam
14'7" (4.44 m.)

Draft
5'6" (1.67 m.)

Ballast
12,000 lbs. (5,443 kg.)

Displacement
50,000 lbs. (22,680 kg.)

Sail Area
1,310 sq. ft. (122 sq. m.)

Construction
Aluminum

Disp./Length Ratio
159

Sail Area/Disp. Ratio
15.1

STEPHEN DASHEW
550 Del Oro Rd.
Ojai, CA 93023

nators. There also is a spare refrigeration compressor and spare alternator that can be driven by either a five-hp. Yanmar diesel or a second propeller shaft. This "charging shaft" is used under sail and is powered by the propeller being turned by the water flow. There is also a 200-gallon-per-minute pump driven by the smaller diesel.

The engine room has five foot six inch headroom, a workbench and sound insulation all around. This appears to be an extremely versatile and reliable arrangement. Range under power is 1,200 miles at eight knots on 250 gallons of fuel.

A hull with the volume of this boat obviously allows great flexibility of interior arrangement. In the one shown, there is an apartment-size owners' cabin aft, with double berth, head/shower with washing machine, settee and fantastic locker space.

Forward of this stateroom is an enormous galley to port and "navigator's station/ship's office" to starboard. The galley contains a microwave oven, propane stove, 20 cubic feet of refrigerator and freezer space and a large vegetable bin. Reverse-cycle air conditioning is also installed.

Forward of the main cabin are mirror-image double cabins port and starboard, each with upper and lower berths and private head. Sail bins and a pipe berth are found in the large forepeak.

The double spreader cutter rig is on the small side but this is in keeping with the slippery hull and easy sail handling. A mainsail of 543 square feet is just about at the upper limit of what can be handled by one or two active people.

To eliminate chafe and other problems with the topping lift, it has been replaced by a compression strut (not shown) from the underside of the boom to the base of the mast. All sail controls, including mainsail reefing lines, are lead to the cockpit.

On the passage from Capetown to Antigua, a distance of 5,860 miles, *Intermezzo* averaged 194 miles per day. Over the last 1,000 miles she averaged 230 miles per day, or nine-and-a-half knots.

ACADEMY 76

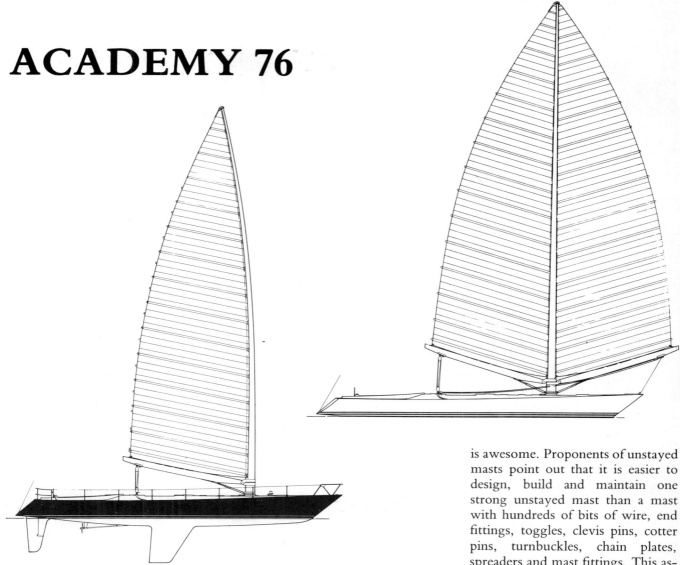

The adjective that comes to mind when looking at this design is "awesome." By combining the latest high-tech building techniques and state-of-the-art materials with efficient aerodynamic and hydrodynamic design, Fred Madlener has created what must be one of the fastest modern monohull sailboats.

Madlener was asked to design a sailing vessel "to carry 16 cadets and two officers with speed, safety and simplicity." He chose a modified Ljungstrom rig as the "easiest to handle and maintain, and so least likely to fail." The carbon fiber S-glass hull was specified for its high strength-to-weight ratio.

It is difficult to imagine a faster, more efficient hull form: ultra-light displacement, deep fin keel, fine entry, straight run, low wetted surface. It should be very easily driven in light airs and heavy, and should be able to approach speeds of about 12 knots before it starts surfing.

Power this hull with a huge and efficient sail plan and the result truly is awesome. Proponents of unstayed masts point out that it is easier to design, build and maintain one strong unstayed mast than a mast with hundreds of bits of wire, end fittings, toggles, clevis pins, cotter pins, turnbuckles, chain plates, spreaders and mast fittings. This assumes that designers and builders have the knowledge and experience to produce strong, easy to handle, long-lasting, self-supporting spars and steps. If this point has indeed been reached, then more cruising sailors should consider these spars for their boats.

Madlener's rig has twin tracks on the 95-foot spar, which is 26 inches in diameter at the deck and tapers to six inches at the head. The two mainsails are fully battened and each has its own boom and gooseneck. When sailing to windward the mast

ACADEMY 76

LOA
76′3″ (23.24 m.)

LWL
61′1″ (18.62 m.)

Beam
16′9″ (5.11 m.)

Draft
10′6″ (3.20 m.)

Ballast
22,400 lbs. (10,160 kg.)

Displacement
44,800 lbs. (20.321 kg.)

Sail Area
1,610 sq. ft. (150 sq. m.)

Construction
Fiberglass

Disp./Length Ratio
88

Sail Area/Disp. Ratio
20.5

MADLENER & SONS
CONSTRUCTORS
1923 Ke'eaumoku St.
Honolulu, HI 96822

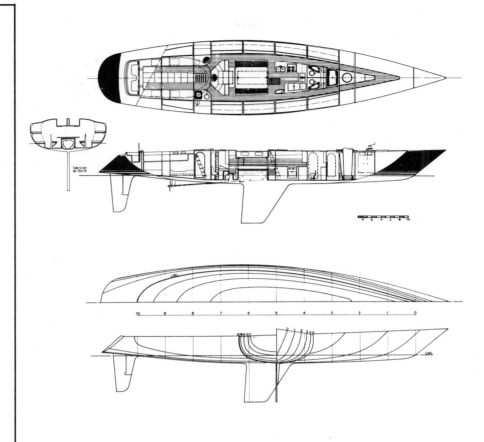

can be rotated slightly, the windward sail tightened and the leeward sail eased to achieve a good airfoil shape. Running, the sails can be winged out, doubling sail area. Booms are canted up to avoid dipping while sailing downwind. Hydraulic vangs are fitted. A backstay stabilizes the spar in heavy running conditions.

Accommodations consist of 16 berths in uppers and lowers on both sides of the main cabin, with two quarter cabins aft for officers. On centerline are the navigator's station (with 3.5 kw generator underneath), saloon table (with 124-hp. diesel under), galley, double heads, mast step and forepeak. Provision is made for carrying up to 600 gallons each of fuel and water. A water maker also is fitted.

This certainly is a boat worth keeping an eye on.

ANTONIA

One often hears of a naval architect combining traditional design with modern building techniques. It may be that Jay Benford has created the ultimate marriage of the two in this breathtaking design.

Antonia was designed for Armando Vasone Filho, a native of Brazil, who wanted a large sailing yacht constructed of the abundant and reasonably priced woods available in South America. Originally, he considered conventional carvel planking as a construction technique, but after reading John Guzzwell's *Modern Wooden Yacht Construction* he became sold on cold-molded wood, and also sold on Guzzwell, whom he hired as a construction consultant. *Antonia* is being built in Porto Alegre, Brazil, by Interamericana Construcoas Navais, Ltd.

Benford submitted a preliminary design to Filho, who selected it from a number of proposals. Guzzwell and Benford had just collaborated on a smaller Benford design.

Interesting changes take place as sailing vessels are made larger and larger. The "Law of Mechanical Similitude" shows that if the size of a boat is doubled, the heeling force of the wind increases by a factor of 8 while the stability increases by a factor of 16. This means that large sailboats are stiffer than small ones and can thus carry proportionately more sail or less ballast.

Another factor favoring large yachts is that the weight of engines and other equipment and luxuries becomes a less significant part of the total displacement. By using modern, lightweight construction tech-

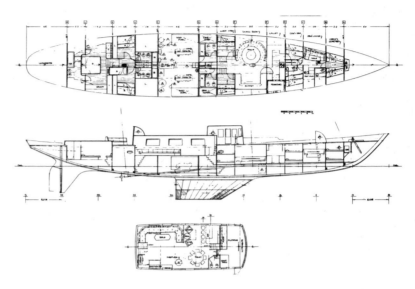

niques, which take full advantage of the aforementioned physical principles, Benford was able to design an ultra-light displacement, ultra-high performance cruising yacht with accommodations for 18 in Sybaritic luxury.

The hull is very narrow for its length and, with a fin keel and skeg-mounted rudder, it will be easily driven at both low and high speeds. An elegant and functional feature seldom seen today is the eliptical counter stern. Hull construction consists of five layers of Honduras mahogany, four laid diagonally with the outside layer longitudinal, for a total thickness of 46mm (1.77"). Framing is longitudinal, on about 16-inch centers amidships, over widely spaced transverse frames and bulkheads. Five watertight bulkheads are fitted.

Three cockpits are found on deck, one on the fantail and one at the base of each mast. There is provision for carrying three tenders on deck.

Shown on the drawing are a 15-foot pulling boat and two 20-foot powerboats amidships and forward.

A raised pilothouse and sunken deckhouse are located amidships. The deckhouse contains a bar, organ, freestanding fireplace and a head. Aft are three double cabins for the owner's party with two guest cabins amidships. Each has its own head with bathtub, shower, toilet and bidet.

Forward of the dining and galley areas is the crew accommodation area, with four double cabins, galley and lounge.

Power is supplied by two Caterpillar turbocharged, aftercooled diesels, with reverse reduction gears and coupled to Hundested variable-pitch propellers. By using a reverse gear, the 90 degrees of available propeller pitch rotation can be used to rotate the blades from full neutral to full feathering. Thus, performance under sail and power is improved. With the reduction gear, larger and

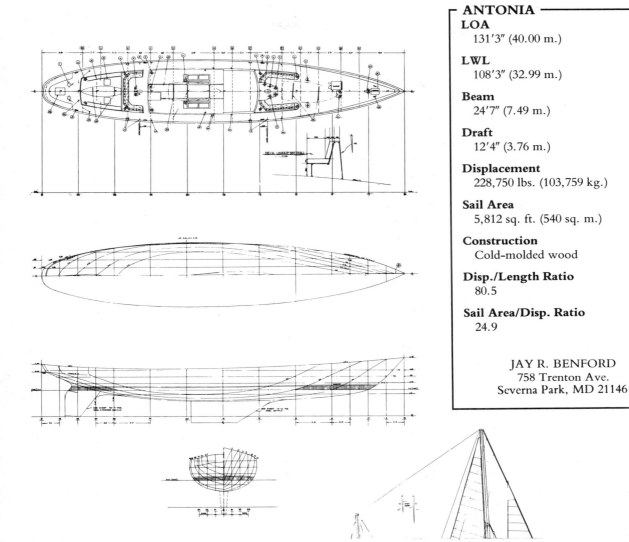

ANTONIA

LOA
131'3" (40.00 m.)

LWL
108'3" (32.99 m.)

Beam
24'7" (7.49 m.)

Draft
12'4" (3.76 m.)

Displacement
228,750 lbs. (103,759 kg.)

Sail Area
5,812 sq. ft. (540 sq. m.)

Construction
Cold-molded wood

Disp./Length Ratio
80.5

Sail Area/Disp. Ratio
24.9

JAY R. BENFORD
758 Trenton Ave.
Severna Park, MD 21146

more efficient propellers can be used.

The owner specified a cruising range of 3,000 miles at 10 knots, requiring 10,000 liters (2,642 gallons) of fuel, weighing over 16,500 pounds. To reduce the quantity and weight of water carried, Benford decided to use the heat of the exhaust of the 25-kw generator to power a water distillation plant, which could supplement the 4,800-liter (1,268-gallon) water capacity. This permits full use of the bathtubs, washing machine and dishwasher. A second 15-kw generator is mounted in the forepeak.

A tall (130-foot) ketch rig spreads nearly 6,000 square feet of sail, with a mainsail of over 2,000 square feet. The main and mizzen have hollow leeches and no battens. Foresails are roller furling. All winches are electrically powered.

With its slippery hull form and powerful rig, *Antonia* will easily reach speeds of 10 knots and often exceed 14 knots. Cruising at that speed with the level of comfort and luxury found on this boat is an experience reserved for a privileged few.

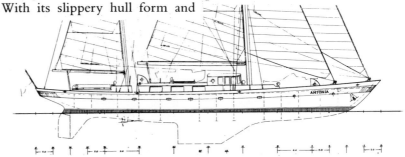

Index